A Clinician's Guide to Think Good – Feel Good

A Clinician's Guide to Think Good – Feel Good

Using CBT with children and young people

Paul Stallard
Consultant Clinical Psychologist, Royal United Hospital, Bath, UK
Professor of Child and Family Mental Health, University of Bath, UK

JOHN WILEY & SONS, LTD

Other Wiley Editorial Offices

John Wiley & Sons Inc., 111 River Street, Hoboken, NJ 07030, USA

Jossey-Bass, 989 Market Street, San Francisco, CA 94103-1741, USA

Wiley-VCH Verlag GmbH, Boschstr. 12, D-69469 Weinheim, Germany

John Wiley & Sons Australia Ltd, 33 Park Road, Milton, Queensland 4064, Australia

John Wiley & Sons (Asia) Pte Ltd, 2 Clementi Loop #02-01, Jin Xing Distripark, Singapore 129809

John Wiley & Sons Canada Ltd, 22 Worcester Road, Etobicoke, Ontario, Canada M9W 1L1

Wiley also publishes its books in a variety of electronic formats. Some content that appears in
print may not be available in electronic books.

Library of Congress Cataloging-in-Publication Data
Stallard, Paul.
   A clinician's guide to think good – feel good : using CBT with children and young
people / Paul Stallard.
        p. cm.
   Includes bibliographical references and index.
   ISBN-13: 978-0-470-02508-6 (pbk. : alk. paper)
   ISBN-10: 0-470-02508-5 (pbk. : alk. paper)
  1. Behavior therapy for children. 2. Cognitive therapy for children. 3. Behavior
therapy for teenagers. 4. Cognitive therapy for teenagers. I. Title.
   RJ505.B4S718 2005
   618.92'89142—dc22
                                                                        2005008602

British Library of Cataloguing in Publication Data
A catalogue record for this book is available from the British Library

ISBN-13 978-0-470-02508-6 (P/B)

Typeset in 10/13 Scala and 12/15 Scala Sans by MCS Publishing Services Ltd, Salisbury, Wiltshire
Printed and bound in Great Britain by TJ International Ltd, Padstow, Cornwall

Contents

About the author

Dr Paul Stallard graduated as a clinical psychologist from Birmingham University in 1980. He worked with children and young people in the West Midlands before moving to the Department of Child and Family Psychiatry, Bath, in 1988. He has a part-time appointment at the University of Bath as Professor of Child and Family Mental Health, and has received a number of research grants exploring the effects of trauma and chronic illness on children. He has published over 70 peer-reviewed papers and his current research interests include the use of cognitive behaviour therapy with children, post-traumatic stress disorder and the psychological effects of chronic illness.

Acknowledgements

There are many people who have contributed, in one way or another, to the ideas contained within this book. Instead of providing an endless list of names I would quite simply like to thank everyone who has helped to shape and develop the ideas that are presented here.

There are however those who have made particularly significant or sustained contributions and to them I would like to express my specific thanks. To my family, Rosie, Luke and Amy for their patience, encouragement and support and, during the final stages of this project, for simply putting up with me! To my colleagues, Julie, Lucy, Kate and Helen for our helpful discussions and their constant enthusiasm and interest. Finally, this book would not have been possible without the children and young people I meet. The creativity and fun of children never fails to inspire me.

On-line resources

All the worksheets and psychoeducational materials are available free and in colour to purchasers of the print version. Visit the Wiley website at http://www.wiley.com/go/cliniciansguide to find out how to access and download relevant sections of the workbook, which can then be used in clinical sessions with your clients. The materials can be accessed and downloaded as often as required.

CHAPTER ONE

Overview

Child-focused cognitive behaviour therapy (CBT) is a popular form of psychotherapy that is now widely used with a range of mental health problems presented by children and young people. The empirical basis of child-focused CBT has been demonstrated through a number of randomised controlled trials that have resulted in a growing conviction amongst clinicians that CBT is the treatment of choice for many disorders. While research evaluating the efficacy and effectiveness of child-focused CBT is more substantive than that evaluating other psychotherapies, the research base is still limited. The first randomised controlled trial (RCT) of child-focused CBT was not reported until the beginning of the 1990s and it is only recently that RCTs evaluating child-focused CBT for obsessive-compulsive disorder (OCD) (Barrett *et al.* 2004) and chronic fatigue syndrome (Stulemeijer *et al.* 2005) have been published. Similarly there is only one published RCT of child-focused CBT for specific phobias (Silverman *et al.* 1999a) and social phobias (Spence *et al.* 2000) and none have yet been published exploring the efficacy of child-focused CBT in the treatment of anorexia nervosa.

The results of RCTs are generally positive and highlight that child-focused CBT results in considerable post-treatment and short-term gains when compared with a waiting list or attention placebo condition. However, the longer-term benefits or the superiority of child-focused CBT over other active interventions has received comparatively less attention and has not yet been consistently demonstrated. Similarly the core features that differentiate CBT from behaviour therapy have not been defined; the extent and specific focus within interventions upon the cognitive domain and assumed dysfunctional cognitive processes varies considerably; little is known about the effective treatment components or their sequencing; the optimum way of involving parents in child-focused CBT and their specific role is unclear.

Despite these limitations the interest in child-focused CBT continues to grow and has resulted in a range of materials and structured workbooks becoming available to help the Clinician undertake CBT with children. These include specific manuals such as the Coping Cat programme for children with anxiety (Kendall 1990); Stop and Think workbook for impulsive children (Kendall 1992); Keeping your Cool: the anger management workbook (Nelson & Finch 1996); the Freedom from Obsessions and Compulsions Using Special tools (FOCUS) programme (Barrett *et al.* 2004) and the Adolescent Coping with Depression Course (Clark *et al.* 1990). In addition there are materials to help children with social skills problems (Spence 1995), chronic fatigue syndrome (Chalder & Hussain 2002) and through anxiety and depression prevention programmes such as FRIENDS (Barrett *et al.* 2000a). There are also books that provide the Clinician with general practical ideas about how CBT can be adapted for use with children and young people (Friedberg & McClure 2002; Reinecke *et al.* 2003; Stallard 2002a).

Materials such as these provide the Clinician with a rich source of ideas that can inform and facilitate their clinical practice of child-focused CBT. This increase in the availability of child-friendly materials is welcomed and serves to highlight the current focus upon what to do (i.e. specific strategies) rather than how (i.e. the process). It is, perhaps, surprising to note that comparatively less attention has been paid to the process of undertaking child-focused CBT. Attending to the process of child-focused CBT is essential and ensures that the theoretical model and the core principles that underpin it are at the forefront of the Clinician's thinking. This will help the Clinician adapt and use CBT in a coherent and theoretically robust way and prevent the simplistic approach in which Clinicians simply dip into the model by taking and using individual strategies in a disconnected and uninformed way.

Think Good – Feel Good (Stallard 2002a) provided a number of practical ideas about how some of the specific techniques of CBT could be conveyed to, and adapted for use by, children. The book uses three characters to explore the three domains of CBT, cognitions (Thought Tracker), emotions (Feeling Finder) and behaviour (Go Getter). *A Clinician's Guide to Think Good–Feel Good* looks behind these strategies to focus upon the process that underpins their use. This book is not intended to be prescriptive and does not advocate a particular model or style for undertaking child-focused CBT. Instead it aims to promote increased awareness of some of the key issues that need to be considered and integrated into therapy in a way that is helpful for the Clinician, the child and the child's carer while maximising the effectiveness of the intervention.

This book will therefore consider a number of key clinical questions including:

- Is the child ready to actively engage in CBT?
- Can the child's motivation to change be increased?
- How does one develop a CBT case formulation?
- What sort of formulation framework should be used?
- Should parents be involved in child-focused CBT?
- How should they be involved and does it make a difference?
- What are the core elements of CBT programmes for particular disorders?
- Where does one start?
- How can Clinicians work in partnership with children?
- How can the process of guided discovery be facilitated?

In the course of this book the reader will be referred to some of the materials in *Think Good–Feel Good* (referred to as TGFG). This is done to provide examples of how some of the techniques and ideas of CBT can be adapted to facilitate the process of working with children. Once again the author is not being prescriptive but is instead attempting to direct the reader to materials and practical examples that can be modified and used to inform their clinical work.

▶ Engagement and readiness to change

At the beginning of the therapeutic process the Clinician meets with the child and the child's carers in order to assess the extent and nature of the current concerns and the outcomes they would like to achieve. This starting point is somewhat easier for Clinicians who work with adults since their clients are often already motivated and prepared to engage in therapy. Children do not usually refer themselves, may not share the concerns identified by their carers, and therefore may not have any ownership in securing any change. The child may therefore present as anxious, unmotivated or disinterested with no agenda for change.

An important first task is to assess the child's readiness to change and to identify whether they have any problems they would like to address or goals they would like to achieve. The *Stages of Change* model (Prochaska *et al.* 1992) provides a helpful framework that conceptualises change as a process rather than a dichotomous decision. This framework can be used to clarify where the child is in the change cycle and to inform the primary therapeutic focus. At the *pre-contemplation* stage the child will not have considered the possibility or, indeed, the need to change. This awareness begins to develop during the *contemplation* stage so that by the *preparation* stage the child has become interested and prepared to make some small change. The major change occurs during the *action* stage with these newly acquired skills being consolidated during the *maintenance* stage. The final stage is that of *relapse* where the child has to cope with any new setbacks or the return of their previous problems, dysfunctional behaviours or cognitive processes.

The model suggests that the primary therapeutic focus will depend upon where the child is in the change cycle. The main therapeutic work, where the child is ready to actively engage in CBT, occurs during the preparation, action and maintenance stages. During the relapse, pre-contemplation and contemplation stages the Clinician is primarily concerned with increasing the child's motivation, interest and commitment to change. During these stages *motivational interviewing* can provide the Clinician with a number of helpful ideas. Motivational interviewing provides a framework that helps the child to vocalise and resolve their *ambivalence* about possible change. Motivational interviewing is based on the central premise that the desire for change needs to come from the child rather than as a result of external pressure or persuasion. This is achieved by helping the child to *develop discrepancy* between where they currently are and where they would ideally like to be. Confronting or challenging the *child's resistance is avoided* since attempts at direct persuasion, argument or challenging result in a polarisation of views, which only serves to strengthen the child's position. Instead the Clinician aims to *reinforce any signs of self-efficacy* or behaviours that might indicate possible self-motivation.

During motivational interviewing the Clinician will be assessing the child's perception of the *importance* of change, their *readiness* to embark upon an agenda of change and their confidence in *achieving* this.

▶ Formulations

Once the child has identified possible goals and is prepared to engage in CBT the assessment process continues until a formulation has been developed. The formulation is the *shared understanding* of the child's problems presented within a cognitive behavioural framework. The formulation serves an important *psychoeducational function* and provides the current *working hypothesis, which informs the intervention.* The formulation is developed collaboratively and provides as much or as little information as necessary to help the child and their carers understand their problems.

There are many different types of formulations. The simplest are *mini-formulations*, which highlight the connection between two or three components of the cognitive model. These can be particularly helpful with younger children who may find it easier to attend to two or three elements at a time rather than simultaneously attempting to grapple with multiple elements spanning different time frames (e.g. important past experiences or current triggering events), concepts (e.g. distinguishing between different levels of cognitions such as core beliefs and assumptions) or domains (e.g. cognitive, emotional and behavioural). A mini-formulation could therefore help a child to see the connection between a situation and how they behave or between their thoughts and feelings. Simple mini-formulations can be developed separately and then combined to provide a descriptive summary of how a child thinks, feels and behaves in a particular situation.

General cognitive formulations use the key components of the general cognitive model to organise and structure the formulation. The simplest is the general *maintenance formulation* in which individual *triggering events* are identified and the resulting *thoughts, feelings and behaviours* tracked. An example of a framework that can be used to develop a simple maintenance formulation is provided in 'The Negative Trap' template. This is developed further in 'The 4-part Negative Trap' template in which feelings and *physiological symptoms* are separated. This is particularly helpful with children who misperceive the physiological changes associated with their feelings as signs of being physically unwell.

General onset formulations provide a historical account of the child's problems by highlighting important experiences and their role in shaping the child's cognitive framework. Important *early experiences* are summarised and *core beliefs, assumptions, triggering events, automatic thoughts, feelings and behaviours* specified. Onset formulations can be relatively simple or complex in which a number of specific early events/experiences or parental behaviours are linked to the development of particular core beliefs. An *onset formulation template* is provided.

Problem-specific formulations provide a framework in which a cognitive explanatory theoretical model is used to structure and organise the information related to the onset and maintenance of the child's problem. Recent advances in research have resulted in greater knowledge about the specific cognitions, feelings and behaviours associated with particular problems. A problem-specific formulation would, for example, highlight and bring together in a coherent way any of the specific attributions, beliefs, biases and parental behaviours that have been found to be associated with the onset and maintenance of the child's problems.

▶ The Socratic process and inductive reasoning

A key task of CBT is to facilitate the process of guided discovery by which the child is helped to reappraise their thoughts, beliefs and assumptions and to develop alternative, more balanced, functional and helpful cognitions and cognitive processes. This process of self-discovery and the promotion of self-efficacy are facilitated by *Socratic questioning*, a dialogue in which the child is helped to discover and attend to new or overlooked information. The Socratic dialogue utilises a range of questions, each with a different focus, that help the child systematically identify and test their thoughts. The first are *memory questions*, which are concerned with establishing facts and clarifying information about specific events and feelings. *Translation questions* then explore the meaning the child attributes to these events with *interpretation questions* seeking possible similarities, connections or generalisations between and across other events or situations. *Application questions* help the child to draw upon their previous knowledge and to consider past information that might be helpful in considering these current events. *Analysis questions* are then used to help the child systematically evaluate their thoughts, assumptions and beliefs with *synthesis questions* being used to help them consider new or alternative possibilities. The process is completed by the use of *evaluation questions*, which help the child re-evaluate and reappraise their cognitions in the light of their newly discovered knowledge.

Useful ways of helping the child engage in the process of *inductive reasoning* in which they learn to set appropriate boundaries around their universal cognitive definitions or biases are discussed. Inductive reasoning helps the child to consider new or overlooked information and can involve helping the child to consider a *third party perspective*, highlighting *past experiences*, or the use of *metaphors* as a way of engaging in *analogical comparisons*. A second method of inductive reasoning involves a structured process of *eliminative causal comparisons* in which the assumed relationship between events is systematically evaluated. This can involve either *confirming* or *disconfirming* the assumed relationship. A visual way of undertaking this task, the *Links in the Chain* worksheet is provided.

▶ Involving parents in child-focused CBT

Important systemic influences that contribute to the onset and maintenance of the child's problems or which will positively or negatively effect treatment outcome need to be considered and addressed during the intervention. The most important influence is that of parents/carers and Clinicians are increasingly recognising the need to involve parents in child-focused CBT. However, the role of parents and their involvement in child-focused CBT has varied considerably. The most limited role is that of a *Facilitator* in which the parent attends one or two psychoeducational sessions designed to educate them in the cognitive model and to inform them about the skills their child will be learning. The next role is that of the *co-Clinician* where the parent participates in the same treatment programme as their child. The primary focus of the intervention remains the resolution of the child's problems with parental involvement being concerned with facilitating transfer and use of skills to the child's everyday environment. Some programmes have involved parents as *co-Clients* in which their behaviour becomes a direct target of the intervention. In addition to the child receiving CBT to help address their own problems, parents receive help with their own difficulties or learn new skills such as managing or resolving conflict. They may also be helped to address any of their behaviours that have contributed to the development or maintenance of their child's problems. The final model is that where the *parent is the Client* and thus the primary target of intervention and change. The child does not necessarily attend any treatment sessions with the intervention being focused upon addressing important dysfunctional parental cognitions. These may be related to their child, the reasons for their child's behaviour or their parenting efficacy. This may be a precursor to a subsequent intervention which, once important parental distortions and biases have been addressed, may be more likely to be successful.

While there is widespread acceptance amongst clinicians that parental involvement in child-focused CBT is essential, comparatively few studies have examined the important question of whether this enhances the efficacy of the intervention. The results of randomised controlled trials that have investigated this are surprising. Additional gains are sometimes modest but overall provide some limited support that child-focused CBT can be enhanced by parental involvement.

Despite the considerable variability in the role and involvement of parents in child-focused CBT, most interventions share a number of features. All involve *psychoeducation* in which the parents are provided with an understanding of the cognitive model and a cognitive explanation of the child's problems. A psychoeducational handout for children ('What is Cognitive Behaviour Therapy (CBT)?') and parents ('What Parents Need to Know about Cognitive Behaviour Therapy (CBT)') that explains the model, goals and process of CBT are provided. *Contingency management* is emphasised and in particular the need for parents to praise and attend to their child's use of new skills while ignoring any inappropriate cognitions, feelings or behaviours. Those programmes addressing childhood anxiety typically involve a component designed to reduce the *parents' own anxiety*. Important biased and dysfunctional parental cognitions that interfere with or limit the parents' ability to support their child are systematically addressed and challenged as part of a process of *cognitive restructuring*. Finally, many aim to improve *parent–child relationships* by teaching new skills such as conflict resolution, problem solving or general behaviour management.

▶ The process of child-focused CBT

The specific nature of the therapeutic relationship within which child-focused CBT is undertaken has received comparatively little attention. While generally recognised as an important moderator of treatment outcome, the specific relationship skills that are important have not been identified. A model based upon the *PRECISE* process is proposed as a way of conceptualising some of the skills that will promote the key principles underlying CBT of collaboration and guided discovery.

The first principle is concerned with developing a *Partnership* between the Clinician and child in which an open and collaborative way of working is promoted and the important and active contribution of the child to the therapeutic process is highlighted and encouraged. The intervention then has to be pitched at the *Right developmental level* so that the child can fully engage with the process of CBT. This requires the concepts and strategies of CBT to be adapted so that they are compatible with the child's linguistic, cognitive and social development. *Empathy* is an important part of the process in which the Clinician conveys interest and aims to understand as fully as possible how the child perceives their world and the events that occur. This also conveys a message to the child that their views are important and that the Clinician wants to hear them. *Creativity* is the process by which the Clinician engages and maintains the child's interest as the concepts and strategies of CBT are carefully crafted to the child's particular interests. The idea of guided discovery is promoted through the idea of *Investigation* in which the child is encouraged to identify their beliefs and assumptions and to use behavioural experiments to objectively test them. *Self-discovery and efficacy* promotes the notion of empowerment and encourages the child to build upon their own ideas and to find their own solutions. This involves helping the child to identify and acknowledge previous successful experiences, their strengths or skills and to consider whether they can be used to help with the current situation. Finally, CBT with children needs to be *Enjoyable* so that the process is fun, entertaining and engaging.

▶ Adapting CBT for children

There has been considerable debate about the age at which children can participate in CBT. Essentially this argument focuses around the issue of whether young children have the cognitive platform necessary to engage in CBT or whether CBT has not been sufficiently adapted for them to access. This argument is briefly reviewed and the cognitive demands and capacity of children to engage with CBT discussed.

The need to adapt CBT by using more non-verbal techniques is highlighted. *Games* provide a familiar medium for children, which can be used to highlight some of the key concepts of CBT or to teach and practise specific strategies or problem-solving skills. *Puppets* provide a safe and engaging way of communicating with young children. They can be used for the purposes of *assessment,* to *highlight common problems* or to *model new skills* and to engage the child in role-plays in which they can *practise* using more helpful coping skills. *Story telling* is another familiar way of communicating with children and can be used for different purposes. *Guided* or *open stories* can be used for the purpose of assessment to identify potentially important thoughts or feelings. *Therapeutic stories* can be used to help the child consider and attend to new information that will help them to reappraise and re-evaluate their cognitions. *Visualisation* and imagery also provide a useful medium with imagery being used for *assessment* and *psychoeducation.* Pictures can, for example, serve as visual prompts to elicit possible thoughts or to highlight the connection between thoughts and feelings. Visualisation can also be therapeutic when the image helps to *change the emotional content* of problematic situations. *Emotive imagery* helps the child to develop images incompatible with anger or fear, such as calming or humorous images. Finally, there are a range of other non-verbal methods that can be used to complement and enhance the verbal component of the treatment. *Cartoons and thought bubbles* can be used to assess cognitions or feelings; *diagrams* to highlight helpful and unhelpful ways of coping; *pie charts and rating scales* to quantify feelings or to identify and reassess attributions; *externalising* problems by drawing them helps to separate the child from their problems and provides a way of making the problem less abstract.

'The Thought Tracker Quiz' provides an example of a simple quiz that can be used to help children to identify the different thinking errors that they might make. Prepared worksheets that list the common emotional and behavioural changes associated with the emotions of *worry, anger and sadness* are provided. An example of a *responsibility pie* and a worksheet to help younger children understand that a thought bubble represents their thoughts ('Sharing our Thoughts') are also included.

▶ Core components of CBT programmes for internalising problems

There is significant variation in the specific treatment components, sequencing and cognitive emphasis of interventions that fall under the general label of CBT. CBT is not a homogeneous intervention delivered in a standardised way but instead embraces a multitude of strategies combined and delivered in different ways to a heterogeneous client group of differing ages and differing cognitive, linguistic and social development. Comparatively little is known about the effective components or whether CBT can be enhanced by directly focusing upon the key cognitions assumed to underlie the child's problems. The number of sessions involved in child-focused CBT vary and little attention has been paid to assessing cognitive change or the assumed relationship with problem resolution.

A three-level approach to undertaking individual CBT is suggested. *Level 1* interventions are primarily *psychoeducational* and aim to develop a clear CBT formulation explaining the onset and/or maintenance of the child's problems. *Level 2* interventions are the next stage of treatment and aim to develop and promote particular skills and strategies that will help the child to *cope with particular problems. Level 3* interventions are concerned with identifying, testing and reappraising *general dysfunctional cognitions* and behaviours that pervade a number of situations. In addition, they prepare the child for potential relapse.

The core components of standardised treatment programmes that have been evaluated and used with *anxiety disorders, depression, obsessional compulsive disorder and posttraumatic stress disorder* are reviewed and potentially important cognitions highlighted. Psychoeducational summary sheets for each of these problems which give an overview of common symptoms and some of the specific strategies that might be helpful are provided in 'Beating Anxiety'; 'Fighting Back Depression'; 'Controlling Worries and Habits'; and 'Coping with Trauma'.

CHAPTER TWO

Engagement and readiness to change

▶ Engaging with children

The process of engagement and the readiness of the child to actively participate and remain in therapy are important issues that need to be assessed. Graham (2005) suggests that engagement requires the child to acknowledge:

- that there is a difficulty or problem;
- that this problem could be changed;
- that the form of help offered could bring about this change;
- that the Clinician is able to help the child develop the skills they require to secure this change.

The process of engagement with children is particularly complex and many potential barriers have to be acknowledged and overcome before the child is ready to collaborate in CBT. In particular:

- Children do not typically refer themselves for help. They are often referred by others and thus their ownership of any problems or motivation to engage in any form of therapy may initially be extremely limited.
- Children may not share the concerns of those who referred them. This is often exemplified with school non-attendance where the objective of the parent and school in securing the child's attendance may not be the main priority, or indeed a priority shared by the child.
- Children may see responsibility for the referred problem as residing in someone else. An adolescent, for example, referred with problems of anger management clearly described his temper outbursts as the responsibility of his teacher, commenting, 'If she didn't pick on me, I wouldn't get angry and lose it.'
- Children may be unable to think about how things could be different or identify any particular targets. This is a common problem with children who become very familiar with their current situation and are unable to think about how this could change or be different. This could be reflected by comments such as, 'I don't know; it has always been like this'.
- Previous experience with adults may lead children to assume a passive role. They expect others to identify their problems and to tell them how they need to change without necessarily having any ownership of either the problem or the change process.

For reasons such as these, children may initially present as reluctant, anxious, unmotivated, disinterested or bored. Careful attention therefore needs to be paid to the process of engagement and in assessing the child's readiness and commitment to change. The process of engagement may take time as the aims, goals and priorities of the intervention are elicited, negotiated and prioritised as an acceptable starting place for both the child and carers.

> Engagement and the identification of a shared agenda needs careful consideration since children:
>
> ▪ do not typically refer themselves for therapy
>
> ▪ may have no ownership of the identified concerns
>
> ▪ may believe that responsibility for change resides elsewhere
>
> ▪ may be unable to think about how the present situation could be different.

▶ The Stages of Change (Prochaska *et al.* 1992)

A useful framework for considering the child's readiness for actively participating in therapy is provided in the Stages of Change model (Prochaska *et al.* 1992) that has been extensively used in the drug and alcohol field. The model highlights how the client's readiness to change is a process that develops gradually, varies over time and is not simply a dichotomous decision. The clinical assumption implicit in the model is that the Clinician's behaviour needs to reflect where the child is in the change cycle. The model therefore provides a framework that can potentially help the Clinician to guide and pitch the focus of the therapeutic process at the most appropriate level.

The framework conceptualises the individual as moving from being unwilling or unmotivated to make any change through to considering possible targets and then deciding and preparing to make some small change. More determined and significant changes then follow with these new skills being incorporated into everyday life and maintained over time. Inevitably this will be followed by some degree of relapse. At this stage confidence may need to be rebuilt and so reflection upon past experiences and helpful strategies is encouraged.

Understanding the child's readiness to change and where they are in the cycle can help to determine the type and main focus of the intervention. As highlighted in Figure 2.1, in the initial stages the Clinician may be more concerned with securing and increasing the child's commitment to change by the use of motivational interviewing techniques. It is only in the latter stages after the child has identified the change they would like to secure that CBT is appropriate.

▪ Pre-contemplation

It is at this stage that many children have their first contact with the Clinician. Often they attend appointments because of pressure from others, have little or no ownership of the presenting problem and will usually not have considered the need for, or indeed possibility of, change. The child may appear angry or in denial stating, 'I don't have a problem' or 'There is nothing wrong with me'. They may appear disinterested, 'I don't need to be here' or resigned to the current situation, 'I have always felt like this'. Alternatively they may appear unmotivated, feeling that they have no control over what happens, 'There is nothing I can do about this'. Statements such as these indicate hopelessness or resistance. They signal that the child has not identified a problem, has no possible agenda for change or does not believe that the current situation could be different.

Therapeutic pitfall

In situations such as this there is a natural tendency for the Clinician to work hard to convince or persuade the child that change is needed and is indeed possible. The Clinician therefore engages in an active process of argument or debate as a way of demonstrating that

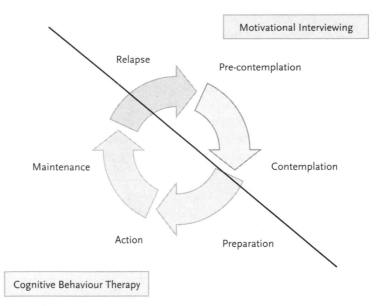

Figure 2.1 The Stages of Change model and primary therapeutic focus
Source: From Prochaska *et al.* (1992). In search of how people change. *American Psychologist*, **47**, 1102–1104.

the child has a problem that needs to be addressed. Often this results in growing resistance or overt scepticism from the child who may enter into arguments with the Clinician and become increasingly polarised in their respective positions. Alternatively resistance may be covert as the child adopts a more passive role and appears quiet, withdrawn and disinterested, as they feel that their views are increasingly ignored or dismissed as unimportant.

In order to prevent this negative situation from developing, the Clinician should aim to elicit from the child their views about potential targets and the possibility of change. This may require careful assessment of the child's knowledge in order to assess whether their apparent passivity is due to a lack of information. Putting the child's difficulties in context and highlighting how the situation could possibly be different may provide the child with new information upon which they could consider possible goals and the need to change.

- 'A number of young people struggle with written school work but sometimes they can be helped to get their ideas down by using computers.'
- 'Children often worry about their parents but many can be helped to control these worries so that they can do things like sleeping over at a friend's house.'
- 'I hear that you think your teacher picks on you and this is her problem. But you told me that you are the only one in the class she picks on. Is there something you do that means she notices you more than the others?'

Identifying possible gaps in the child's knowledge by providing new information may therefore help them to reconsider the need for, and possibility of, change.

Questions during the pre-contemplation stage should aim to identify discrepancies between where the child is now and where they would like to be in the future. Questions should emphasise that the Clinician is interested in learning more about the child's views such as:

- 'Is there anything at home or school that **you** would like to be different?'
- 'What are the biggest worries for **you** at the moment?'
- 'When would this become a worry or problem for **you**?'
- 'What would have to happen for **you** to want things to change and be different?'

It should, however, be noted that some children find it very difficult to contemplate future change. Children tend to be more present- than future-orientated in their outlook. They may find it difficult to identify a different future or the potential benefits of engaging in any intervention that might take a little time to secure (Piacentini & Bergman 2001).

If the child continues to be unable to identify any potential goals, then the Clinician should acknowledge this. The Clinician should reflect what the child has said, emphasise the importance of the child's views while highlighting that the Clinician is available to provide the child with any help and support whenever the child wishes. The Clinician therefore remains optimistic and accessible but acknowledges that the time may not be right to engage in a programme of active change.

> ■ The therapeutic aim at the pre-contemplation stage is to promote discrepancy between the current situation and what the child would like to achieve

■ Contemplation

By this stage the child has begun to identify some potential areas that they would like to change but may appear unsure about the possibility that this can be achieved. They may appear ambivalent and will often follow any positive statements with a number of obstacles and barriers as to why this could not be pursued or achieved.

- I suppose it would be good ... **but** ... it will take too much time.'
- 'It would be nice if this was different ... **but** ... I can't be bothered.'
- 'It would create less hassle ... **but** ... it just won't work.'

Therapeutic pitfall

The Clinician, often heartened by the growing motivation within the child, attempts to build upon their growing conviction by helping the child to recognise that they can be successful and bring about change. Often this results in the introduction of assignments or behavioural experiments as positive empowering ways of objectively testing the child's predictions and demonstrating that change is indeed possible.

The therapeutic pitfall at this stage is too jump in too quickly with experiments and targets without fully working through the potential barriers and obstacles. Instead the Clinician should undertake a full exploration with the child of the potential benefits and barriers to change before any experiments are undertaken. Thoroughly working through these issues provides opportunities to highlight and acknowledge uncertainties, discuss any ambivalence and prepare the child for any potential problems, thereby increasing the likelihood of success.

Questions that might help the child to articulate their ambivalence and to begin to identify potential solutions include:

- 'What **might stop you** from trying this?'
- 'What **might go wrong**?'
- 'What **might help** you to give this a try?'
- 'What **has helped** in the past?'

> ■ The therapeutic aim at the contemplation stage is to undertake a thorough analysis of ambivalence and potential obstacles in order to maximise the likelihood of subsequent success.

■ Preparation

By this stage the child is ready to make some small change. They will have identified potential targets, worked through their ambivalence, discussed potential barriers that might prevent their achievement and are prepared to experiment. The child may not, however, feel very confident about the likelihood of success and may focus upon and recount previous episodes where they have tried and failed.

The aim of the Clinician is to continue to build upon the child's growing motivation and confidence by maximising the possibility of a successful experience. This will involve drawing upon previous experiences and focusing the child's attention upon some of the skills, thoughts and behaviours that have been important and helpful in the past. The Clinician adopts a positive focus emphasising the child's useful skills and strategies while highlighting other potential pitfalls that need to be thought through and addressed.

Therapeutic pitfall

The first steps in the process of change are clearly important. In order to increase the child's motivation and confidence it is important that they experience some degree of early success. The first steps and targets therefore need to be small and achievable so that this positive momentum can be built upon. Larger targets are enticing and can be positively viewed as the child's determination to secure significant change but this enthusiasm needs to be tempered whilst the child's fragile confidence is built upon.

The potential pitfall is to select targets that are too large or ambitious, take time to achieve or are outside of the child's influence and thus ability to change. Large targets increase the likelihood that the child will fail or be unsuccessful. In the early stages it is important for the child to gain some fairly immediate positive feedback that will fuel their growing motivation. Goals that will take some time to achieve or which will result in some delayed gratification should therefore be avoided at this stage. Similarly a child may select a goal of initiating social contact with a group of children only to find that they are snubbed and rejected. The outcome of this experiment is dependent upon others and so should be avoided. Early failure may reinforce potential beliefs about powerlessness or lack of control and discourage any further attempts at change.

It is therefore important that the Clinician ensures that potential targets are:

- realistic
- short-term
- achievable so that the child experiences early success
- within the control of the child/parent to bring about
- result in some form of reward or positive reinforcement.

> ■ The therapeutic goal at the preparation stage is to help the child identify small, realistic and achievable targets.

■ Action

This is the stage at which the child is ready to fully engage in therapy and to secure significant change. The child is now ready to actively participate in CBT and to build upon their early successes. The Clinician provides the CBT framework, skills and guidance that will educate the child in the cognitive model, will provide a cognitive explanation of their difficulties and will enable the child to develop and apply new skills to their particular problems.

Therapeutic pitfall

The main problems at this stage are that the child's agenda and targets can become lost, the intervention is inappropriately paced or the collaborative and active process of guided discovery that underpins CBT is not maintained. It is therefore important that the Clinician builds in regular review meetings in which the agreed targets are clearly agreed and the progress towards their attainment reviewed. The nature of the therapeutic process needs to be made explicit so that the child is aware they have an active role and will be engaged in experimentation to discover what might be helpful. Similarly the Clinician needs to attend to the process of CBT and to ensure that the process and techniques have been adapted so that they are congruent with the child's development.

> ■ The action stage is where CBT is undertaken and significant change is achieved.
>
> ■ The goals and process of securing their achievement need to be made explicit and regularly reviewed.

■ **Maintenance**

During the maintenance stage the child is encouraged to generalise their new skills to different situations and to monitor and reflect upon their practice. The aim of the Clinician is to encourage integration of these skills into the child's everyday life so that positive change is maintained. In addition, the child is helped to consider and expect future difficulties and to develop problem-solving skills that can be used to plan and cope with any future relapses.

Therapeutic pitfall

Problems at this stage tend to focus around two main areas. Firstly, withdrawing too early, resulting in the child receiving insufficient support in implementing, testing and using their new skills. This problem is common and is often a consequence of the child's newly found confidence and enthusiasm resulting in them being keen to end therapy and to 'go it alone'. Possible problems may not have been encountered or fully resolved as the child remains focused upon their success and does not have an opportunity to experience and be supported and guided through possible setbacks and difficulties.

The second potential problem is that the child has not been sufficiently prepared for any potential setbacks and how they will cope with them when they arise. Once again, this is often a result of therapeutic enthusiasm where the clinical sessions remain focused upon celebrating current success rather than planning for potential future problems.

Both these issues need to be directly addressed during the maintenance stage so that the child is prepared and helped to plan and cope with future difficulties. A simple and easy solution is to ensure that one session is explicitly devoted to coping with future problems and setbacks. In addition, routinely scheduling a three month review provides an opportunity to monitor progress, resolve problems and reinforce useful skills.

> ■ During the maintenance stage the child is helped to integrate their skills into everyday life and to plan for future setbacks.

■ **Relapse**

Inevitably the child will experience future problems and setbacks and encounter situations when their old patterns and difficulties return. At times such as these the child may question the usefulness and effectiveness of their new skills. The aim of the Clinician is to maintain the child's confidence and to encourage reflection about how they coped with previous situations and what they found helpful. It is also important to challenge any beliefs about the permanency of the setback and in particular to emphasise that while difficult, the child has been able to positively change the situation in the past and probably can do so again. The Clinician remains hopeful and optimistic as they help the child attend to information and skills that have proven to be useful.

> ▪ During the relapse stage the therapeutic aim is to help the child reflect upon previous helpful skills and strategies and to encourage their use.

The stages of change model provides a way of understanding the child's readiness to change which in turn informs the main therapeutic focus. The child is more able to benefit from CBT during the preparation, action and maintenance stages. By these stages the child will have identified possible goals and will be sufficiently motivated to secure their achievement. However, in the relapse, pre-contemplation and contemplation stages the Clinician will primarily be concerned with increasing the child's motivation. During these stages the Clinician many find the techniques of motivational interviewing useful.

▶ Motivational interviewing

Motivational interviewing has been defined as 'a directive client-centred counselling style for eliciting behaviour change by helping clients to explore and resolve ambivalence' (Rollnick & Miller 1995). The aim of motivational interviewing is to develop discrepancy between the current situation and what the child would ideally like. In turn this discrepancy is hypothesised to motivate the child to secure their goal.

▪ Principles of motivational interviewing

Rollnick & Miller (1995) emphasise the need to distinguish between the techniques used in motivational interviewing and the philosophy that underpins the process. The therapeutic style is embedded within the philosophy and is based upon the following seven principles.

Motivation to change is elicited from within not imposed from without

The early stages of motivational interviewing are concerned with helping the child to identify their potential targets for change. Attempts to elicit motivation by external threats (e.g. 'you know that you will be excluded from school if you don't try to control your temper') or persuasion ('I am sure this can be different so why don't you give it a try') should be avoided.

Ambivalence needs to be articulated and resolved

During motivational interviewing the Clinician aims to facilitate a process that allows the child to express both sides of their ambivalence. Children may not have engaged in this sort of discussion before and may find such an opportunity helpful. The child can weigh up the potential advantages or disadvantages of action or inaction. This can help them to become clearer and make an informed choice as to the path they would like to pursue. This process can be done verbally or as a visual exercise using 'The Scales of Change'.

Sam (14), for example, was keen to become friends with Surinder but was very reluctant to talk with her. 'The Scales of Change' exercise was used to help Sam communicate his ambivalence.

Although it looked as if there were more reasons for Sam to talk with Surinder, this changed when Sam was asked to rate the importance of each item. Sam was very worried about being shown up and ignored and this far outweighed all the potential benefits.

Direct persuasion is not effective and serves to increase resistance

Attempts to motivate the child by persuading them to try a particular course of action are often unsuccessful. If the child has no ownership of a problem then they will have no commitment or investment to change. With adolescents, direct attempts at persuasion can be counter-productive. Therapeutic persuasion often results in increased verbal hostility as the young person counters the Clinician's persuasive attempts by adopting a more rigid position, which they feel obliged to defend and justify.

The process takes as long as necessary for ambivalence to be expressed, clarified and resolved

The process of motivational interviewing can feel slow and at times frustrating. The process cannot however be rushed. It is only after the child has identified the need to change and resolved issues regarding their readiness and confidence to secure this that therapy can begin. This leisurely, exploratory approach may often conflict with the expectations and time frame of others, resulting in the Clinician having to manage competing pressures from other vested parties (e.g. parents, schools, etc.) keen for some immediate change. The Clinician therefore needs to remain focused upon the child as the key partner in the therapeutic relationship while managing and containing the demands of others.

Readiness to change fluctuates over time

During motivational interviewing the Clinician needs to pay particular attention to signs of resistance and denial and to use these to alter the focus and pace of the interview. A child may, for example, seem committed to securing change at the end of one session but appear resistant during the subsequent session. This may be due to a variety of intervening events that have served to increase the child's uncertainty. Alternatively the Clinician may have misjudged the child's behaviour. The previous positive signals of agreement may have been misread as signs of self-motivation rather than as a passive acceptance to please the Clinician and end the session. Readiness to change will fluctuate over time and the Clinician needs to continue to assess possible signs of resistance that might suggest that they have moved too far ahead in the change process.

The Clinician actively facilitates the expression of ambivalence

Motivational interviewing is a focused and directive technique in which the child's ambivalence is viewed as the central obstacle that needs to be resolved in order to initiate change. It is assumed that insufficient attention is paid to this task with Clinicians often moving towards the agreement and establishment of intervention programmes before the child's ambivalence has been fully explored. In turn this increases the likelihood that the child will feel 'unheard', have no ownership of the process, become increasingly passive or hostile during sessions and prematurely drop out of therapy. The Clinician needs to remain focused upon the goal of actively facilitating the child's expression of ambivalence. Their uncertainty needs to be acknowledged and openly and directly talked about.

Motivational interviewing takes place within a partnership model

The key features of the therapeutic relationship are the same as those in which CBT is undertaken and are described more fully in Chapter 6. The relationship is a positive and supportive one in which the child is viewed as a partner. Their ideas are welcomed and respected even if they conflict with those of the Clinician or others. Responsibility for determining and securing change resides within the child and the Clinician attends to, and reinforces, any positive signs, such as the child attending appointments, talking about problems, sharing their ambivalence and feelings. Motivational interviewing helps the child identify and notice their strengths and any positive indications that suggest a growing motivation to change.

Motivational interviewing is based upon the following principles:

- Motivation for changes comes from within the child, not by external persuasion.
- The child's ambivalence needs to be articulated and resolved.
- The Clinician works in partnership with the child to actively facilitate this process.
- Resistance is a reaction to Clinician behaviour and is not the child's problem.

■ Readiness, importance and confidence

The child's motivation to change is multidimensional and according to Rollnick *et al.* (1999) incorporates the dimensions of importance, readiness and confidence.

- Importance is the recognition and need the child ascribes to securing a different outcome.
- Readiness relates to how prepared the child feels to embark upon an active process of change.
- Confidence is the child's ability and perceived self-efficacy to achieve the desired change.

As part of the process of motivational interviewing, children can be asked to rate themselves on each of these dimensions using a simple 10-point visual analogue rating scale. This provides a useful way of quantifying the child's motivation which can be reviewed in each session to highlight variations and any positive shifts. This can also help the Clinician focus more specifically upon those dimensions of the child's motivation that are low.

- Low importance – the Clinician needs to focus upon providing information that will help the child to recognise that different outcomes are possible and in developing discrepancy between the current situation and their future plans.

- Low readiness – the Clinician needs to explore with the child when the timing would be right to embark upon a process of change and how they can best prepare themselves for achieving it.
- Low confidence – the Clinician needs to help the child discover the skills they have previously found useful and to develop a systematic plan that will increase the likelihood of success.

> ■ The child's motivation to change depends upon their perception of how important change is, how ready they are to change and how confident they are to achieve it.

■ Techniques of motivational interviewing

The process of motivational interviewing employs a number of specific counselling skills in order to achieve the following four aims:

- To help the child feel understood.
- To develop discrepancy between where the child is now and where they ideally would like to be.
- To avoid confronting and challenging resistance.
- To highlight and support self-efficacy.

Help the child feel understood

Empathy is used to gain a full understanding of how children view themselves, their world and their future. When someone feels understood and valued they are more prepared to engage in a full and open discussion about their concerns and worries. It begins to feel safe to voice uncertainty and ambivalence and, in turn, this will help the Clinician to understand the child's position and the meaning they attach to events.

Summaries are a useful way of demonstrating empathy and clearly demonstrate that the Clinician has listened to, and heard, what the child has said. This is particularly helpful during the initial stages and highlights to the child that they are important, have useful things to say, and that the Clinician wants to hear them. It can be useful to start summaries with an invitation to the child to 'tell me if I have got this wrong' so that they are encouraged to correct any misunderstandings, thereby minimising potential arguments. This also encourages the child to adopt an active role in the sessions and explicitly defines the nature of the relationship as a partnership where the Clinician does not have all the 'right' answers.

Develop discrepancy

The development of discrepancy creates a gap that highlights how the child's current behaviour is unlikely to lead them towards the goals they desire, thereby increasing their motivation to engage in a process of change.

Open-ended questions can be particularly useful in helping the child to volunteer their own goals and explore uncertainties. In motivational interviewing these are seen as creating a self-initiated impetus for moving forward. Closed questions encourage the child to adopt a more passive role, although they can be helpful with less communicative children and are easier for younger or less able children to answer. They are, however, prescriptive and provide a range of Clinician-identified options which may not necessarily reflect the child's issues. In turn this sets up a demand characteristic where the child might feel under pressure to passively agree with the provided options.

Similarly, the Clinician might develop discrepancy by reflecting back to the child's apparent contradictions in what they are saying. A child may, for example, say that they don't want any friends (present time focus) but in the longer term talk about going in to town at the weekend with a group of mates (future time focus). The aim is therefore to highlight the child's own internal contradictions rather than introducing an alternative external viewpoint. The former requires children to resolve their own ambivalence; the latter encourages argument.

Avoid challenging and confronting resistance

Rolling with resistance rather than challenging it minimises the possibility of the Clinician being drawn into potential arguments where positions can become polarised. Instead the Clinician can positively use the child's resistance as a way of discovering more about their ambivalence. This can lead to the child developing their own solutions and plans which they themselves will be able to defend.

When the Clinician becomes aware of the child's resistance they should stop, stand back and carefully listen to what the child is saying. Reflective listening is a useful strategy that allows the Clinician to reflect upon what the child is saying and provides opportunities to focus upon and emphasise any change talk. The child's view is therefore acknowledged but not challenged and if necessary the interview can shift into a different area in an attempt to find possible areas of change.

Alternatively the child's view can be under-emphasised or over-exaggerated as a way of encouraging them to challenge their own statements. Undershooting minimises the child's motivation to change 'so there is nothing at all that could be better in your life at the present moment' while overshooting encourages them to challenge their own views, e.g. 'what you are telling me is that you will **never ever** be able to have any friends'.

Highlight and support self-efficacy

Self-efficacy can be supported by attending to and reinforcing signs of motivation from the child that change is possible. Statements that suggest the possibility of change are important motivators that need to be reinforced. Similarly, the child needs to be helped to develop a belief that they have ideas and skills that can bring this about and that change can be achieved in many different ways. This may be particularly important with children who may be anxious and reluctant to commit to a particular course of action, fearing that they may have chosen the 'wrong plan'.

Affirmation is a useful method in which the Clinician selects and reinforces the child's strengths. The child is helped to attend to their possible skills and successes rather than their failures or inadequacies. This is a useful way of countering perceived feelings of hopelessness that change is possible and feelings of helplessness that this can be brought about by the child. While it is often helpful, Schmidt (2004) highlights that some young people dislike being praised, and so it is important to do this in a low-key or humorous way.

Motivational interviewing uses techniques to:

- promote empathy by using summaries and reflective listening
- develop discrepancy by using open-ended questions and highlighting the child's contradictions
- roll with resistance by standing back and using reflective listening
- highlight self-efficacy by affirmation and selective attention.

■ **Define the approach**

The philosophy and style of motivational interviewing with an emphasis upon curiosity, respect, minimisation of conflict and acknowledgement of choice and ambivalence works particularly well with adolescents (Schmidt 2004). The focus upon the child's individual goals as opposed to those of parents or the wider system again highlights the importance and centrality of the child in the process. However, this position may feel unusual for the child and be viewed with some degree of suspicion. Similarly, the equality of the Clinician–client relationship will probably be a new experience for many children. They may appear reticent and may expect the Clinician to take the lead role, to ask questions, rather than feeling able to openly and equally contribute their views. The Clinician therefore needs to make time during the first meeting to distinguish themselves from other adults and to explicitly state the philosophy of their approach.

■ **Dealing with serious and concerning behaviour**

A dilemma posed by interventions that aim to increase self-motivation and achievement relates to the issue of challenging, rather than passively colluding with, concerning behaviour. There will be situations when the child needs to be confronted with the seriousness of their behaviour (e.g. deliberate self-harm) irrespective of whether they see it as a problem or share this view about its seriousness. This does not, however, need to become the focus for any argument or conflict. Instead the Clinician's view can be conveyed in a clear, factual statement, 'I am concerned that you continue to feel so low that you keep cutting yourself'. Similarly, children may not see the potential benefits of some targets or share the objectives of their parents or statutory authorities. School-refusing children, for example, often see returning to school as a low priority. In situations such as this, Schmidt (2004) suggests using the concept of a 'higher authority'. The concept brings to the child's attention important information that acknowledges the context within which they operate but limits the choices that they, and the Clinician, can make. The Clinician could, for example, explain that 'the law says that you have to go to school, so let's look at how you would like to make this happen'.

Rollnick & Miller (1995) suggest that Clinicians need to be clear when they are using motivational interviewing as a method of increasing readiness to change and when they are confronting concerning behaviour. There will undoubtedly be times when the child has to be confronted with the reality of their behaviour, e.g. 'If you do not increase your food intake, you will have to be admitted to hospital.' However, while attempts to persuade, use professional authority or provide direct advice may increase the child's motivation to pursue a course of action, this is different from motivational interviewing.

■ **Dealing with resistance or counter-motivation**

Motivational interviewing is concerned with resolving ambivalence and reducing resistance. The term resistance is often viewed as a negative or pejorative term implying that someone is perhaps being intentionally stubborn or challenging. Construing ambivalence in this way can result in the Clinician becoming more challenging and confrontational as they try to convince the child of the 'error of their ways'. This negative connotation has resulted in some preferring to use the less emotive term, counter-motivation.

Signs of counter-motivation include active strategies such as denial, arguing, changing the subject or talking about comparatively trivial issues, or more passive strategies such as appearing bored or disinterested or refusing to talk. In motivational interviewing these are seen as signals for the Clinician to reflect upon and check their own behaviour. The Clinician might need to consider:

- Is the pace appropriate?
- Has the Clinician moved to planning for change before the child is ready?
- Is the child frustrated at feeling unheard or by being unable to vocalise their ambivalence?

Once checked, the Clinician can identify the possible trap they have fallen into and to rectify their behaviour.

The question and answer trap

This can be a common difficulty with children who are perhaps unfamiliar with volunteering or spontaneously expressing their views. This results in the Clinician adopting a more active role, which in turn results in the child becoming more passive as they await the next question. The child does not therefore volunteer their own thoughts, resulting in the interview being largely guided by the Clinician's hunches as to what possible areas need to be vocalised and explored. In these situations the Clinician may consider experimenting with more non-verbal materials.

The confrontational and denial trap

Clinicians will be aware that they often react to apparently reasonable justifications for no change with increased attempts to persuade the child or challenge their reasons. Rather than enter this confrontational trap, the motivational interviewer attempts to steer the conversation towards helping the child voice their views as to the sort of change they may desire and when this could be achieved. Simply pushing people to justify their position results in more entrenched positions developing, which attempts to change prove pointless. The Clinician may find it helpful to spend a few minutes at the end of each session reflecting on their own behaviour.

The expert trap

In some situations Clinicians may find themselves providing expert advice and direction to the child without having fully clarified the goals the child would like to achieve. This may be due to inappropriate pacing or over-enthusiasm on the part of the Clinician who misinterprets the child's ambivalence as resolved. Similarly the Clinician may feel that the child needs some guidance and so takes a more active role in developing treatment goals. Reflections and summaries provide regular opportunities for the Clinician to check that the child's agenda and goals are being addressed.

The blaming trap

Children may blame others for their problems, resulting in the Clinician becoming drawn into a challenging position as they attempt to highlight the child's potential responsibilities. The inevitable outcome is the child and Clinician becoming locked into an unhelpful dispute. In motivational interviewing, blame is viewed as irrelevant as the Clinician helps the child to focus upon what they would like to change and how they might achieve it rather than who is responsible for causing it. Adopting a no-blame solution-focused approach is a helpful way of avoiding this trap.

Counter-motivation can occur for four common reasons:

■ The Clinician promotes child passivity with the question and answer trap.

■ The Clinician attempts to persuade the child in the confrontational and denial trap.

■ The Clinician rushes ahead without any child ownership in the expert trap.

■ The Clinician and child become locked in unhelpful disputes in the blaming trap.

▶ When would CBT not be indicated?

In addition to assessing the child's motivation and readiness for change, the clinician also needs to determine the appropriateness of using child-focused CBT. There are a number of occasions when CBT may not be the intervention of choice, the main therapeutic focus or the immediate requirement of the intervention. This may be related to:

■ the nature of the presenting problem;

■ the characteristics of the presenting problem;

■ multiple problem presentations;

■ the systemic context in which the problem presents;

■ the child's linguistic and cognitive development.

■ The nature of the presenting problem

There is strong and growing evidence to suggest that child-focused CBT is the treatment of choice for many internalising disorders, including generalised anxiety, depression, OCD and PTSD. However, the evidence for child-focused CBT in the treatment of externalising disorders such as attention deficit hyperactivity disorder, aggression or conduct disorder is weaker. While a number of interventions for these disorders include what could be considered to be a cognitive component, this is typically delivered as part of a more eclectic package rather than the cognitive approach being the prime therapeutic intervention. Thus the multi-systemic approach that has proved helpful in the treatment of antisocial youth uses cognitive interventions as part of a series of interventions that target the range of factors that contribute to the development or maintenance of the child's problems (Henggeler *et al.* 2002). Similarly behavioural parenting programmes are effective in the treatment of conduct disorders, although recently researchers have explored how these can be enhanced by the addition of a cognitive component for those families who traditionally respond less well to these interventions (White *et al.* 2003). Clinicians therefore need to recognise the strengths of child-focused CBT as well as acknowledging the limitations of majoring upon, or adopting, a singular cognitive approach.

■ The characteristics of the presenting problem

Child-focused CBT is an active process in which the child embarks upon a process of guided discovery, experimentation and practice. This is an important feature of CBT that allows the child to find solutions to their problems and, through a process of practice and systemic exposure, learn to overcome them. This approach can be difficult with low-frequency behaviours such as a fear of sickness that manifests, for example, once every six to eight weeks. While the problem may have a significant effect upon the child's everyday life resulting, for example, in the avoidance of sleepovers at friends in case someone is sick, the child may have few real-life opportunities to practise using their newly acquired skills. Low-frequency behaviours do not preclude the use of child-focused CBT since imaginal rehearsal and exposure can be undertaken. However, the final step of in vivo exposure and mastery can be difficult to achieve.

■ Multiple problem presentations

It is not unusual for children to present with a range of difficulties and for these to become increasingly dominant at various times throughout the course of the intervention. This can result in clinical sessions losing their impetus or focus as the latest problem or crisis is addressed. In these situations CBT can help to maintain the clinical focus. The other problems are acknowledged and 'parked' as clinical sessions focus upon the problem that was initially agreed as the target of the intervention. Once successfully resolved, the 'parked' problems can be revisited and the next one selected and worked through.

While CBT can be helpful in these situations there will be other occasions when the prime task is liaison not therapy, i.e. to liaise with other professionals and agencies to coordinate a range of inputs and supports to address the multiple needs of the family. There may be educational issues, a need for practical support or help for the parents with their own mental health problems necessitating liaison with schools, social services, the family doctor or community adult mental health team. While this can be very time-consuming it is nonetheless essential that a supportive framework is built around the multiple needs of the family. Once this is in place, child-focused CBT can be more readily undertaken.

■ The systemic context in which the problem presents

Assessment of the systemic influences that contribute to the onset or maintenance of the child's presenting problem may highlight that child-focused CBT is not the preferred intervention. Within the family, the child's problems may be a manifestation of inappropriate family patterns (e.g. scapegoating) or may reflect inappropriate processes within the wider system (e.g. problems adhering to boundaries). The child's behaviour may also become the focus that unites and diverts the parents' attention away from more important difficulties within, for example, their own relationship. Similarly, what may be presented as the child's biases and distortions about being unloved, rejected or overly criticised may prove to be a reality. On these occasions, pursuing child-focused CBT without addressing the wider systemic influences runs the danger of colluding with the dysfunctional family system and pathologising the child. A more systemic approach would be indicated to address these wider issues rather than child-focused CBT.

■ The child's linguistic and cognitive development

There will be regular occasions where the Clinician needs to be creative and flexible in adapting and presenting the ideas and strategies of child-focused CBT so that they are cognisant with the child's linguistic and cognitive development. This will involve greater use of non-verbal methods and materials, the use of more specific concrete strategies or methods that involve fewer decision choices. In all instances the Clinician aims to ensure that child-focused CBT is pitched at a level the child can access.

There will, however, be times when, despite considerable creativity on the part of the Clinician, it becomes clear that the child does not possess sufficient cognitive or linguistic skills to engage in even a limited version of child-focused CBT. As a general principle there is a widely accepted consensus amongst Clinicians that children under the age of seven will find it difficult to engage with child-focused CBT. While this is a helpful guide, it highlights the need for careful assessment since there will be occasions when the child's cognitive or linguistic limitations would suggest that child-focused CBT is not the treatment of choice.

Child-focused CBT may not be the prime therapeutic intervention if:

- the child presents with externalising problems
- the problem is low frequency
- there are multiple presentations and needs
- there are overriding systemic influences
- the child's cognitive, linguistic or memory capabilities are limited.

The Scales of Change

Sometimes you need to weigh up the benefits or disadvantages of trying to do something new.

Write down what you are thinking about doing at the top of the scales. Write down on one side of the scales all the positive reasons/benefits and on the other side all the negative reasons/disadvantages.

| Reasons for doing it | Reasons for not doing it |

Formulations

Once the child is motivated and ready to engage in CBT the initial task is to develop a problem formulation. The formulation is a shared understanding of the onset and maintenance of the child's presenting problems described within a cognitive behavioural framework. The formulation is a prerequisite of any individual intervention and provides the explicit, shared, working hypothesis that is used to direct and inform the specific content of the intervention.

The formulation represents a shared understanding and is therefore developed in partnership with the child and their carers. The process is descriptive in which the child is encouraged to use their own words to describe their feelings and the meanings they attribute to events. The information provided by the child and their carers is then structured and organised by the Clinician, using a cognitive framework, to highlight and explore the possible relationships between cognitions, feelings and behaviour. This is a collaborative process during which the emerging formulation is discussed, tested and revised until a mutually agreed explanation is obtained. Once agreed, the formulation provides the current working model that informs the content and focus of the cognitive programme. The formulation provides a dynamic and evolving understanding that will be modified during the course of therapy. The resulting formulation is constantly checked, evaluated and revised to take account of any new information that might emerge. Formulations are therefore a useful alternative to static diagnostic classifications and provide a functional, coherent and testable way of bringing together important variables that explain the onset of the child's difficulties and/or current maintaining factors.

The clinical formulation is at the heart of good clinical practice and serves important functions for both the child and the Clinician. From the child's perspective, the formulation is the vehicle by which they understand and make sense of their difficulties. Individual symptoms, thoughts, behaviours and experiences that often feel unconnected are brought together in a coherent and understandable way through the formulation. The development of this shared understanding during the early stage of treatment models the active, open and collaborative process that will continue throughout therapy. The construction of the formulation also clearly acknowledges the importance of the information the child and their carer possess and introduces the concepts of self-discovery and self-efficacy.

For the Clinician, the formulation is used to assess the onset and development of the child's problems against theoretical explanatory models. Formulations therefore provide the mechanism by which theory and practice are bound together (Butler 1998; Tarrier & Calam 2002). The formulation provides the empirical model that directs and informs the content of the treatment programme. This ensures that the Clinician remains focused and that the effectiveness of the intervention is maximised. As highlighted by Kuyken & Beck (2004), the formulation 'guides the practitioner in planning and delivering the right intervention, in the right way at the right point towards the collaboratively agreed goals for therapy'.

Formulations therefore serve important functions for both the child and the Clinician. However, the content and specific detail required by the child and their carers may not necessarily be the same as that required by the Clinician. It is important to ensure that the child and their carers receive the level of detail they require without over-burdening them with too much information. The Clinician, however, may be keen to identify different levels of cognitions or to specify, in detail, particular cognitions associated with theoretical models. This level of sophistication and analysis is often not required by children or their carers. Different levels of formulation with varying degrees of specification will be required for different purposes.

Once developed it is very helpful if the working formulation can be summarised diagrammatically. This provides a powerful, permanent visual representation that can be referred to during each session and revised accordingly. The child and their carers can take a copy home, which allows them to reflect upon the accuracy of the formulation and to discuss and share it with others. In addition, it can facilitate the development of self-efficacy by providing the carer and child with the opportunity to consider and explore potential ways in which the current unhelpful patterns can be changed.

> ▪ Formulations provided a shared understanding of the onset and maintenance of the child's problems.
>
> ▪ The formulation is testable and informs and guides the subsequent intervention.

▶ Key aspects of a formulation

The process of developing a formulation involves the elicitation and identification of relevant information, which is then arranged according to some theoretical or explanatory model in order to understand the origins, development and/or maintenance of the presenting problem (Tarrier & Calam 2002).

A good formulation therefore depends upon the careful identification and selection of key information. This process has the potential to become overly inclusive and complex as attempts are made to assimilate the wealth of information gathered during an assessment into a single formulation. This can result in the Clinician and child becoming overwhelmed and confused. The tendency to try to incorporate all the assessment information into a single comprehensive formulation should be avoided. As a guiding principle, formulations need to be kept simple so that they are readily understandable and do not exceed the cognitive capacity of the child. The aim is therefore to provide the minimum amount of information necessary to summarise the problem and provide the rationale for the action plan (Charlesworth & Reichelt 2004). In order to achieve this, the Clinician needs a framework that will help them identify, select and organise salient information.

There are many ways that formulations can be structured. The simplest are mini-formulations that highlight the relationship between two elements in the CBT cycle. This could involve, for example, tracking the cognitions and emotional reaction associated with a particular event. A more comprehensive model could be based around the general cognitive model and focus upon either a maintenance (e.g. event, thoughts, feelings, behaviour) or onset (e.g. early experiences, core beliefs, assumptions, triggering events, automatic thoughts) formulation. Finally there are problem-specific formulations whereby information is organised around the key aspects identified in specific theoretical explanatory models.

Formulations can be:

- simple mini-formulations highlighting relationships between two factors
- general cognitive models that provide a cognitive onset or maintenance formulation
- problem-specific formulations.

▶ Mini-formulations

These are the simplest formulations that serve to highlight the association between two or three elements of the CBT cycle. These are particularly useful during the early stages of therapy, or when the child and their parents are new to the cognitive model, and can facilitate the development of a collaborative relationship between the Clinician and child (Charlesworth & Reichelt 2004). Similarly, their simplicity is helpful for young children who may have a limited cognitive capacity and find the abstract relationship between the multiple elements of the CBT cycle difficult to immediately understand. Focusing upon each relationship in turn (i.e. cognitions and associated emotional reaction; emotional reaction and associated behavioural response) provides a more understandable and staged approach. These can then be joined together to help the child develop a fuller formulation.

■ Rhiannon is unhappy and scared

A mini-formulation was used to help Rhiannon (8) understand how her worries about the other children at school resulted in her feeling frightened and playing on her own. The first step was to help Rhiannon describe what happened in the school playground during play-times. This was summarised in Figure 3.1.

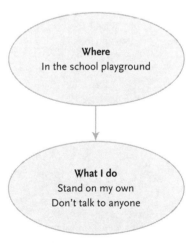

Figure 3.1 Rhiannon's where and what link.

The next stage was to help Rhiannon identify the thoughts and feelings she had when she was in the school playground (Figure 3.2). Unidirectional links are often used in models with children. These are less complicated than bidirectional relationships and therefore easier for the children to understand. This does not negate the bidirectional nature of the relationship between variables but simply highlights the primary direction of the relationship.

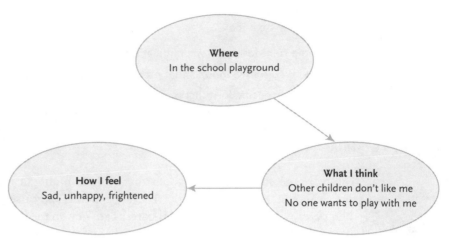

Figure 3.2 Rhiannon's situation, thoughts and feelings link.

The two diagrams, Figures 3.1 and 3.2, were then combined to provide Rhiannon with a simple formulation that highlighted the link between what she thought, how she felt and what she did in the school playground (Figure 3.3).

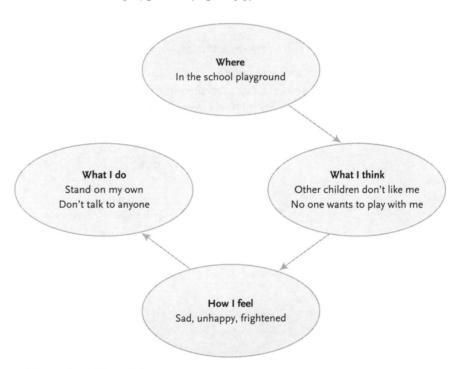

Figure 3.3 Rhiannon's mini-formulation.

- Mini-formulations highlight the link between two or three parts of the cognitive cycle.
- Mini-formulations can be joined together to build a fuller formulation.

▶ General cognitive formulations

The general cognitive formulation uses the key elements of the cognitive framework to provide the child and their family with an understanding of why their problems may have developed (onset formulation) or why they keep happening (maintenance formulation). These formulations tend to identify the important early experiences and events that have led to the development of the child's beliefs, assumptions. Triggering events are highlighted and the associated automatic thoughts and resulting feelings and behaviours described.

■ Maintenance formulations

The simplest of the general models is the maintenance formulation. This links together triggering event/situations, thoughts, feelings and behaviour. A worksheet that can be used with children to identify this dysfunctional cycle, 'The Negative Trap', is provided at the end of this chapter.

Naomi cuts herself

Naomi was a 14-year-old girl referred with problems of depression and self-harming. The self-harming involved Naomi cutting her arms and the tops of her legs with a razor blade approximately twice per week. During an assessment meeting Naomi reported that she had cut herself twice over the last week. These events were tracked through and summarised in the negative trap formulation in Figure 3.4.

Mum, Dad and brother Jake went out on Saturday night. I was left alone.

Figure 3.4a   Naomi's negative trap.

The first diagram (Figure 3.4(a)) helped Naomi to recognise the importance of her negative thoughts and how they had made her feel sad. The second (Figure 3.4(b)) highlighted how Naomi found it difficult to cope with any unpleasant feelings. When she felt angry or sad she would cut herself and this took her unpleasant feelings away.

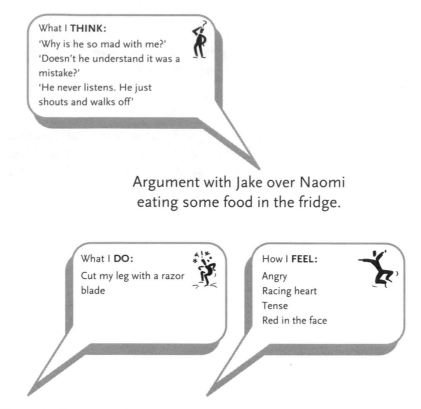

Figure 3.4b   Naomi's negative trap.

Maintenance formulations such as these often provide enough information, particularly for younger children. They highlight the important relationships between thoughts, feelings and behaviour and, with the here and now focus, help the child to make sense of their current difficulties. In some instances it can be helpful to differentiate between feelings (moods) and somatic symptoms (bodily changes). A worksheet, 'The 4-part Negative Trap', is provided at the end of this chapter. This can be particularly useful if a child is misperceiving anxious physiological changes as an indication of being physically ill. Helping the child to understand that the bodily changes they notice are normal anxiety reactions can be reassuring and help them to challenge assumptions that they are seriously ill and thus unable to undertake or participate in activities.

> ■ General maintenance formulations identify triggering events and track the associated cognitions, feelings and behaviour.

▶ Onset formulations

Onset formulations provide a developmental explanation of the way past experiences have shaped important cognitions. The onset formulation therefore highlights how significant events and experiences result in the development of important beliefs/schemas/assumptions that determine how children perceive themselves, their performance and their future. In developing onset formulations it is important to consider potentially significant family factors and relationships, important or traumatic events, school experiences and relationships with peers. This is in contrast to the maintenance formulation that has a more 'here and now' focus in which the thoughts, feelings, physiological symptoms and behaviour associated with specific triggering events is tracked.

The key elements of the cognitive model proposed by Beck (1976) provide a helpful way of structuring an onset formulation and for disentangling the different levels of cognitive processes. Important elements to consider in the development of onset formulations include:

- significant early experiences and events;
- important core beliefs/schemas;
- the assumptions children use about themselves, their performance and future;
- automatic thoughts that arise from activating events;
- the emotional responses that are generated;
- the behaviour that follows.

Early experiences

Early experiences are hypothesised to be central to the development of maladaptive core beliefs and schemas. Important negative experiences could cover a wide range of events including:

- family factors – death, illness, poor or violent parental relationships, parental separation, parental mental/physical health;
- relationship issues – separation from parents, poor or ambivalent attachment, rejection, failed relationships, multiple carers;
- medical factors – persistent health problems, disability, chronic illness, repeated or prolonged hospitalisation;
- educational issues – school failure, learning problems, bullying;
- social factors – rejection from friends/peers, isolation, delinquent/criminal behaviour;
- trauma – abuse, single or multiple traumatic events, discrimination.

Some events may not objectively appear particularly significant to a third party. There is a danger that these could readily be dismissed as unimportant or irrelevant. It is therefore important to assess the meaning the child ascribes to these events so that their potential significance can be determined. For example, a girl of 16 was referred with a long-standing history of OCD related to germs and health. During the assessment a range of possibly important events emerged, although most appeared comparatively trivial. However, further questioning clearly revealed the personal significance of one event in which the girl fell and cut her knee while on holiday in France. The vividness of the memory and her associated thoughts, 'this is not going to stop bleeding', 'no one will know I am hurt', 'I am going to die', clearly highlighted the importance she had ascribed to this comparatively minor everyday event.

Core beliefs/cognitive schemas

Core beliefs and schemas are deep-seated, fairly fixed and rigid ways of thinking. Models developed with adults hypothesise that unhelpful core beliefs or dysfunctional schemas develop during childhood and are assumed to underpin many psychological problems (Beck 1967; Young 1990). Comparatively little is known about core beliefs and schemas in children and, since the cognitive development of children is evolving, it is unclear when these core beliefs develop, become established and enduring or are activated.

Downward arrow

Core beliefs/schemas tend to be expressed as absolute statements such as 'I am a failure', 'no one loves me', 'I am a bad person'. Core beliefs and schemas are often not directly voiced during interview and so the Clinician will need to actively seek them. The downward arrow technique can be useful ('Identifying core beliefs', TGFG, page 94). With this method one of the child's common automatic negative thoughts is identified and they are then repeatedly asked, 'So what? If this was true what does this mean about you?', until the underlying core belief emerges.

Questionnaires

Another way of identifying core beliefs is to supplement information obtained during the clinical interview with a questionnaire such as the Schema Questionnaire for Children.

The Schema Questionnaire for Children is also known as 'Common beliefs' (TGFG, page 97). This was designed to assess the 15 early maladaptive schemas, identified by Young (1990) in his work with adults, which have received support from psychometric evaluation (Schmidt *et al.* 1995). The questionnaire has 15 statements, which relate to each of the early

Table 3.1 Correlation between the Schema Questionnaire for Children (Core Beliefs) and the Young Schema Questionnaire

Schema Questionnaire for Children – questionnaire Item	Young Early Maladaptive Schema	Correlation and significance
It is important to be better than others at everything I do	Unrelenting standards/ Hypercriticalness	$R = 0.615, p = 0.0001$
No one understands me*	Social isolation/ Alienation	$R = 0.548, p = 0.0001$
Others are out to get or hurt me*	Mistrust/Abuse	$R = 0.594, p = 0.0001$
People I love will never be there for me	Abandonment/ Instability	$R = 0.202, p = 0.179$
I need other people to help me get by*	Dependence/ Incompetence	$R = 0.393, p = 0.007$
Bad things happen to me*	Vulnerability to harm or illness	$R = 0.418, p = 0.004$
No one loves or cares about me*	Emotional deprivation	$R = 0.439, p = 0.002$
It is more important to put other people's wishes and ideas before my own*	Subjugation	$R = 0.274, p = 0.066$
Other people are better than me*	Defectiveness/Shame	$R = 0.407, p = 0.005$
I am more important/special than others	Entitlement/ Grandiosity	$R = 0.352, p = 0.016$
People will be cross or upset if I say the things I really want to say*	Self-sacrifice	$R = 0.279, p = 0.060$
I must not show my feelings to others*	Emotional inhibition	$R = 0.718, p = 0.0001$
It is important that my parents/carers are involved in everything I do	Enmeshment/ Undeveloped self	$R = 0.015, p = 0.922$
I am not responsible for what I do or say	Insufficient self-control/ self-discipline	$R = 0.031, p = 0.839$
I am a failure*	Failure	$R = 0.671, p = 0.0001$
Total score*		$R = 0.775, p = 0.0001$

* Children attending a community child and adolescent mental health team score significantly differently from a non-referred community sample on these items.

maladaptive schemas proposed by Young (1990). The child rates their strength of belief for each statement on a visual 10-point scale ranging from 'I don't really believe at all' to 'very strongly believe'.

Preliminary psychometric assessment of the Schema Questionnaire for Children has recently been undertaken (Stallard & Rayner 2005). A community sample of children aged 11–16 attending a secondary school ($n = 47$) completed the short form Young Schema Questionnaire and the Schema Questionnaire for Children. Table 3.1 summarises the results and highlights that there were significant correlations for 10 of the 15 items, with a further two approaching statistical significance.

A subsequent analysis was undertaken comparing the results of the community (non-referred) sample ($n = 46$) with those of children ($n = 41$) referred to a community child mental health service. There were statistically significant differences on 10 of the 15 items as well as the total score. The significant items are marked with an asterisk in Table 3.1.

■ **Cognitive assumptions**

Assumptions operationalise the child's cognitive framework and describe the relationship between their thoughts and behaviour. These are typically referred to as 'if/then' or 'should/must' statements (Padesky & Greenberger 1995). Often these are not apparent or clear during the assessment and again are not typically vocalised in a direct way.

The 'I wonder what happens' question

A useful way of eliciting assumptions with children is to use the 'I wonder' question in which the Clinician wonders with the child how their core beliefs might lead them to behave. The following highlights how Kate's assumptions became clear.

PS:	Kate, you have told me that it is very important that everything you do has to be right. So, I wonder what happens when you have to do a piece of homework for school?
KATE:	I get really worried and it seems to take me ages to finish it.
PS:	Is that because you work slowly?
KATE:	No, not really.
PS:	So why does it take so long?
KATE:	Well it never seems good enough. I have to keep going over it, checking, and changing and it takes me ages.
PS:	Have you tried doing it one night and then handing it in the next day?
KATE:	No. That wouldn't work. It wouldn't be good enough.
PS:	What would be wrong with that?
KATE:	Well I probably wouldn't have done enough work.
PS:	So does that mean that if you spend lots of time on your work, then you will get better marks?
KATE:	Yes. That's why I have to keep doing it again and again.

Kate's assumptions were now becoming clear. For her it was important to get everything right, leading her to assume that **if** she spent a lot of time on her work **then** she would be successful.

The if/then quiz

Another way of teasing out the child's assumptions or predictions is through the use of quizzes. The child is asked to play a game in which the Clinician provides an 'if' statement and they are asked to complete the sentence by saying what they expect will happen. The Clinician can generate specific questions in order to assess assumptions that they suspect might be particularly important for the child

- IF I get things wrong, THEN . . . . . . 'people will be angry'
- IF I am successful, THEN . . . . . . 'I'm lucky'
- IF people like me, THEN . . . . . . 'they are just being kind'

Behavioural experiments

Behavioural experiments provide another way of identifying the child's assumptions. The process requires the child to identify their experiment; predict what will happen; undertake the investigation; record the result; compare the results against their prediction and then re-assess their initial assumptions and beliefs. The prediction provides an insight into the way the child perceives their world and will help to discover some of the assumptions they use to operationalise their beliefs. Children are often familiar with the idea of experimentation and are increasingly encouraged at school to undertake investigations.

The child's assumptions still are not clear

At other times it may not be possible to identify the child's assumptions or beliefs. At these times it can be useful to acknowledge this. The use of question marks in formulations can be helpful. This signals that there are some things that are not fully understood and can be checked again in later sessions to see if the operational relationship has become clearer.

■ Automatic thoughts

Diaries

Automatic thoughts are the most accessible level of cognitions. The Clinician is interested in those negative automatic thoughts that accompany problematic situations and uncomfortable feelings and may ask children to keep diaries or thought records. Some children are motivated and able to keep diaries. Others may prefer to design their own computer records or to send an email after any difficult situations. However, if a child is unwilling or unable to keep any form of diary or record, then their thoughts can still be assessed during the next clinical session. Any difficult situations can be tracked through and the Clinician can elicit any accompanying thoughts. While this does not provide the detail that can be obtained in a diary or record sheet and may not totally capture the specific thoughts, it does nonetheless provide the Clinician with an insight into the nature of the child's thoughts.

The thought catcher

During clinical sessions children indirectly volunteer a great deal of information about their thoughts. Clinically, the Clinician may not want to disrupt the flow of conversation or to focus upon these too early and so may prefer to simply note and revisit them at a more appropriate time. The Clinician adopts the role of the 'thought catcher', and can feed these back to the child with comments such as 'Last time we met I heard you say ...' or 'You told me that when that happened you remembered thinking ...'. When catching thoughts, it is important to record exactly what the child says, rather than paraphrasing or summarising. Using the child's own words ensures that the meaning they attribute to events is accurately captured and demonstrates empathy, strengthens the therapeutic relationship and helps to maximise understanding.

Other questions

More direct attempts to elicit automatic thoughts by asking, 'What were you thinking when that happened?' may not always be helpful and often results in a fairly short and abrupt response of 'Nothing' or 'I don't know'. Friedberg & McClure (2002) suggest some alternative ways of phrasing this question that they have found helpful such as:

- What raced through your head?
- What did you say to yourself?
- What popped into your mind?

■ Emotional responses

Feelings worksheets

In terms of emotions children are not always good at distinguishing the different feelings they experience. The Clinician may therefore need to spend time helping the child to identify and express different emotions. A number of worksheets are available which help the child focus upon the three main aspects of emotional identification, facial expression, body posture and activity (TGFG, pages 129–132). It can also be useful to help the child identify and understand some of the physiological changes or behaviours that are associated with their feelings. Presenting the child with worksheets like 'When I feel anxious', 'When I feel sad' or 'When I feel angry' (included at the end of Chapter 7) provides an overview of some of the possible physiological changes or behaviours that might be associated with the feeling. The child does not have to engage in the more difficult tasks of generating possible physiological changes. Instead the worksheets can be used as a way of highlighting and prompting possible reactions whilst the child selects those that are relevant for themselves.

Emotional dictionaries

Pictures cut from newspapers and magazines of people expressing different emotions are also useful visual prompts that can be used to help the child label their emotions. Alternatively, children can create their own emotional dictionary by cutting and pasting pictures into a book that highlight the feelings they experience.

Feeling charades

Similarly, feeling charades can be an entertaining way of helping the child express and identify different emotions. The child is presented with a series of cards, each with a different feeling. The child then acts each feeling while the observer tries to identify it. Games such as this will help the Clinician to identify how the child expresses their feelings, the labels they use to name them and which are most commonly experienced by the child.

■ Onset formulation: Marco's depression

Marco (16) was urgently referred by his GP with possible depression. The current problems started when he was expelled, totally unexpectedly, from school for repeated minor misbehaviour. Marco was devastated and although he admitted that he was often in trouble at school, he had tried hard and thought that this had been his best term yet. Throughout the interview he conveyed a sense of failure making comments such as 'I'm rubbish, I've let everyone down'.

Marco felt tearful most days and had thoughts about self-harming but had not made any attempts to hurt himself. He had lost his appetite, felt tired and lethargic but couldn't sleep. He woke early but found it difficult to get out of bed. Before his first appointment Marco had started a new school. On the first day he experienced a panic attack and felt unable to return. Marco reported a number of anxious symptoms including a churning stomach, racing heart, sweating, hot flushes and difficulty concentrating. Marco was clearly frightened by these symptoms commenting, 'What if I have another panic attack?' and was now reluctant to go out and only felt 'safe' when at home.

Marco had a close and caring family, living with mother and sister (Jessica). There were a number of significant events. His father died from a heart attack when Marco was 7; when

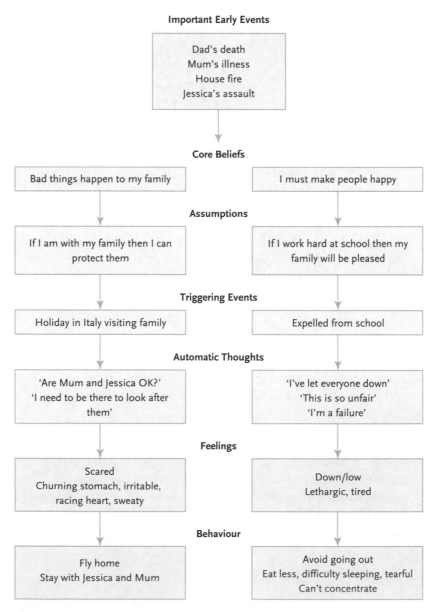

Figure 3.5 Marco's depression.

he was 8 his mother was diagnosed with cancer; when he was 10 Jessica was assaulted; at the age of 11 the family were involved in a house fire in which the kitchen was destroyed.

Marco could recall his first panic attack when he was 9, coinciding with him starting a new school. These also occurred when he changed schools at age 13; but he could recall a particularly bad series of panic attacks when he went on holiday on his own to visit his family in Italy (aged 15). Marco could remember feeling concerned for the safety of his mother and sister making comments such as 'I need to be there to look after them'. After two days he returned home. During the next appointment we built up a formulation to explain the onset of Marco's problems of anxiety and depression, identifying and agreeing important core beliefs and assumptions. This is summarised in Figure 3.5.

There are many different ways of structuring and presenting a formulation. In this case it would have been possible to develop separate formulations for each of Marco's problems (i.e. anxiety and depression). However, in view of the overlap and in order to provide some continuity between this visual representation and Marco's real-life experience, we agreed to combine them. This provided a strong visual representation for Marco of how he continued to be troubled by two main problems although the intensity and dominance of each fluctuated over time.

The onset formulation helped Marco to realise how the past experiences of his father dying, mother developing cancer, house fire and sister being abused had led to the development of his belief that 'bad things happen to my family', a situation he felt obliged to correct by his need to 'make people happy'. These beliefs were operationalised through his assumptions. If Marco was always with his family then he thought he could protect them from bad things. Similarly, if he worked hard at school then he knew that his mother and sister would be pleased and that he would live up to his father's hopes. Marco's beliefs were activated by being separated from his family (e.g. holiday in Italy) and by being expelled from school. These events resulted in various automatic thoughts and these had the effect of making Marco feel extremely anxious and depressed. Marco's way of coping with these negative

---

- Onset formulations provide an overview of the important events and experiences that have shaped the development of the child's cognitive framework.
- Key elements of the cognitive model, i.e. core beliefs, assumptions, triggering events, automatic thoughts, feelings and behaviour are included.

---

thoughts and unpleasant feelings was to return home, avoid going out and stay in the house where he felt safe.

▶ Complex formulations

Clinical experience suggests that the development of a formulation can be a very powerful way of helping the child and their carers to understand the significance of past events and to explain why current problems are occurring and how they are being maintained. The formulation therefore needs to be understandable and, as previously mentioned, needs to provide the child and their carer with sufficient information to be helpful. With young children this can be quite simple. Often a maintenance formulation (e.g. Figure 3.3) is all that is required to provide the child with the understanding they need and a framework for exploring how this can be changed. There are, however, times when it is helpful to develop a more complex formulation in which important events or experiences and their relationship with particular beliefs or assumptions are specified in more detail.

Ben's OCD

Ben (17) was referred by his GP with a long-standing problem of obsessional behaviour and repetitive hand-washing. He washed his hands 10–15 times each day, and on each occasion would wash his hands three times, a process that took between 5 and 10 minutes. Ben would need to wash his hands every time he went to the bathroom or if he touched something he felt was 'dirty', e.g. computer keyboard or door handles. This was affecting Ben's college work since he would not hand in his assignments for fear that he would pass germs to his teachers and infect them.

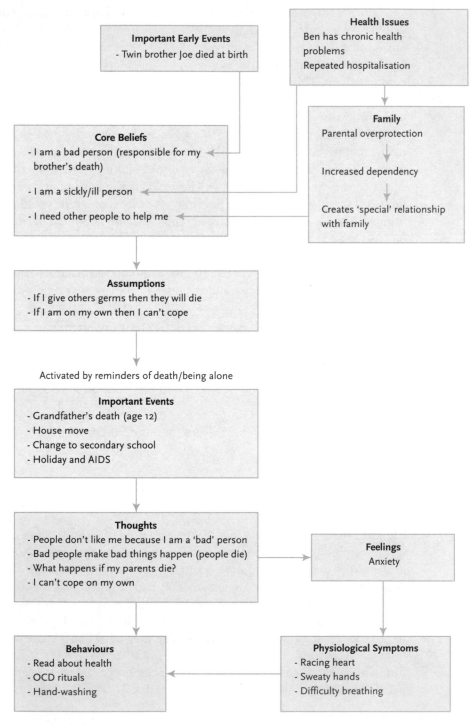

Figure 3.6 Ben's OCD.

Ben was a twin with his brother (Joe) unfortunately dying at birth. The labour was premature and the birth traumatic, with Ben being born at 25 weeks' gestation. Ben had many medical problems that resulted in him spending a great deal of time in hospital and undergoing many corrective operations. Ben and his mother had a very close relationship, with his mother feeling that she had become very protective, over-compensating for the loss of her younger son, Joe.

Ben's obsessional behaviours had been present for many years but became particularly noticeable at times of change and worry. Upon starting secondary school at age 11 he was subject to regular bullying. His grandfather, whom Ben was very fond of, died unexpectedly of a heart attack the following year. On-going peer problems resulted in Ben changing schools when he was 14. At age 15 the family went on holiday to South Africa and Ben became very concerned about AIDS. The next year the family went on holiday to India and Ben was very concerned that he might bump into people and be infected with germs and spent a great deal of time in his hotel room.

Throughout the assessment Ben expressed a number of comments and concerns about germs and his own health, and that he might infect others. He saw himself as responsible for causing bad things to happen and blamed himself for his brother's death (he was born first and survived).

The formulation developed with Ben and his mother is summarised in Figure 3.6. This formulation highlights two important categories of important events (i.e. health issues and the role of his family) and how they contributed to the development of Ben's specific core beliefs.

> ■ Complex onset formulations that relate important carer behaviour and/or events with specific core beliefs can be developed.

▶ Problem-specific formulations

There have been a number of recent advances in the development of theoretical cognitive models to explain specific childhood problems. Barrett & Healy (2003), for example, have demonstrated how many of the key features of Salkovskis's (1985; 1989) cognitive theory of OCD apply to children. Children with OCD reported higher ratings of harm responsibility, potential harm severity, thought–action fusion and less cognitive control compared to a non-clinical group. Similarly, the Ehlers and Clark (2000) cognitive model of PTSD developed with adults has recently been applied to children. Ehlers *et al.* (2003) found that negative interpretation of intrusive memories, rumination, thought-suppression and persistent disso-ciation were associated with PTSD severity at 3 and 6 months.

Theoretical models such as these can provide useful frameworks to structure formulations and to identify and highlight important variables and cognitive processes. By way of an example, information about children's cognitions and family factors that are associated with the development and maintenance of anxiety will be briefly summarised and used to structure a case formulation.

■ Generalised anxiety

Children with generalised anxiety disorders tend to display a number of common cognitions and biases. In terms of cognitive content, children with generalised anxiety disorders tend to report worries that are focused upon what will happen in the future (e.g. 'Will I get there on time?') or about events that have occurred (e.g. 'I am not sure if I said the right thing'). The predominant content of their worries differs, for example, from children with social phobia who are particularly concerned about social embarrassment or negative evaluation from others, or from those with phobias who have a marked fear of a particular situation or object. In addition, children with generalised anxiety disorders tend to display a number of common cognitive biases. They make more negative evaluations about themselves and their performance, have more negative expectations and focus more upon threat-related cues and information (Barrett *et al.* 1996a; Bogels & Zigterman 2000). Rapee (1997) has highlighted how these thinking patterns and biases are often encouraged and reinforced by the child's family. Parents of anxious children have been found to model anxious behaviour, to identify more threats in ambiguous situations and to encourage their children to cope with challenges or new situations by avoidance. The parents are often over-involved, which conveys to the child that the world is a threatening place, which they cannot cope with on their own (Hudson & Rapee 2001). Finally, they tend to be overprotective, which results in the child having fewer opportunities to develop and practise using more appropriate coping skills. When confronted with new or demanding situations, anxious children report significant anxiety symptoms, which they will try to reduce by avoidance.

This model was used to structure a formulation about a young girl with generalised anxiety. The formulation incorporated important contextual information about the family and also the role of the parents in the onset and maintenance of Yung Ming's problems.

Yung Ming's anxiety

Yung Ming (8), the only daughter of her parents, was referred with concerns about excessive worrying and generalised anxiety. These difficulties were particularly noticeable at school, both in the classroom and the playground. Yung Ming was described by her teacher as academically very able, a girl who set herself very high standards and who became upset if her performance fell short of these. From her perspective, Yung Ming did not like her teacher, reporting that she didn't listen to her worries and that she was always shouting, something that made her worry. She felt anxious when she had to undertake work assignments, fearing that she would make errors and be told off. Socially she had two friends but she did not see them outside of school. Yung Ming was regularly teased at school, with this consisting of name-calling. The family was very close, had few family friends or contact with relatives and so spent most of the time together, on their own. The relationship between Yung Ming and her mother was especially close and her mother would spend considerable time listening to her daughter's worries and would regularly take up any of her issues with the school. She would not let her daughter play with the other children because they might tease her or say unkind things.

On the basis of this and other information that emerged during the assessment, the following formulation (Figure 3.7) was developed with Yung Ming and her mother to explain her difficulties.

The formulation that was developed attempted to include and highlight important background information and experiences that contributed to Yung Ming's anxiety (i.e. Yung Ming was an only child, family socially isolated, spent lots of time together). The consequences of this were identified (i.e. Yung Ming and her mother spend the majority of their time together, resulting in a very close 'protective' relationship). In turn this led Yung Ming to perceive the world to be a 'frightening place' and one in which she needed her mother to help. These beliefs were activated by triggering events (e.g. friendship issues and schoolwork) that resulted in Yung Ming having a number of biased negative automatic thoughts. These biases were consistent with some of those found with children with generalised anxiety. Yung Ming had general worries that often predicted failure (e.g. 'What if I get it

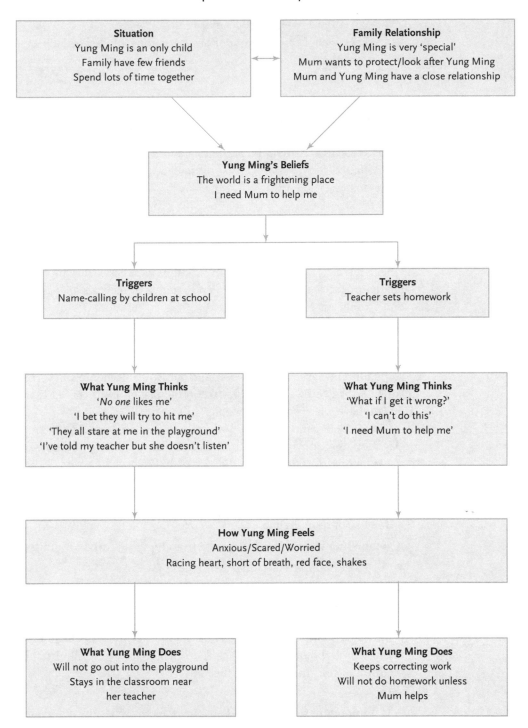

Important Events and Experiences

Situation
Yung Ming is an only child
Family have few friends
Spend lots of time together

Family Relationship
Yung Ming is very 'special'
Mum wants to protect/look after Yung Ming
Mum and Yung Ming have a close relationship

Yung Ming's Beliefs
The world is a frightening place
I need Mum to help me

Triggers
Name-calling by children at school

Triggers
Teacher sets homework

What Yung Ming Thinks
'*No one* likes me'
'I bet they will try to hit me'
'They all stare at me in the playground'
'I've told my teacher but she doesn't listen'

What Yung Ming Thinks
'What if I get it wrong?'
'I can't do this'
'I need Mum to help me'

How Yung Ming Feels
Anxious/Scared/Worried
Racing heart, short of breath, red face, shakes

What Yung Ming Does
Will not go out into the playground
Stays in the classroom near
her teacher

What Yung Ming Does
Keeps correcting work
Will not do homework unless
Mum helps

Figure 3.7   Yung Ming's anxiety formulation.

wrong?') and made negative evaluations about her ability ('I can't do this') and herself ('No one likes me'). She had a tendency to perceive situations as potentially threatening ('They all stare at me in the playground') and to expect people to be aggressive ('I bet they will try and hit me'). These thoughts resulted in a number of physiological anxiety symptoms and resulted in Yung Ming avoiding situations (e.g. playground) and not having opportunities to learn how to socialise with her peers. This avoidance was also encouraged by her mother (e.g. would not let Yung Ming play with children outside of school).

> ■ Problem-specific formulations provide a framework that can incorporate important contextual and family factors.
>
> ■ They highlight and link important cognitions and behaviours associated with specific problems.

▶ Common problems

A good case formulation is a prerequisite for any individual treatment programme. However, developing a formulation can be difficult with Clinicians reporting a number of common problems.

■ What if the child has difficulty identifying their thoughts?

Sometimes Clinicians find it difficult to identify any of the child's cognitions or feelings. The child seems to talk in a descriptive matter-of-fact way in which events are objectively and factually described. Attempts to elicit thoughts or feelings are met with silence or a simple 'I don't know' or 'Nothing'.

In terms of communication, many children are able to engage in a verbal dialogue. Direct questions can be helpful, particularly for adolescents who are often ready to volunteer their ideas. Embedding questions in specific events or situations often makes them clearer, understandable and easier to answer. A child may find it easier to answer, 'What was going through your head as you walked up to Mike in the playground?' rather than 'What sort of thoughts do you have when you meet people?'

Carefully listening to a child will often reveal that apparently factual descriptive accounts are often littered with a wealth of statements indicating the child's automatic thoughts and assumptions. At other times the use of indirect or non-verbal approaches can be helpful. Children often feel more relaxed and able to volunteer their thoughts when engaged in an activity. Useful methods to consider are:

- ■ the use of thought bubbles;
- ■ wondering what a third party/best friend might think in a similar situation;
- ■ the use of puppets to act out a situation;
- ■ drawing a picture about the difficult situation;
- ■ telling a story.

If the appropriate means of communication is found, it is uncommon for children not to volunteer some thoughts or feelings. The challenge for the Clinician is to find an appropriate medium to communicate with the child.

■ Is it important to distinguish between different levels of cognitions?

Padesky & Greenberger (1995) highlight the importance of the Clinician being aware of the different levels of cognitions since they will require different methods of assessment and interventions. Automatic thoughts are the most accessible and are often amenable to assessment through thought diaries or become apparent when talking through difficult situations. These can be modified by the commonly used method with children of replacing negative and dysfunctional automatic thoughts with positive self-talk. The child is therefore encouraged to practise alternative, more helpful, thoughts that can be used in difficult situations.

Assumptions are rarely directly verbalised but can be identified through behavioural experiments in which the child is asked to predict (i.e. operationalise their cognitions) what will happen. Behavioural experiments also provide a useful way of challenging and testing assumptions and can lead to cognitive restructuring. However, while behavioural experiments may provide information that challenges the child's core beliefs, this alone will not be sufficient to change them. By definition, core beliefs are the deepest and most enduring cognitions and are typically resistant to new or conflicting information. If working with core beliefs, the therapeutic aim is to develop an alternative belief rather than attempting to disprove the existing belief. This process can be facilitated by the use of ratings so that subtle changes in the strength of existing beliefs can be highlighted.

■ I can't seem to put this together in a formulation

A key challenge for the Clinician is to identify important information and to organise this in a cognitive framework that helps children to understand their problems. Clinicians can feel overwhelmed by the amount of information collected during the assessment and struggle to incorporate this into a simple, understandable or coherent formulation. Often this difficulty arises for two main reasons.

Firstly, the Clinician may not have identified the relevant or necessary information required to develop the formulation. This may be due to a variety of factors, such as the inexperience of the Clinician to focus and attend to key information or the assessment questions not being sufficiently specific or detailed. Enormous amounts of information are obtained during a clinical interview and much of this may not be directly relevant to the formulation. It is therefore helpful to carefully consider the structure of the interview to ensure that relevant areas are assessed. Similarly, if the information is not sufficiently detailed, then paying greater attention to the type and content of the questions may help to elicit clearer and more specific information. If these difficulties persist, then clinical supervision will be particularly important and will help the Clinician to identify different ways in which key information can be obtained and how the required distinctions can be determined.

The second common reason is that the Clinician has not identified a clear formulation framework to help them select and organise the information. The mini-formulation provides the simplest structure and helps the Clinician to focus upon identifying a triggering event and tracking through each of the accompanying key elements of the CBT cycle, i.e. thoughts, feelings and behaviour. If necessary, feelings can be further subdivided into the emotional reaction and physiological/somatic changes. Once practised it will become easier to develop the onset formulation and to distinguish between different cognitions.

■ I'm not sure if the formulation is right

Clinicians are understandably concerned to ensure that the ideas and information they provide during therapy are accurate and that the agreed formulation is 'correct'. It is, indeed, essential to ensure that the formulation is consistent with a cognitive explanatory model since this will inform the nature and content of the intervention. There are, however, times when this preoccupation with getting it 'correct' can be counterproductive and can result in the Clinician failing to explicitly share the formulation. The opportunity to educate the child and their family into the cognitive model is missed. The process of therapy starts to change from an open collaborative model to one that becomes closed and more secretive. The failure to freely share information implicitly shifts the process of CBT away from shared empiricism towards more of an 'expert-led model'.

Formulations are not static and therefore can never be totally 'correct'. They are dynamic, constantly updated and revised during the course of therapy as new information emerges or behavioural experiments confirm or disprove aspects of the model. However, at any one time the formulation is the shared understanding that links together important information. Children and carers therefore need to understand that the formulation is a current working model and that it may change over time. Adopting such an approach ensures that the formulation is developed and shared early in therapy and that the Clinician and child work together to test, revise and develop the formulation. The dynamic nature of the formulation does not imply that the Clinician has failed to get it right. Instead it suggests that in the light of greater knowledge the understanding of the child, carers and Clinician has changed.

■ I can't seem to find all the information to complete the formulation

In developing a formulation there will inevitably be times when it may prove difficult to identify certain pieces of the model. Core beliefs are the deepest cognitions and often the least accessible. Assumptions can prove difficult to access and children may not have the language to adequately describe their emotions. At these times the Clinicians can still organise the information they have obtained within a CBT framework but they can highlight where information may be missing. This is often useful to do visually so that the incomplete boxes are clearly visible, and sometimes this can help to focus the discussion. At other times it might be helpful to simply acknowledge that 'we don't know what to put in this box yet' and to leave a question mark. The missing section of the formulation is therefore highlighted and this can be returned to during subsequent sessions to explore whether new information has emerged that will allow the missing section to be completed.

> ■ Non-verbal methods can be used to identify thoughts.
> ■ Different levels of cognitions require different methods of assessment and intervention.
> ■ Simple mini-formulations often provide a useful way to structure a formulation.
> ■ Formulations evolve and change over time. Share early and flag up any missing or incomplete information.

The Negative Trap

Think about one of your **most difficult situations** and write/draw:

▶ what **HAPPENS**

▶ how you **FEEL**

▶ what you **THINK** about when you are in that situation.

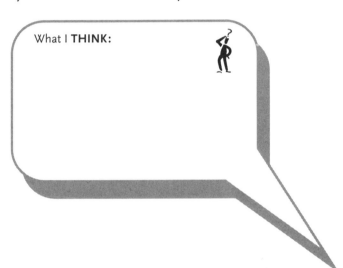

What I **THINK:**

What I **DO:**

How I **FEEL:**

The 4-part Negative Trap

Think of a recent situation or event that was difficult and draw or write it in the 'What Happened' box

When this happened draw or write down:

▶ what did you **THINK** – the thoughts that rushed through your mind?

▶ how did you **FEEL?**

▶ how did your **BODY CHANGE?**

▶ what did you **DO?**

What **HAPPENED?**

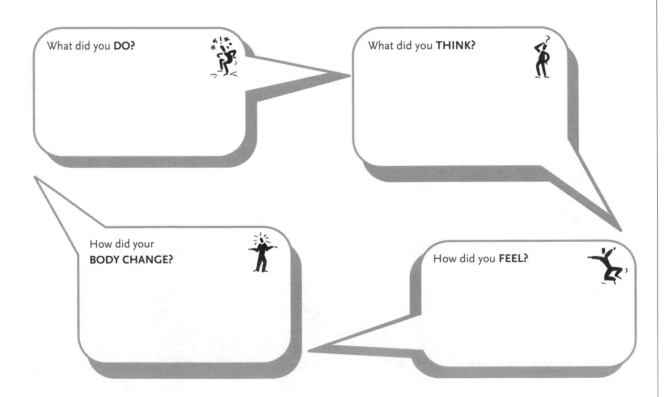

What did you **DO?**

What did you **THINK?**

How did your
BODY CHANGE?

How did you **FEEL?**

Onset Formulation Template

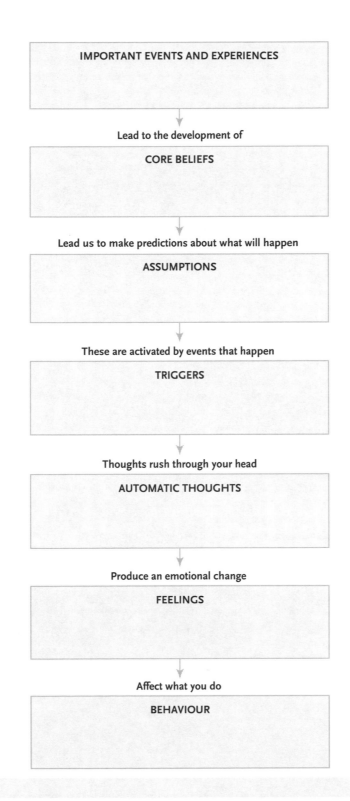

IMPORTANT EVENTS AND EXPERIENCES

Lead to the development of

CORE BELIEFS

Lead us to make predictions about what will happen

ASSUMPTIONS

These are activated by events that happen

TRIGGERS

Thoughts rush through your head

AUTOMATIC THOUGHTS

Produce an emotional change

FEELINGS

Affect what you do

BEHAVIOUR

CHAPTER FOUR

The Socratic process and inductive reasoning

CBT aims to help children develop skills and processes that enable them to identify, understand, challenge and reappraise their thoughts, beliefs and assumptions. The important cognitions that are used to explain events and predict future outcomes are therefore identified and systematically examined in order to identify potential biases or inappropriate generalisations. This structured examination results in the child setting more appropriate limits around their beliefs and assumptions which in turn leads to the development of an alternative, more balanced cognitive framework.

▶ Facilitating self-discovery

A common misapprehension amongst Clinicians inexperienced in CBT is that this process of self-discovery and redefinition is achieved by encouraging the child to simply think in rational or logical ways. Inevitably such a naive approach involves the Clinician asking a series of 'clever' questions designed to challenge, disprove or discredit the child's cognitions. The Clinician therefore has a preconceived idea about the outcome they would like the child to obtain and uses questions to guide the child to this conclusion. The process is neither empowering nor collaborative as Clinicians use their more developed verbal skills to highlight the irrationality of the child's thoughts and prove them wrong. This becomes a negative, abstract and intellectual exercise in which the child has no ownership of the process or outcome. Adolescents will find such an approach particularly unhelpful. It will typically result in the Clinician becoming locked into an increasingly adversarial relationship as the adolescent is forced to maintain and defend their beliefs and assumptions in the face of this external challenge.

In contrast, child-friendly CBT is firmly embedded within a Socratic process, which helps the child to discover, assess and reappraise their cognitions. The process is positive, enabling and supportive and is based upon genuine, open questions that convey interest and highlight that the Clinician is keen to understand how the child thinks, feels and behaves. This sense of curiosity encourages the identification of their universal definitions, the cognitive generalisations the child applies to their life. Important thoughts, beliefs, assumptions and experiences are made explicit as the meaning the child attributes to them is clarified. Questions are carefully crafted to direct and maintain the therapeutic momentum. These guide the child to systematically question their universal definitions and to engage in a process of inductive reasoning through which important cognitions are explored and reappraised. Clinician-initiated questions help the child attend to, and consider, information that they had previously overlooked or considered unimportant. Attending to this new information helps the child to consider a broader range of factors and possibilities. It highlights how there may be a variety of different ways of thinking about and explaining events and that the child's universal definitions have limits.

The Socratic process is collaborative and enables the child to establish a new understanding that both makes sense and is helpful. It is not concerned with simply proving the child's thinking wrong or encouraging them to change their mind. The Clinician's questions therefore need to both model and facilitate the process of guided self-discovery.

- The Socratic process **is not** about proving the irrationality of the child's cognitions.
- It is about creating a positive, empowering and supportive dialogue, which enables the child to identify, test and reappraise their assumptions and beliefs.

▶ The structure of the Socratic process

The Socratic process provides the framework by which the child identifies, tests and reappraises the important cognitive generalisations they use to interpret and understand their world. The process is structured and involves a number of discrete steps, each with a particular purpose.

Rutter & Friedberg (1999) identify a five-stage process that leads to the final step of logical deduction and systematic evaluation of key cognitions. The initial stages involve identifying important cognitions and then secondly the feelings and behaviours associated with them. The third stage is psychoeducational whereby the thought–feeling–behaviour link is highlighted. The child is educated in the cognitive model as the relationship between what they think, how they feel and what they do is clarified. The fourth stage is concerned with reassessing and developing the collaborative relationship. The child's view about the formulation is sought and their agreement to move towards the final stage of Socratically questioning/testing their cognitions obtained. This process highlights the need to ensure that the child is conversant with the cognitive model, a problem formulation has been agreed, and a collaborative therapeutic relationship established before inductive reasoning is undertaken.

Padesky (SQ1 audio tape) describes a similar four-stage process. The first stage is concerned with psychoeducation, eliciting and identifying important cognitions/assumptions and the feelings and behaviours associated with them. Stage two involves empathic listening on the part of the Clinician, resulting in the child's language being incorporated into the dialogue and potentially important, but overlooked, information drawn to their attention. The third stage involves summarising the child's cognitions/assumptions. Key information that has been obtained through the dialogue that supports or challenges their current way of thinking is summarised. The use of summaries and reflections are important in maintaining the collaborative relationship and provides regular opportunities for any misunderstandings to be corrected. They also provide the child with regular commentaries about the relationships they have ascribed between events. This can act as a catalyst for the child to engage in more critical analysis through inductive reasoning. The final stage is concerned with reflecting on this new information (e.g. 'What do you make of this?') and using this to re-evaluate existing cognitions. Cognitions are therefore reappraised, the new information synthesised into the child's cognitive framework and an alternative set of beliefs or assumptions developed.

Finally, Overholser (1994) describes a process based upon the three steps of identification, evaluation and redefinition. During the identification stage the Clinician is concerned with identifying important 'universal definitions', the cognitive generalisations and biases the child uses to filter, interpret, guide and predict what happens in their life. Once elicited the Clinician attempts to clarify the definition and to secure a clear and unambiguous shared understanding of the meaning the child ascribes to it. Inevitably this starts to highlight some degree of confusion and leads the dialogue to the second stage, that of evaluation. This is concerned with testing the definition and, in particular, identifying any exceptions or limitations. Universal definitions need to be stable and consistent over time and to account for all eventualities. Evaluation is concerned with systematically challenging this universality and typically involves searching for counter-examples or evidence of logical inconsistencies. This process helps the child to set limits around their definitions and leads to the final stage of redefinition. This involves the integration and assimilation of this new information within the child's cognitive framework and a new definition or set of cognitions being developed.

The Socratic process involves:

- eliciting and identifying important cognitions and associated feelings and behaviours
- helping the child attend to new or overlooked information
- synthesising and integrating new information
- reappraising old cognitions and developing a new more balanced cognitive framework.

This occurs within a collaborative context that involves the use of:

- empathic listening
- summaries and reflections.

Inductive reasoning

The process by which the child is helped to explore and analyse similarities and differences between events is that of inductive reasoning. This helps the child to identify and test any over-generalisations, selection biases or dichotomous thinking that result in general beliefs or assumptions being inappropriately applied. In turn this leads to the establishment of appropriate limits and the development of alternative more balanced cognitions.

Over-generalisation involves the extrapolation of specific individual experiences to a wide range of different situations. Subtle but important differences between events are unnoticed as the universal definition is uncritically applied. This difficulty is common and indeed many of the cognitive biases encountered in CBT are based upon inaccurate over-generalisations (Ellis 1977). Typically these over-generalisations become self-perpetuating as the child seeks and attends to confirmatory information while negating or ignoring information that would challenge or contradict their views. This may result in the child developing extreme and polarised dichotomous beliefs in which events are considered from two mutually exclusive positions while overlooking any intermediate graduations.

Inductive reasoning with children typically involves two main approaches:

- Helping the child attend to new or overlooked information that allows them to reconsider and revise their generalisations and biases.
- Systematically assessing the relationships that underpin their cognitive assumptions and beliefs.

■ Acquiring new information

Inductive reasoning helps the child to set limits on their generalisations by helping them to accumulate supporting or disproving evidence for their beliefs or assumptions. The child is therefore encouraged to consider and draw upon a broader body of knowledge or to consider alternative viewpoints. This typically involves three methods:

- considering the belief or assumption from a different perspective;
- drawing attention to new or overlooked information;
- the use of analogical comparisons to help the child consider important but not immediately obvious differences.

Considering a third-party perspective

To counter the inherent self-selection and subjective bias that underpins many generalisations the child is helped to consider their cognitions from a different perspective. The introduction of a third-party perspective promotes objectivity and helps the child to distance themselves from the emotional component of their cognitions while allowing them to recognize and acknowledge alternative and possibly conflicting views. For example, a child who regularly describes themselves as a 'failure' may be asked to consider whether their best friend would see them in this way. What might they say if they heard them using such a statement? If the child was unable to consider this from a different perspective, the task could be developed into a behavioural experiment. The child could ask those people they value and feel safe talking with to identify what they thought the child was good at. This positive focus (i.e. what they are good at) upon success is also a direct challenge to the belief of being a 'failure' and will help the child to recognise that their negative generalisation may have limitations. This may help the child to define their 'failure' more specifically, e.g. 'I often fail my maths test at school', while developing an alternative cognition, 'I often win races with the local swimming team'.

Attending to new or overlooked information

A second way of limit-setting is to help the child attend to new information, past experiences or events that they may have overlooked. A child who believes that people are unkind and want to hurt them may be helped to consider previous times when this has occurred. This may help them to discover that the bullying they experienced was inflicted by a small and specific group of children. Similarly, exploration of current events might highlight examples where friendships have developed and helpful acts occurred. This helps to set some appropriate limits around their universal beliefs that 'others are unkind'.

A worksheet that provides a structure that can be used to help the child participate in the process of deductive reasoning by seeking new evidence is included in TGFG (page 83). This involves the following steps:

- Identify the negative thought/universal definition that will be tested.
- Rate the strength of belief in the thought.
- Find the evidence that supports this thought.
- Find the evidence that does not support this thought.
- Consider another perspective by asking a valued person (parent, friend) what they would say if they heard these thoughts.
- Depersonalise the situation and consider what they would say to their best friend if they heard them thinking this way.
- After considering this, rate how much the child now believes this thought again.

Analogical comparisons

In a number of situations generalisations are made on the basis of one observed similarity, which is then used to assume the presence of other factors that have not been identified. A child may, for example, have experienced some episodes of bullying that led them to believe that other children are unkind. This belief is then generalised to other situations where they encounter other children. Analogical comparisons bring to the child's attention a broader range of information that can help them to identify important differences between events.

Analogical comparisons involve mapping the conceptual structure of the child's ideas onto another set of ideas taken from a different domain. Two events or situations are then compared on a number of relevant but not immediately obvious variables. Thus children can be helped in a concrete manner to develop new and wider perspectives by looking beyond single or surface similarities (e.g. all other children) in order to identify and understand some of the other factors that may result in them being unkind (e.g. familiarity, gender, age, nature of their relationship, etc.).

A common way in which analogical comparisons are undertaken with children is by the use of metaphors. For example, the child who assumes that other children are unkind could be helped to think about cars. While most cars share a number of observable similarities it is only once the bonnet is opened and the person looks inside that the differences become clear. Children may therefore look similar but it is only once you get to know them (get inside or lift up the bonnet) that you discover that some are nicer or better than others. Metaphors such as this can be used to broaden the child's perspective and to challenge the over-generalisation of their cognitions.

Inductive reasoning helps children place limits around their generalisations by acquiring new information. This can be acquired by:

- thinking about events from a different perspective
- attending to new or overlooked information
- using analogical comparisons that typically involve metaphors.

■ Systematically testing the assumed relationship

Children often make assumptions about the relationship between events, where one event is assumed to be the cause of another. A child with OCD may, for example, assume that they will cause their parents to be involved in a car accident if they do not repeat a set of words or carry out some form of compulsive behaviour. In these situations it can be useful to help the child systematically test this assumed relationship. This can be achieved through causal reasoning, which involves a logical analysis of these assumptions by either confirming or disproving the assumed relationship. For the child with OCD,

- confirmation would involve exploring both aspects of the assumed relationship, i.e. whether performing the ritual prevented accidents and secondly whether failure to perform them resulted in accidents happening.
- disconfirmation would involve an exploration of other factors that could cause an accident that are independent of whether or not the ritual was undertaken (e.g. mechanical failure, hit by another driver, poor road surface). Similarly disconfirmation can occur by looking at the many steps involved in order for an event to happen.

Confirmation

In terms of confirmation this could be undertaken as a behavioural experiment in which the child investigates the assumed relationship. This could involve the child checking with their parents whether:

- performing the rituals made the parents safe. The child might predict that their parents would not have had any car accidents since they started their compulsive behaviour.
- not performing the rituals results in accidents. The child might predict that accidents would occur if they did not engage in their rituals. So have the parents made car journeys that the child was not aware of or were there any times that the child forgot or did not engage in their rituals before the parent went out?

Disconfirmation

Disconfirmation involves the child discovering the complexity of the relationship they assume by detailing the multiple steps that would need to occur before their cognitions could possibly come true. A useful visual way of undertaking this with children is through an exercise such as 'The Chain of Events'. This helps the child to detail all the links in the chain

Figure 4.1 Marla's Chain of Events.

that need to be in place before the event could happen. If one of the many links is missing, the chain is broken.

Marla was an 11-year-old girl with OCD who feared that she would be responsible for infecting other people and that they would die. She engaged in a variety of compulsive behaviours in order to neutralise these thoughts. Inductive reasoning was undertaken in one session using 'The Chain of Events' to highlight some of the many steps that would be involved before this could possibly happen. Figure 4.1 is the Chain of Events that was constructed with Marla.

Disconfirmation can help children acknowledge the possible contribution of other factors and the complexity and impossibility of their assumptions. However, this alone is not always sufficient and children may continue to overemphasise their own importance. At these times the use of responsibility pies (see Chapter 7) can be a helpful visual way of determining and quantifying the respective contribution of each component to the overall outcome. The child's responsibility pie can be compared with that of another person as a way of highlighting different perspectives and helping the child to challenge and reappraise the strength of their cognitions.

> ■ Eliminative causal comparisons systematically help the child to explore and test the assumed relationship between events.

▶ The Socratic process

The Socratic process relies upon the careful use of systematic questioning to guide the child through a process where their universal definitions can be identified and critically assessed. Overholser (1993a) identified seven types of questions, each with different functions that can be used at various stages to facilitate the process of self-discovery, understanding, appraisal and re-evaluation. The process is summarised in Figure 4.2.

■ Memory questions

The first, and perhaps the easiest, for the child to engage with are descriptive memory questions. These are concerned with clarifying facts or details and are designed to help the child focus upon and recall information relevant to the present discussion. Overholser (1993a) highlights that memory questions are designed to facilitate the development of a shared understanding in which the Clinician gains an insight into the child's experiences, feelings and thoughts. Memory questions have a factual and descriptive focus such as:

- When did this start?
- What do you do when you feel like this?
- How often does this happen?

■ Translation questions

The next level of questioning uses translation questions to discover the meaning the child attributes to these events. The Clinician reflects back to the child what they have heard and inquires about the meaning.

- What do you make of this?
- Why do you think you get those funny feelings?
- Why do you think this happens to you?

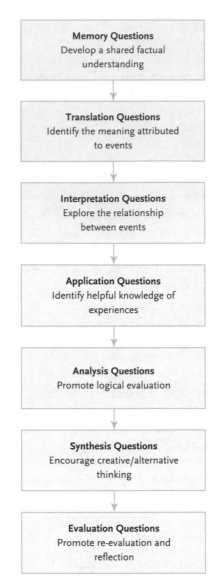

Figure 4.2 The seven question formats of the Socratic dialogue.

Translation questions start to identify some of the attributions and assumptions the child makes. These provide the Clinician with an insight into the child's cognitive framework and begin to highlight important distortions and biases that might need further evaluation.

■ Interpretation questions

Interpretation questions logically follow and are used to explore possible relationships or connections between events. They are designed to help the child identify possible patterns and similarities for themselves rather than the Clinician providing their views about possible connections. Typically this involves the Clinician summarising two or more events and asking the child to consider whether there are any similarities or connections between them.

■ Is the feeling you get when you go into school the same as the one you get when you meet up with your friends in town?

■ Have you noticed a link between those negative thoughts and how you feel?

■ Are there any times that you notice those negative thoughts more?

■ **Application questions**

The fourth type are application questions, which are designed to draw upon the child's previous knowledge or skills. These questions are used to identify relevant or important information that may have been overlooked or forgotten.

■ What have you done in the past when you have felt like this?

■ You told me that the last time this happened it didn't seem so bad. Was there anything you did differently that may have helped?

■ You don't seem to have these worrying thoughts at school. Is there anything different at school that helps you to ignore these thoughts?

■ **Analysis questions**

The next type of questions are designed to help the child systematically and logically think through their problems, thoughts and coping strategies. This is the process of rational analysis or inductive reasoning. Analysis questions are designed to foster logical conclusions by promoting objectivity and the use of inductive reasoning to critically evaluate and challenge beliefs, assumptions and inferences.

As mentioned previously, inductive reasoning helps the child to consider and attend to new or overlooked information or to systematically test the assumed relationship between events.

■ When you think like that, what is the evidence that supports your thoughts?

■ Is there any evidence that you have overlooked?

■ What would your best friend say if they heard you thinking this way?

■ You tell me this always happens, but are there any times when it doesn't?

Similarly gentle questioning can help the child to test the assumed causal relationship between events.

■ Are there any times when this hasn't happened?

■ Are there times when it did happen but it was due to something else?

■ **Synthesis questions**

Synthesis questions take the discussion to a higher level and encourage the child to think 'outside of the box' in order to identify new or alternative explanations and solutions. Overholser (1993a) cautions that the Clinician needs to retain an open mind during this process and not to have a single preconceived idea about what they want the child to 'discover'.

■ Let's list all the different ways we could cope with this, even if some might sound a little odd or silly.

■ What do you think your best friend would do?

■ Are there any other ways we could explain what has happened?

■ **Evaluation questions**

The completion of the Socratic process is achieved by the use of evaluation questions. The initial thoughts, beliefs and assumptions are now reappraised and modified in the light of the discussion.

- So what sense do you make of this now?
- Do you still see yourself as a failure?
- Is there another way of thinking about this?

The prime focus of the questions will therefore depend upon the stage of the Socratic dialogue. For example, in the five-stage process identified by Padesky, memory and translation questions will be used more often during Stage 1 when the Clinician is establishing information and meaning. During Stage 2, interpretation and application questions will be used to help the child focus on overlooked information and to explore the connection between events. Stage 3 is concerned with deductive reasoning and will draw heavily upon analysis questions. The final stage will focus more upon synthesis and evaluation questions as the child considers the new information and reappraises their thoughts.

The Socratic process and question focus	
Identification of thoughts and feelings	— Memory and Translation questions
Exploring meaning and relationships	— Interpretation and Application questions
Rational analysis and deductive reasoning	— Analysis questions
Reappraisal and reassessment	— Synthesis and Evaluation questions

▶ The Socratic process and collaborative empiricism

Collaborative empiricism, the foundation of CBT, is developed and nurtured through the Socratic process. During this the Clinician encourages the child to suspend their preconceived ideas and to keep an open mind as they test and evaluate the accuracy of their beliefs and assumptions. The child's cognitions are therefore viewed as hypothesises that are open for empirical validation rather than established facts. Through the Socratic process the child is encouraged to draw upon their past knowledge and empowered to discover new information that can help them re-evaluate and reappraise their cognitions. In essence, the child is helped to become their own therapist and to learn a process that can be applied to future problems in order to foster more adaptive and functional ways of thinking and behaving. The Clinician facilitates this process by helping the child to discover a framework that allows them to question and reappraise their thoughts rather than providing the child with a prepared set of alternative or preconceived views. Carefully crafted questions guide the child through the framework and keep the discussion focused and progressing until the child has evaluated and reappraised their thoughts and reached their own conclusions.

- The Socratic process is based upon a cooperative inquiry between child and Clinician.
- The process aims to facilitate the child's self-discovery.

For the Socratic process to be genuinely collaborative the Clinician needs to be open and non-judgemental in their approach. The Clinician and child need to cooperate in an open investigation and as such each partner needs to be aware of their own assumptions and preconceived ideas. The child's thoughts are not therefore automatically assumed to be dysfunctional. Instead the Clinician positively uses the Socratic process as a way of understanding the child's way of thinking. Once understood, the Clinician can adopt a gentle and curious approach in which questions and prompts are used to help the child reappraise and test their thoughts. Once again the philosophy of self-discovery is important and the

Clinician needs to avoid asking questions designed to directly criticise or challenge the child's thoughts (e.g. 'I think you've got that wrong'; 'No, it isn't really like that') or indeed by imposing their own preconceived ideas (e.g. 'I think it may be more like this').

> ■ Adopt an open, curious and non-judgemental approach in order to understand the child's way of thinking and to facilitate their development of appropriate limits.

▶ What makes a good Socratic question?

■ Clear and specific

Evaluating and reappraising thoughts can be an abstract process, especially for younger children, and so it is important to make Socratic questions as clear and specific as possible. The initial stages of the Socratic dialogue are concerned with establishing facts and so simple, specific and concrete questions are useful. Questions that are helpful tend to be:

- ■ 'What' questions – what did you do?; what did he say?
- ■ 'How' questions – how did you feel?; how did he do that?
- ■ 'Where' questions – where did you go?; where does this happen most?
- ■ 'When' questions – when does this happen?

■ Answerable

The Socratic process is designed to be empowering by highlighting how the child already possesses useful knowledge or has the ability to discover helpful information. It is then essential for the Clinician to ensure that their questions are answerable and that they do not ask what may seem to the child to be impossible questions. In particular 'why' questions, which require the child to make some interpretation or judgement rather than recounting factual details, are important but their use should be carefully monitored. Similarly, complex and multiple-component questions should be avoided while abstract and hypothetical questions are used with care.

■ Uses the child's language

Questions need to be phrased in the child's language and be consistent with the child's developmental level. The Clinician needs to carefully listen to what the child says and the words or metaphors they use so that these can be incorporated into the Socratic dialogue. This validates the child's use of language and constructs a dialogue based upon their words and meaning.

■ Attends to overlooked information

Inevitably the child's maladaptive or dysfunctional thoughts will arise from some bias or distortion in cognitive processing. The child may, for example, be selectively attending to information that supports their thoughts while overlooking that which might provide a different perspective. Socratic questioning brings to the child's attention relevant information that is currently being overlooked. By helping the child attend to this new information the Clinician is providing the child with new opportunities to question and reappraise their beliefs.

■ **Remain focused**

In many instances the child will be in possession of a great deal of information that could be used to reappraise and challenge their thoughts. Often the child will be unaware of this and will not have made the relevant links that will help them to piece this together in a coherent and helpful way. Socratic questioning helps the child to remain focused upon relevant information that will enable them to make the links and connections that will allow them to systematically evaluate their thoughts. It is all too easy to allow the dialogue to meander across subjects or to become distracted by interesting but non-relevant information.

> Good Socratic questions should:
>
> ■ be clear and specific
>
> ■ answerable
>
> ■ use the child's language
>
> ■ remain focused
>
> ■ help the child attend to relevant information that has been overlooked.

▶ How does it work?

Mike was 12 years of age and had many obsessive behaviours and thoughts. His current preoccupation was with the safety of the family cat that resulted in him insisting that the cat was locked in the house each night. This preoccupation was based upon his assumption that **If** the cat goes out at night **then** she will be knocked down by a car. This was discussed during our next meeting and Mike was helped to discover, evaluate and challenge this assumption.

PS:	Mike, Mum tells me that you are very worried about your cat.
MIKE:	Yes. I am. I don't like her going outside.
PS:	**When** do you most worry about her going out?
MIKE:	At night-time when it is dark.
PS:	OK, so **what** do you think will happen if she is out at night?
MIKE:	She'll have an accident.
PS:	**What** type of accident do you think she could have?
MIKE:	Don't know. Knocked down by a car and killed, I suppose.
PS:	I remember you telling me about how things always seem to go wrong and that you expect bad things to happen to you and your family.
MIKE:	Yeah, that's right.
PS:	So now you are worried that something bad will happen to your cat. **How** do you cope with this worry? **What** do you do each night when your cat wants to go out?
MIKE:	I have to go and find her and lock her in the house.
PS:	**What** time do you usually shut her in?
MIKE:	When I get home from school usually.
PS:	Does she mind being locked in?
MIKE:	Yeah, she hates it. She scratches me and tries to get out again.

PS:	So **how** does it make you feel when she is locked in?
MIKE:	Relieved, I suppose. I know she is safe.
PS:	So let me check that I've got this right. You worry that if your cat goes out at night she will get knocked over by a car. It seems to you that bad things often happen to your family. So to make sure this doesn't happen you keep her locked in where you know she is safe. She doesn't like this and wants to be outside but locking her in makes you feel better.
MIKE:	Yes, that's right.
PS:	**What** happens during the daytime?
MIKE:	What do you mean?
PS:	Well, I wondered whether you had to lock her in during the daytime?
MIKE:	No. She goes out.
PS:	**How** do you feel about her being out during the daytime?
MIKE:	It doesn't bother me.
PS:	Is your road not so busy during the daytime?
MIKE:	Oh yes, it is still quite busy.
PS:	**When** is it busier, day- or night-time?
MIKE:	Daytime, I suppose. Lots of people drive up and down to school and there is that big office block at the top of our road.
PS:	But you aren't so worried about your cat going out in the daytime even though the road is busier?
MIKE:	No, I'm not so worried during the daytime.
PS:	**When** would she be more likely to be hit by a car?
MIKE:	Don't know. I hadn't really thought about it.
PS:	Yeah I know, sometimes we just end up with an idea in our heads. But now we are thinking about this, when would she be most likely to be hit by a car?
MIKE:	I suppose it would be during the daytime when there are more cars about.
PS:	I think I am a bit confused, Mike. It sounds as if your cat is more likely to be knocked over during the daytime and yet you keep her locked in at night. Is there something else we need to think about or can you help me make sense of this?
MIKE:	Well there isn't anything else I am worried about but this doesn't really make sense. I hadn't thought about the road being busier during the daytime before.
PS:	Now we know that, does it help you to think about this differently?
MIKE:	It tells me that if she is safe being out during the daytime, then I suppose she should also be safe at night-time.

This example highlights how the Socratic process helped Mike to evaluate and reappraise the assumption that resulted in him locking his cat in the house each night. This assumption was based upon the premise that night-time was more dangerous and that his cat was more likely to be knocked down by a car The questioning process used clear and specific what, when, how questions that Mike was readily able to answer. The questions remained focused upon helping Mike discover and challenge his thinking by helping him to attend to new information that highlighted how his cat would be more likely to be hit by a car during the day rather than the night. In turn this helped him to reassess his behaviour and his need to lock his cat in at night.

In terms of process, the interview progressed through the first stage of identifying Mike's assumption and the feelings and behaviours associated with it. Through the use of empathic listening and summarising, the Clinician checked Mike's understanding of events and helped him consider new information that he had overlooked. Finally, he was helped to synthesise this new information and to reappraise his cognitions.

▶ Common problems

■ The Socratic process becomes an unpleasant question-and-answer inquisition

A Socratic dialogue is constructed around many Clinician-initiated questions. If not undertaken sensitively it can feel like a question-and-answer session with the Clinician acting as an inquisitor, firing question after question for the child to answer. With children this form of questioning may be associated with past situations where they have done something wrong or where they have needed to justify themselves. The inevitable outcome of such a process will be to alienate the child and to make them increasingly defensive and passive. Adolescents may, for example, appear irritated and refuse to talk; they may lose interest, become bored and stop participating in the dialogue; younger children may become worried, concerned about whether they are providing the Clinician with the 'right' answer.

The Clinician needs to ensure that this potentially unpleasant situation is avoided. A gentle, curious approach can reduce the possibility of an inquisition. Summarising provides a useful break from questions and can take the form of a fun activity in which the child and Clinician draw or write up where they have got to on a black/white board or a piece of paper. Similarly the Socratic dialogue could be conducted over more than one session. If the process feels uncomfortable, then stop and break it up.

If these problems continue, then this needs to be directly raised and discussed with the child. The Clinician should emphasise that they need to ask questions in order to understand how the child views events and experiences. They should explicitly state that there is no right answer and that there are many different ways of looking at and understanding events and each is important. The emotional reactions of the child should be acknowledged and lead into a discussion about how the Clinician and child can work together in a comfortable and fun way in order to gain a shared understanding. Finally, if you become aware that the Socratic process is resulting in the child continuing to appear angry, bored or worried, then examine the way therapy is being undertaken. Consider whether it remains collaborative, fun and relaxed and whether it is being undertaken at an appropriate speed. Pacing is an important consideration so that the potentially unpleasant quickfire question-and-answer cycle is prevented.

> ■ Clarify that you want to hear the child's views and ideas.
>
> ■ Adopt a gentle and curious approach.
>
> ■ Break up questions with summaries and take a break if it feels like an inquisition.
>
> ■ Use non-verbal methods.

■ The child cannot seem to understand or answer the questions

Socratic questioning is designed to help the child discover and explore their thoughts, feelings and behaviour. There will, however, be times during any interview when the child seems unable to find or access the information to answer questions. If this becomes a repeated problem it may be useful to reflect upon your questioning and whether you are asking the child questions that they have the information or knowledge to answer. This is particularly important with younger children who may find complex, more abstract or open questions difficult. At these times it may be better to experiment with more concrete and narrowly defined questions. These may help to ground the child and place your question in a context to which they can relate. Thus instead of asking a very general question such as 'How would you like things to be different?', you may want to ask a series of more defined questions such as 'What would you like to start doing?'; 'Would you like to go to any new clubs?'; 'What would change at school?'; 'How would Mum be different?' If the child still found it hard to answer, then you could become even more specific, 'Would you like to have more friends, see your friends more often or play outside more?' This presents the child with firm options while highlighting that there can be more than one answer. It also gives the child opportunities to say 'No', this does not apply to me. Alternatively the Clinician can more actively involve a parent or other family member in the discussion and ask them to suggest some ideas. However, this needs to be carefully monitored to ensure that the child does express their own views rather than simply agreeing with the options that are being provided.

> ▪ Make questions simple, clear and unambiguous.

■ The child cannot identify any new information

The Socratic process helps the child attend to relevant information that they may have overlooked. In many situations the child will already be in possession of this information but there will be occasions when they need to actively seek the information they require. This could be obtained by simply asking someone else (e.g. Mum, Dad, friends) or alternatively through a behavioural experiment. Experiments are powerful and enjoyable ways of objectively seeking new information. The child can be encouraged to act as a scientist, 'Private I' (Friedberg & McClure 2002), 'Social Detective' (Spence 1995) or 'Thought Tracker' (Stallard 2002a), who sets out to discover information and to test their cognitions.

There are many ways in which behavioural experiments can be used, but before embarking upon one it is important to ensure that all relevant parties are aware of and support the experiment. Without this support the experiment may inadvertently be undermined. Once the support is agreed the process involves a number of simple steps:

- ■ Specify the negative cognition that will be tested.
- ■ Rate the strength of belief in the cognition.
- ■ Devise an experiment that can be used to test this cognition.
- ■ Agree when the experiment will be undertaken.
- ■ Describe what the child predicts will happen.
- ■ Carry out the experiment and specify what actually happened.
- ■ Rate the strength of belief in the cognition after completion of the experiment.

> ▪ Encourage the child to discover new information by using behavioural experiments.
> ▪ Involve carers in treatment sessions so that they can provide a different perspective.

■ **The child cannot synthesise the new with the old information to reappraise their thoughts**

Some children may actively engage in the Socratic process, but it becomes a rationale exercise that does not lead them to the final step of reflection and reappraising their own cognitions. New and challenging information is identified but is viewed as somewhat separate and detached and not synthesised into the child's cognitive construction of their world.

On these occasions the Clinician needs to be patient. The Socratic process continues, the child is helped to discover more new information and their attention is brought back to that which they have overlooked. Reviews and summaries where the Clinician and child write or draw what the Socratic process has helped them to discover are useful. These non-verbal summaries can be added to during each session and provide a powerful and objective way of highlighting important information. Summaries and reviews should be followed by a discussion in which the child is encouraged to reflect on this information. Regularly asking the child to reconsider their cognitions in light of this new knowledge provides opportunities for the old and new information to be integrated and cognitions to be reappraised.

> ▪ Keep the child focused upon information they have overlooked and continue to help them to discover new information.
>
> ▪ Written summaries are powerful visual reminders of newly acquired information.
>
> ▪ Provide regular opportunities for reflection.

The Chain of Events

Sometimes we worry that if we don't do something then bad things will happen. Because we think it, we believe that it is true without checking out whether it is possible.

Start at the bottom and write down the bad thing that you think will happen. Go back to the top of the chain and fill in all the links that would have to be there before this could happen.

CHAPTER FIVE

Involving parents in child-focused CBT

▶ The importance of involving parents

The theoretical model that guides CBT needs to consider and incorporate both the internal and the external environments that surround the child (Krain & Kendall 1999). In terms of the external environment there are many potentially important influences including the child's school, peers, family, social and cultural context. Many interventions are context-specific and while they may acknowledge these important influences they do not necessarily fully involve or actively address them through the intervention. One notable example of an evidence-based multi-component intervention is multi-systemic therapy (MST). MST considers the role of family, school and peer group on the development and maintenance of adolescent antisocial behaviour. Although not primarily CBT, a variety of interventions including behavioural, family and cognitive therapy (e.g. self-instruction training) are used to address each factor contributing to the child's difficulties. The results are encouraging and the longer-term outcomes with severely antisocial delinquents have now been reported (Henggeler *et al.* 2002).

The relative importance of each environmental influence will vary, depending upon the age of the child. Peer and social factors are more important during adolescence while family factors play a more significant role with younger children. However, one of the most important influences that requires particular attention in child-focused CBT is that of parents. Indeed, Kendall & Panichelli-Mindel (1995) note the importance of parental psycho-pathology, parenting styles and parental management in the development and maintenance of many child disorders. Child-focused CBT therefore needs to consider the wider systemic context and, in particular, the potential role of parents and carers in the onset, maintenance and treatment of their child's problems.

During assessment the Clinician needs to gain an understanding of important family beliefs, the systemic structure and context within which the problems present, and parental behaviours that may encourage and reinforce the child's difficulties. This will involve the identification of any deficient skills, perhaps in parenting or conflict resolution; distorted parental expectations and beliefs about their child; or dysfunctional cognitions the parents may ascribe to their child's behaviour or their ability to effect positive change. In turn this will inform both the focus (e.g. directly working with child and/or parent) and content (e.g. addressing child cognitions, parental management skills or important parental cognitions and beliefs) of the intervention.

Despite the widespread recognition amongst Clinicians about the need to involve parents in child-focused CBT, the precise role of parents has received comparatively little attention (Barrett 2000). This may in part be due to the early tendency for Clinicians to download and apply intrapsychic models developed for use with adults, a tendency which resulted in children often being treated as little adults and the important family context being overlooked.

■ The Clinician needs to consider the systemic context in which the child operates and to involve key influences in the intervention.

■ Externalising disorders

Parent training

There is strong empirical support to indicate that externalising problems such as conduct disorder and oppositional defiant disorders respond positively to interventions that aim to directly modify parenting practice (Brestan & Eyberg 1998; Kazdin 1997; Kazdin & Weisz 1998). These interventions target important parental behaviours that are associated with the development and maintenance of the child's problematic behaviours. New skills are taught to replace deficient parenting skills and inappropriate parenting practices modified through parent training programmes (Forehand & MacMahon 1981; Patterson 1982; Webster-Stratton 1992). These interventions pay little direct attention to parental cognitions, although undoubtedly cognitive change will occur through experience and use of new skills. In these interventions:

■ The parents rather than the child are the primary focus of the intervention.

■ Child behaviour is changed as a result of changes in parenting practice.

■ The main focus is upon behavioural techniques where parents are encouraged to
  — identify antecedents that elicit, and consequences that maintain, inappropriate behaviour;
  — identify and reward prosocial behaviour;
  — reduce inappropriate behaviour through the use of methods such as timeout or response cost;
  — improve monitoring of the child's activities.

These programmes tend to be primarily behavioural and although parent training does produce positive results these approaches also have a number of limitations. A number of families who start parenting programmes drop out before completion (Prinz & Miller 1994). Data analysis is typically reported for treatment completers rather than for all who enter the trials. Many of the outcome studies have been undertaken with volunteers who arguably present with less severe problems (Scott et al. 2001). It is therefore not surprising to note that outcomes in traditional clinic-based settings are typically poorer. This may be due to a range of factors, including cases that are more severe, cases that exist within a complex social and familial context, cases that have a greater rate of co-morbidity, and cases that receive less empirically supported interventions from staff with heavier caseloads. There is also the important issue of clinical significance. Although significant reductions on symptom measures are reported in many studies, up to 40% of children continue to show clinically significant problems at follow-up (Kazdin 1997). These factors highlight that, while behaviourally based parenting programmes can obtain promising results, there are a significant number of children and parents who are not helped.

Cognitively enhanced parent training

Increased recognition of these limitations has led to the development of more sophisticated programmes in which greater attention is directly paid to important parental cognitions that may impede or interfere with the achievement of positive change. As highlighted by Johnston (1996), parental attributions about the causes of their child's behaviour or in their ability to bring about positive change are important cognitions that need to be assessed and addressed.

Parental cognitions may also affect the motivation of the family to seek help, their commitment to the intervention or their evaluation of change (Durlak *et al.* 2001). In terms of help-seeking, the authors note that the majority of children with significant adjustment problems are never brought for treatment by their parents. A significant factor in determining help-seeking is the parents' perception of the child's behaviour rather than its actual severity. Statements such as 'This is the way he has always been and always will be' or 'No one can make this any different' are clear indications of hopeless cognitions that will limit the parents' desire to seek or engage with any form of help. In terms of the intervention, statements such as 'You can try if you like' or 'Attending these appointments is difficult' begin to signal that the parent is unsure or not yet committed to the possibility that this particular intervention can result in change. Ambivalence such as this needs to be recognised, directly addressed and resolved before the parent is able to fully engage in CBT.

Alternatively the parents' own psychological problems may compromise the intervention. An anxious parent may, for example, have problems encouraging their child to undertake behavioural tasks or a depressed parent may have difficulty recognising and praising their child's success. The ability of some parents to encourage or reinforce their child's new behaviours and adaptive coping strategies may therefore be limited (Shirk 2001). Similarly, parents may find it difficult to see or acknowledge change in their child, particularly if they have their own mental health problems. This could be verbalised by hopeless statements such as 'I can't see any difference' or 'He still plays up when we go to the shops' which may reflect the parents' biased and negative cognitive style rather than the reality of their child's behaviour.

At other times parents may express negative and dysfunctional cognitions about their child ('He hates me'), how they behave ('She does this to wind me up') and the future ('I can't do anything when he has a temper'). Parental cognitions such as these need to be directly addressed since they will adversely interfere with effective parenting and contribute to the maintenance of the current situation. A direct focus upon parental cognitions has been incorporated into some recent parenting programmes. Attributions and beliefs about being a parent are directly assessed and addressed as a way of increasing engagement and enhancing parent training (White *et al.* 2003).

> ■ Greater attention is being paid to identifying and addressing important parental cognitions that might impede or adversely affect behavioural parenting programmes.

■ Internalising disorders

There is growing evidence about the role of parental behaviour and cognitions in the onset and maintenance of child internalising problems. A number of researchers have documented the nature of the relationship between parent and child anxiety and the role of parental behaviour in maintaining the child's anxiety (Dadds & Barrett 2001; Ginsburg *et al.* 1995). For example, Barrett *et al.* (1996a) note that parents of anxious children are more likely to engage in behaviours that communicate a sense of continued threat and danger to their child. Other research suggests that parents of anxious children tend to be more overly controlling, protective and critical, and that this results in the child having fewer opportunities to develop successful coping skills (Krohnc & Hock 1991). These findings would suggest that children of anxious parents become sensitive to the threatening features of their environment. This is encouraged by parental behaviour, which conveys to the child a sense of continuing threat and danger and limits the child's opportunities to develop alternative coping skills.

Similarly, in terms of OCD important family patterns and parental behaviours have been identified. Children with OCD come from families where there are high levels of criticism and over-involvement (Hibbs *et al.* 1991). Parents are less likely to reward independent behaviour in their child and make less use of problem-solving strategies (Barrett *et al.* 2002). The distress of the child can understandably be upsetting for the parents. They may attempt to deal with this by becoming involved in reassuring their child or participating in their rituals and habits, behaviours that serve to reinforce the child's OCD.

The significant contribution of parental behaviour and cognitions to the onset and maintenance of many childhood disorders provides a strong rationale for involving parents in child-focused CBT. Indeed, Spence *et al.* (2000) note that interventions that do not attempt to change parental behaviour would be unlikely to be effective.

■ Parental behaviour and cognitions are associated with the development and maintenance of childhood problems.

■ Greater attention is now being paid to identifying and addressing important parental cognitions that negatively interfere with or limit child-focused CBT.

▶ Clinical benefits of parental involvement

It has been suggested that parental involvement in child-focused CBT results in a number of benefits.

- The important role and influence of parents in the development of their child's functional and dysfunctional behaviours and cognitions is recognised, included in the formulation and addressed as part of the intervention.

- Parents are educated in, and able to support, the treatment rationale. They are able to send consistent messages to the child about the importance and value of the skills they are learning.

- The child's use of new skills outside of clinic sessions can be monitored, prompted and reinforced.

- The transfer of skills from clinical to real-life situations can be encouraged.

- Important parental perceptions, expectations and beliefs about their child can be challenged and reappraised.

- Parental behaviours that may be maintaining the child's behaviour (e.g. reassurance or inappropriate boundaries) can be addressed.

- Continued improvement and maintenance after therapy has ended may be facilitated by parental involvement.

The extent of parental involvement will vary depending upon the nature of the problem and the age of the child. As previously mentioned, CBT interventions that address externalising behaviours through parent management training are primarily directed at the parent with child involvement being limited. Those that address internalising disorders tend to focus more upon direct work with the child. In terms of age, Bailey (2001) notes that with younger children parental involvement is more important. With older adolescents the parents may have a less direct role in therapy sessions, although they will still need access to psychoeducational resources and information that will allow them to support the intervention outside of the clinic setting.

The involvement of parents in child-focused CBT:

- allows important parental behaviours associated with the child's problems to be addressed
- facilitates parental encouragement, reinforcement and the generalisation of the child's newly acquired skills.

▶ Model of change

The way parents participate in child-focused CBT varies. In many programmes parental involvement results in parents being provided with parallel treatment sessions but often separate from their child (Clarke *et al.* 1999; Heyne *et al.* 2002; Lewinsohn *et al.* 1990). In a variation, parental involvement in the study by Spence *et al.* (2000) consisted of parents observing the children's sessions through a one-way screen. In these programmes parents and children work through the same materials but never actually attend any treatment sessions together in the same room. In others, particularly those focusing upon anxiety (Barrett 1998; Barrett *et al.* 1996b; Cobham *et al.* 1998), sessions are scheduled for parents and children to work together.

The underlying model detailing how parental involvement facilitates changes in the child's behaviour or their acquisition of skills has seldom been explicitly stated. Barrett (1998) describes a model in which the Clinician joins with parents and children during joint sessions to form an 'expert team'. This involves the open sharing of information and building upon the existing strengths of family members with a view to empowering parents and children to solve and address their own problems.

Silverman *et al.* (1999b) describes parental involvement as part of a process that involves the transfer of expert knowledge and skills from the Clinician to the parent and then to the child. This 'transfer of control' model informs the sequencing of treatment sessions and application of skills. Thus in their programme, although parents and children learn skills together, the parents are encouraged to implement the skills first. Once mastered, the parents' use of anxiety-reduction strategies is faded out and the child's use of self-control strategies is encouraged.

- The model of change is rarely defined.
- The transfer of control model assumes that parents need to be taught the skills first or simultaneously in order to teach their children.

▶ The role of parents in child-focused CBT

Parents are often involved in CBT, either as treatment collaborators or part of the therapeutic team (Braswell 1991). While their involvement appears to have clinical, theoretical and pragmatic substance, their actual role and the extent of their involvement varies considerably. Parents have been involved in child-focused CBT in various roles including as facilitator, as co-Clinician or as a client in their own right. The focus and emphasis of interventions have ranged from directly working on the child's problems through to separate parent-focused sessions. Similarly the balance between child, parent and family work, and the way in which it is conducted and sequenced, has varied.

■ Parents as facilitators

The most limited role for parents in child-focused CBT is that of the facilitator. Typically parents attend two or three parallel sessions in which they are provided with the rationale for using CBT and information about the techniques and strategies that their child will learn. The child is the direct focus of the intervention and the CBT programme is designed to address their problems. This is exemplified in the Coping Cat programme for children with anxiety disorders (Kendall 1994). The 16-week individually administered programme is undertaken directly with the child, with parental participation consisting of two or three separate sessions focusing upon psychoeducation.

A similar model has been described in the Adolescent Coping with Depression Course (Clarke *et al.* 2002) where young people participate in a 16-session course while their parents attend three informational meetings. These meetings are designed to inform parents about the topics being discussed, the skills taught and the rationale for their use. Similarly, the role of parents in the programme by March *et al.* (1994) for children with OCD also falls within this category. The main focus is individual work with the child with parents attending three meetings with their child.

> ■ The facilitator is the most limited parent role.
>
> ■ The prime focus of the intervention is upon direct work with the child.
>
> ■ The parents attend psychoeducational sessions to:
> — educate them in the CBT model and
> — inform them about the skills their child will be acquiring.

■ Parents as co-Clinicians

As co-Clinicians, parents are more extensively involved in the intervention. They participate in the same or a similar intervention programme as their child either together or in parallel. Parents are encouraged to be more active and to act as a co-Clinician outside of treatment sessions by monitoring, prompting and reinforcing their child's use of cognitive skills. Both Mendlowitz *et al.* (1999) and Toren *et al.* (2000) describe joint parent/child interventions for children with anxiety disorders. In these programmes the parents' own behaviour/problems are not directly addressed, the child remains the focus of the intervention and the primary goal is for the parents to help reduce their child's psychological distress.

> ■ The co-Clinician attends a number of the treatment sessions.
>
> ■ The co-Clinician has an active role in encouraging and supervising the child's use of skills out of sessions.
>
> ■ The child remains the target of the intervention.

■ Parents as co-clients

An alternative model involves parents themselves also being the subject of a direct intervention by, for example, learning new parenting skills, managing self/family anxiety or addressing issues related to child abuse (Cobham *et al.* 1998; Cohen & Mannarino 1998). With the co-client model, the child receives CBT to address their own problems while their parents/family acquire new skills in order to address family or personal difficulties that contribute to the onset or maintenance of their child's difficulties. Cohen & Mannarino (1996), for example, describe a 12-session CBT programme for children who have been sexually abused, where the intervention addresses both child and parent issues related to abuse. Child sessions focus upon feelings of helplessness/powerlessness, attributions of blame, anxiety and behavioural problems related to the abuse. Separate parent sessions focus upon parental attributions of blame, parent history of abuse, feelings towards the perpetrator, and the facilitation of child support and management of abuse-related behaviour. Similarly, Cobham *et al.* (1998) describe a programme in which children with anxiety disorders receive 10 sessions with parents receiving four separate sessions. The parents' sessions explore their role in the development and maintenance of their child's problems and explore how to manage their own anxiety and model appropriate anxiety management strategies for their child.

> ■ The child and parent are both targets of specific interventions.
>
> ■ Important parent/family problems that contribute to the child's difficulties are directly addressed.

■ Parents as clients

The final model exemplified in behavioural parent training programmes is where the parents themselves are the direct focus of the intervention. The child typically does not attend the treatment sessions, which are concerned with teaching parents positive behaviour management, problem solving and negotiation skills.

Cognitively enhanced parent training directly focuses upon assessing and challenging important parental cognitions. The focus of the intervention is not the parents' own psychological problems but their attributions and expectations about their child. Durlak *et al.* (2001) suggest that important parental cognitions could be negative or pessimistic attributions regarding the locus of the problem (e.g. lies solely within the child), the reason for it (e.g. she hates me) and the possibility of change (e.g. he will never be able to control his temper). Cognitions such as these are demotivating and adversely effect engagement in therapy. They also tend to increase the powerlessness and hopelessness of the parents, thereby reducing effectiveness.

The potential value of focusing upon the parents' attributions about their child is highlighted in a study by Bugental *et al.* (2002). The simple cognitive intervention they described involved challenging parental attributions relating to either self or child blame for problematic behaviour until a more benign external cause and strategy was generated. The results demonstrated that rates of physical abuse amongst these high-risk mothers were significantly lower in the group who received this cognitive intervention.

> ■ The parent is the target of intervention and the child does not attend treatment sessions.
>
> ■ The intervention focuses upon:
> — teaching new skills to address deficient parenting behaviours or
> — challenging biased cognitions about parenting efficacy or the nature of their child's problems.

► Parental involvement

■ Does parental involvement enhance effectiveness?

This brief overview highlights the need for Clinicians to carefully consider and plan how parents are involved in child-focused CBT. If parents are involved, their role needs to be defined, the focus of the parental sessions needs to be clarified, and the process by which parents facilitate change in their child needs to be defined. In turn this will inform whether parents and children will be seen jointly or separately and the sequencing of the sessions. However, given the different ways in which parents can be involved in child-focused CBT, a key question facing Clinicians is whether parental involvement enhances effectiveness and if

Table 5.1 Randomised controlled outcome studies comparing child-focused CBT with and without parental involvement

Study	Size, age and primary diagnosis	Child only CBT	Child CBT + parents
Barrett (1998)	N = 60 Aged 7–14 Anxiety disorder	12 weekly 2-hr sessions Group administration	12 child sessions + 12 child and parent Family Anxiety Management sessions Group administration
Barrett et al. (1996b)	N = 79 Aged 7–14 Anxiety disorder	12 weekly 60/80-minute sessions Individual administration	12 child sessions + 12 child and parent Family Anxiety Management sessions Individual administration
Clarke et al. (1999)	N = 123 Aged 14–18 Major depressive disorder or dysthymia	16 2-hr sessions over 8 weeks Group administration	16 child sessions + 8 parent sessions Group administration
Cobham et al. (1998)	N = 67 Aged 7–14 Anxiety disorder	10 1.5-hr sessions over 14 weeks Group administration	10 child sessions + 4 parent sessions on Parental Anxiety Management Group administration
Heyne et al. (2002)	N = 61 Aged 7–14 School refusal + anxiety disorder	8 50-minute sessions over 4 weeks Individual administration	8 child sessions + 8 parent sessions Individual administration
King et al. (2000)	N = 36 Aged 5–17 PTSD or severe stress reaction	20 50-minute weekly sessions Individual administration	20 child sessions + 20 parent sessions Individual administration
Lewinsohn et al. (1990)	N = 59 Aged 14–18 Depressive disorder	14 2-hr sessions over 7 weeks Group administration	14 child sessions + 7 parent sessions Group administration
Mendlowitz et al. (1999)	N = 62 Aged 7–12 Anxiety disorder	12 1.5-hr weekly sessions Group administration	12 1.5-hr weekly sessions Group administration
Nauta et al. (2001)	N = 18 Aged 8–15 Anxiety disorder	12 45–60-minute weekly sessions Individual administration	7 45–60-minute fortnightly sessions Individual administration
Nauta et al. (2003)	N = 79 Aged 7–18 Anxiety disorder	12 45–60-minute weekly sessions Individual administration	7 45–60-minute fortnightly sessions Individual administration
Spence et al. (2000)	N = 50 Aged 7–14 Social phobia	12 1.5-hr weekly sessions plus two booster sessions Group administration	12 child sessions + 12 parent sessions Group administration

so, what model of involvement is optimal for which condition? This question is of paramount importance to Clinicians in planning and structuring interventions and yet has received surprisingly little attention.

A literature review of RCTs that have compared child-focused CBT for emotional problems with and without parental involvement identified 11 studies. All provided pre- and post-assessments that allowed the additional contribution of parental involvement to be determined. The studies are summarised in Table 5.1.

The studies used a variety of measures to determine post-treatment outcome. Diagnostic status was assessed in nine studies although only one found a statistical difference in favour of parental involvement (Barrett *et al.* 1996b). Information from a total of 35 different self-report measures was collected but in only one instance was there a significant difference to suggest that parental involvement enhanced the outcome (Mendlowitz *et al.* 1999). Clinician ratings were completed in six studies with two reporting CBT to be significantly enhanced by parental involvement (Barrett 1998; Barrett *et al.* 1996b). Parent ratings were completed in all 11 studies with five finding superior results with parental involvement, mostly on the internalising or externalising sub-scale of the Child Behaviour Checklist (Barrett 1998; Barrett *et al.* 1996b; Heyne *et al.* 2002; Lewinsohn *et al.* 1990; Mendlowitz *et al.* 1999).

In conclusion the results of these studies do not provide the expected support that parental involvement enhanced the effectiveness of child-focused CBT for emotional disorders. Indeed, five of the 11 studies failed to demonstrate any positive significant effect of parental involvement on any measure (Clarke *et al.* 1999; King *et al.* 2000; Nauta *et al.* 2001, 2003; Spence *et al.* 2000).

While the results from the individual studies are disappointing, a number of researchers observed a trend towards better outcomes with parental involvement. In considering the findings from these studies it should be noted that many of the samples were small and were not of a sufficient size to detect small, but significant, differences. Nonetheless, at present the available data do not strongly support the anecdotal views of Clinicians that parental involvement enhances child-focused CBT and aids the use and transfer of skills to everyday situations (King *et al.* 1998; Sanders *et al.* 1994; Toren *et al.* 2000).

> ▪ The results are not always consistent and the gains are sometimes modest.
>
> ▪ At present the evidence from individual studies does not provide strong support for the widely accepted clinical view that parental involvement enhances child-focused CBT.

▪ Are gains maintained over time?

The questions of whether post-treatment gains last, or indeed increase or decrease over time, have been examined in six of the studies detailed in Table 5.1. Once again the results from the individual studies demonstrate that some of the benefits obtained at the end of treatment become less significant. The post-treatment differences reported by Heyne *et al.* (2002) in school attendance disappeared, as did the differences in the Lewinsohn *et al.* (1990) study. The strongest data suggesting the enhanced role of parents in child-focused CBT came from the work of Barrett *et al.* (1996b). However, when these children were followed up 6 years post-treatment there were no differences between the groups on any measure (Barrett *et al.* 2001). Child-focused CBT with or without parental involvement appears effective.

> ▪ The additional long-term treatment benefits of involving parents in child-focused CBT have not yet consistently been demonstrated.

■ How long do child-focused interventions involving parents take to deliver?

The interventions were typically completed within 14 weeks, involved between 8 and 40 separate treatment sessions, with the total length of child-focused CBT ranging from under 7 hours (Heyne *et al.* 2002) to 28 hours (Lewinsohn *et al.* 1990). The total number of hours spent in the programme did not appear related to outcome. The shortest child-focused programme involved a total of 7 hours (Heyne *et al.* 2002) and the longest 28 hours (Lewinsohn *et al.* 1990), both programmes that failed to find any substantive benefits of parental involvement. CBT with and without parental involvement were matched for total clinical time in some studies (Barrett 1998; Barrett *et al.* 1996b; Cobham *et al.* 1998; Mendlowitz *et al.* 1999), whereas others provided parent sessions in addition to child-focused CBT (Nauta *et al.* 2001, 2003). This resulted in some interventions requiring over 30 clinical hours to deliver (King *et al.* 2000; Lewinsohn *et al.* 1990).

> ■ The parental component of some programmes can significantly increase the number of therapeutic hours required to deliver the intervention.

■ How should parents be involved?

Parents were involved in child-focused CBT in different ways. Parents were either involved in the whole (Mendlowitz *et al.* 1999) or part of the treatment session with their child (Barrett 1998), or attended parallel separate sessions (Heyne *et al.* 2002; Nauta *et al.* 2001, 2003). A number of studies used an individual-based approach (Barrett *et al.* 1996b; Nauta *et al.* 2001, 2003), whereas others were delivered in a group format (Barrett 1998; Mendlowitz *et al.* 1999; Spence *et al.* 2000).

> ■ There is no preferred way of involving parents in child-focused CBT.
> ■ Separate or joint sessions, group or individual formats have all been used.

■ Does any additional clinical time outweigh the potential gains?

In view of the high rates of improvement with child-only CBT, the comparative benefits of any additional therapeutic time required to deliver the combined child/parent intervention need to be considered.

A number of studies matched the length of the intervention, so that parental involvement did not result in any increased clinical time (Barrett 1998; Barrett *et al.* 1996b; Cobham *et al.* 1998). Thus, if parental involvement does not result in additional therapeutic time, then this would seem to be the model of choice. However, parental involvement in other child-focused CBT interventions has resulted in clinical time being effectively doubled (Heyne *et al.* 2002; King *et al.* 2000). In this situation, involving parents in child-focused CBT would result in fewer children being treated within the available clinical time. The effective use of limited therapeutic time is an increasing consideration for many child and family mental health services that are struggling to meet increasing rates of referrals. If CBT interventions involving parents result in additional therapeutic time, the relative benefits of this over-providing child-focused CBT need to be considered.

> ■ A large number of children make considerable progress without parental involvement.
> ■ Additional therapeutic time from involving parents needs to be considered against potential reductions in the number of children who can be helped.

■ **Does the effect of parental involvement depend on the child's presenting problem?**

The majority of studies that have explored the additional effects of involving parents in child-focused CBT have been undertaken with children with anxiety disorders, typically aged 7–14 years. Conclusions about the relationship between parental involvement and the child's presenting problem cannot therefore be made. At a purely descriptive level, both studies in Table 5.1 that involved children with depression failed to find positive benefits from involving parents (Clarke *et al.* 1999; Lewinsohn *et al.* 1990). Similarly parental involvement in child-focused CBT to address social phobia (Spence *et al.* 2000), school refusal (Heyne *et al.* 2002) and sexual abuse (King *et al.* 2000) resulted in few additional gains. The most substantive evidence came from studies treating children with generalised anxiety disorders (Barrett 1998; Barrett *et al.* 1996b) although the results are not consistent (Nauta *et al.* 2001, 2003).

> ▪ There is little evidence to determine whether the enhanced benefits of parental involvement in child-focused CBT are associated with the child's problems.

■ **Is the outcome affected by the parent's own mental health?**

When considering the particular role of parents and the focus of any intervention, it is important to consider the mental health needs of the parent. Although this seems self-evident, only one study has explored this issue. Cobham *et al.* (1998) examined whether parental involvement in child-focused CBT was affected by parental anxiety. The results demonstrated that child-focused CBT plus the additional parental anxiety management component resulted in significantly lower rates of diagnosed child anxiety at post-treatment if both the child and parent were anxious. The parental component did not result in additional benefits if the parent was not anxious.

This is clearly an important yet neglected area and further work is required to assess the role of parental mental health upon the effectiveness of child-focused CBT. In addition this will help to clarify the specific focus and content of the parental component.

> ▪ The parent's own mental health needs to be assessed.
> ▪ Parental involvement in child-focused CBT may be helpful if the parent has a mental health problem.

■ **Should parents attend the same or separate treatment sessions?**

The way in which parents have been involved in child-focused CBT has varied. It is surprising to note that in a number of studies parents have not actually participated in the same treatment sessions as their child. Instead, parents attend concurrent sessions and so may not be fully aware of the specific issues, skills or problems that their child is addressing (King *et al.* 2000; Lewinsohn 1990; Nauta *et al.* 2001, 2003). Clarifying the purpose of parental involvement and adhering to an explicit model that defines how parents contribute to their child's learning would determine both the sequencing and way in which they are involved.

Those studies that have involved parents and children in the same treatment sessions have generally found more positive effects (Barrett 1998; Barrett *et al.* 1996b). As reported by Mendlowitz *et al.* (1999), parental involvement provided the parents with more specific opportunities to prompt the child to use, and reinforce, their skills. New skills are practised during treatment sessions and the Clinician is able to identify and intervene to address any parent–child interactional issues that might hinder therapy.

> ■ Parental involvement in child-focused CBT may be more beneficial if parents and children attend and participate in the same treatment sessions.

▶ Common components of parent-focused interventions

Although there are considerable variations in the way parents are involved in child-focused CBT, Ginsburg & Schlossberg (2002) highlight that parental interventions with children with emotional problems tend to focus upon a number of core skills:

- psychoeducation;
- contingency management;
- reducing parental anxiety;
- cognitive restructuring;
- improving parent–child relationship;
- relapse prevention.

■ Psychoeducation

A common aim of all interventions that involve parents in child-focused CBT is to provide parents with information about CBT. Information is typically provided about the underlying rationale of the treatment model, the process of therapy and the content and key skills that will be covered.

Included at the end of this chapter are information sheets for parents and children that explain the basic CBT model and process. The materials highlight the core features of CBT, namely:

- highlighting the link between events, thoughts, feelings and behaviour;
- identifying unhelpful ways of thinking;
- learning to check out and test negative thoughts;
- learning new ways of coping with unpleasant feelings;
- how to solve problems so that difficulties are faced and overcome.

Finally, the key aspects of the process in terms of being collaborative, fun and experimental are highlighted. The parent sheet also contains information about how parents can help their children and uses the acronym SUPPORT to highlight the following key issues:

- S – Show your child how to be successful.
- U – Understand that they have a problem and need your help.
- P – Patient approach.
- P – Prompt them to try.
- O – Observe what they do.
- R – Reward and praise their efforts.
- T – Talk about what they do.

Written summaries such as these provide a permanent reminder that can be referred back to at a later date or discussed with those unable to attend therapy sessions.

■ Contingency management

The major goal of contingency management is to maximise the praise and attention the child receives for displaying positive behaviour and new skills and to minimise the amount they receive for engaging in dysfunctional behaviours. Parents are typically encouraged to reinforce:

- the child's use of new skill or behaviours;
- the child's coping, courageous or independent behaviour;
- signs that the child is approaching and tackling their problems rather than avoiding them;
- each successive step that moves the child closer towards achieving their overall goal.

Parents are instructed to reinforce their child's positive behaviours in a number of different ways, including the use of verbal praise, increased privileges and tangible rewards. Similarly parents are educated about the need to ignore and extinguish dysfunctional behaviours and cognitions. Thus parents would be advised to respond in a caring and empathic way to any of their child's worries or concerns, but not to become involved in reinforcing or simply rehearsing them. Instead parents would encourage the child to try their new skills and coping strategies and to praise and encourage their use. Parents are therefore helped to use simple contingency management techniques of descriptive praise and planned ignoring.

■ Reducing parental anxiety

In view of the significant association between child and parent anxiety, a number of CBT programmes include interventions aimed at reducing the parent's own anxiety. These interventions are essentially concerned with helping the parent to:

- identify their own anxious feelings and specific anxiety response;
- recognise the effect of their own behaviour upon the child;
- replace their anxiety-increasing thoughts with more helpful anxiety-reducing thoughts;
- to face and overcome their own fears and challenges;
- to model courageous behaviour and helpful skills.

■ Cognitive restructuring

Parental cognitions are clearly important and in a number of instances will interfere with treatment and limit the ability of the parents to support their child. Some programmes have therefore included a specific cognitive restructuring programme designed to identify, challenge and reappraise important or dysfunctional parental cognitions. For example, beliefs about parenting ability, expectations about their children's behaviour and attributions about events could become the specific focus of parent sessions. In programmes with sexually abused children, parental attributions about blame (e.g. 'I should have protected her and I didn't'), about responsibility (e.g. 'If I had listened more to his worries he wouldn't have needed to abuse her') or about guilt (e.g. 'If I had given up my job in the evenings I would have spent more time at home') may be specifically addressed.

With children with anxiety disorders, parental beliefs about their child's competence (e.g. 'They just don't know what to do in that situation'), independence (e.g. 'They just wouldn't cope without me') or ability to confront and handle stressful events (e.g. 'That is just too big a step') may be elicited and tested.

Work with parents of children with externalising difficulties may directly address the meaning parents ascribe to their child's behaviour moving from more internal causal attributions (e.g. 'He does that because he doesn't like me') to more external attributions (e.g. 'He probably plays up and cries because he is tired at the end of nursery').

The process of cognitive restructuring typically involves the following six steps:

- elicitation of important or common dysfunctional cognitions;
- identification of common thinking traps and the consequences of these ways of thinking;
- a full exploration of information that supports or does not support these thoughts;
- experimentation to test and check what really happens;
- reflecting upon this new information to arrive at a more balanced view that provides a better explanation;
- implementation of this view and challenging previous beliefs.

■ Improving parent–child relationships

A key aim encapsulated within the parental component of many child-focused CBT programmes is to enhance the relationship between parent and child. This typically involves the development of strategies that reduce conflict and improve communication and problem solving. These build upon the contingency management skills described earlier, resulting in positive messages increasing and negative confrontations decreasing.

In terms of reducing conflict, parents are helped to develop skills that prevent arguments occurring or escalating. Parents may be helped to plot the stages that arguments move through and to identify ways in which this escalation can be stopped, and they can 'bale out' and calm down. Important triggers, common problem areas, de-escalation strategies and important cognitions (e.g. 'I'm going to have the last word') need to be clarified and challenged. The need for between-carer consistency is examined with shared boundaries and consequences agreed. Communication is facilitated by the development of appropriate listening skills that convey interest, such as eye contact, nodding and summarising. Negative communication patterns that involve criticism, blaming, interrupting and talking over are replaced with more positive patterns. Parents are also encouraged to make regular times to talk and review the day with their child and to reinforce the use of important skills and behaviours. Finally a framework that can be used in a step-by-step fashion to solve problems is emphasised. This could be based upon the problem-solving approach described in TGFG (pages 174–176). This involves clearly defining the problem and then identifying a range of potential solutions. The consequences of each solution are explored and, on the basis of this, a preferred solution is chosen and implemented.

■ Relapse prevention

There is a need to prepare the child and their parents for a possible relapse and the return of their previous problems. Inevitably, there will be times when the child's new skills prove less effective and their previous dysfunctional behaviours and cognitions return. Without appropriate preparation the child and their parents may believe that their new skills, like many of the others they have tried in the past, have become ineffective. In turn this can become very negative and demotivating and may reinforce previous beliefs about being unable to effect any positive change.

Preparing the child and their parents for a possible relapse is an important part of the intervention. Relapse is therefore expected and normalised as part of the on-going process of change and is construed as a temporary setback rather than a more permanent indication of failure. As well as explicitly acknowledging and preparing for this eventuality a more proactive approach can be adopted by identifying potential triggers or difficult events. These may include a variety of events such as starting a new school year, joining a new social club or moving house. Their identification allows the parents and child to prepare how they will deal with these events, to be aware of previous dysfunctional patterns and to focus more clearly upon using their new skills.

Parental involvement in child-focused CBT for emotional problems typically involves:

- the provision of psychoeducational material about the treatment rationale, process of therapy and skills and strategies covered

- maximising parental attention and reinforcement for use of new skills and minimising the amount received for dysfunctional behaviour

- directly addressing the parents' own problematic behaviour

- identifying and restructuring dysfunctional parental cognitions that might interfere with or impede progress

- improving family relationships by increasing communication and reducing conflict.

▶ Two final thoughts

■ Differing agendas of child and parent

It is not uncommon to find that a child has a different agenda and thus different goals from their carers. This presents the Clinician with a problem in terms of ensuring motivation and agreeing a treatment plan that is acceptable to, and is 'owned' by, both the child and their carers. On other occasions too many problems and goals will be identified and there is a danger of being overwhelmed by an apparently impossible agenda. This has the potential to act negatively by reinforcing parental and child cognitions about helplessness and the impossibility of change.

In situations such as this, it is important to explicitly identify the goals of all the prospective parties and to ensure that these are recorded. This provides a permanent record that can be referred back to in future meetings and indicates that the views of all relevant parties have been heard. The Clinician maintains an objective and neutral position in which the differing agendas and goals of the parents and child are acknowledged and are recorded.

On other occasions the use of simple methods such as reframing can provide an alternative definition and understanding of the problem that can facilitate a shared agenda that unites both parents and child. Reframing the problems of a child's reluctance to go out as a sign that they are worried and don't know how to cope with new situations provides a very different understanding to one which suggests that the child can't be bothered to do anything to help themselves. The latter provides an explanation in which the child needs help, whereas the former implies that they are deliberately choosing to behave in a difficult way and thus need to be challenged. The understanding and attributions the child and their family ascribe to the presenting problems can therefore either facilitate the development of a shared agenda or result in conflict.

However, in terms of prioritisation it is useful to secure the child's commitment to the therapy process and this can be helped by selecting one of their targets to work upon first. It is important to ensure that the selected target is small, achievable and within the child's ability to bring about, thereby increasing the likelihood of success. The other targets are not lost or forgotten, but are simply left on the list and effectively 'parked'. Once the child has successfully accomplished their first target, the 'parked' goals are revisited and the next one selected.

- In order to maximise engagement with the child it is useful to start with one of the child's targets.
- Ensure that the target is small, realistic and achievable in order to maximise success.
- Multiple problems needs to be 'parked'.

■ Are the parents able to support their child in CBT?

Careful assessment of the parents' psychological functioning needs to be undertaken in order to determine whether they are able to positively support their child through CBT. Parental psychopathology can be a major factor that interferes with or prevents positive change. A parent may, for example, be depressed and have predominantly negative beliefs or assumptions and be unable to reinforce and encourage attempts by their child to secure positive change. If suffering from significant anxiety they may model and reinforce avoidance behaviours in their child and be unable to facilitate behavioural exposure-based experiments. Similarly, if the parent has been involved in similar traumatic events to their child (e.g. traffic accident or domestic violence), they may be experiencing their own post-traumatic response, which prevents them being able to support their child.

Parental psychopathology therefore needs careful assessment to determine whether parental involvement will positively enhance or negatively interfere with child-focused CBT. If the parents' problems need to be addressed, then the Clinician will need to determine how this can best be achieved. Depending upon their significance and extent, the parents' problems may require to be directly addressed before initiating child-focused CBT. Alternatively they may be indirectly tackled or directly addressed during the course of work with the child. Clinicians will also have to be aware of the extent of their skills in order to determine whether they can address the parents' problems or whether a referral to the specialist adult mental health team would provide a more intensive and focused intervention.

Finally, the Clinician needs to be aware of wider issues of child protection. Significant scapegoating, overly hostile and rejecting cognitions or signs of potentially excessive emotional or physical abuse need to be taken seriously and referred to the appropriate agencies. Like all forms of therapy, effective CBT can only occur within the context of a supportive and enabling environment.

- The parents' ability to support their child in CBT needs to be assessed.
- Parental problems that might interfere with CBT need to be identified and appropriate interventions provided.

What is Cognitive Behaviour Therapy (CBT)?

Hassles and problems are part of everyday life. Parents, friends, school, work; in fact everything can cause problems.

Luckily, we are quite good at sorting out many of these problems but there are some that seem very **big and difficult**. They:

- ▶ happen fairly often
- ▶ never seem to get any better
- ▶ feel too big to sort out
- ▶ affect everything you do.

Problems like these can take over and you may end up feeling unhappy or worried. At times like this you need to discover more helpful ways of dealing with your problems and **Cognitive Behaviour Therapy (CBT)** may be able to help.

What is CBT?

CBT is a way of coping with problems that look at the link between:

- ▶ the way you think
- ▶ how you feel and
- ▶ what you do.

Why is this link important?

People with problems often think in unhelpful ways. They are more likely to:

- ▶ Expect things to go wrong.
- ▶ Worry about what has happened or what might happen.
- ▶ Seem to notice more of the things that aren't right.
- ▶ Are very critical of what they do.
- ▶ Blow small things up into big problems.

These ways of thinking are unhelpful and can make you feel **rotten**.

If you expect things to go wrong, then you might end up feeling **stressed or anxious**

 If you think you always get things wrong, you might end up feeling **sad or unhappy**

 If you think that other people don't like you or say unkind things, you may end up feeling **cross or angry**

People don't like to feel like this and so try to find ways of making themselves feel better. Unfortunately some of the things they end up doing actually make them feel worse. They **stop doing things**. They:

Avoid things they find difficult
Give up trying to do things
Stop going out and spend more time at home on their own.

How will CBT help?

CBT will help you find:

▶ the thoughts and feelings you have

▶ the link between what you think, how you feel and what you do

▶ more helpful ways of thinking

▶ how to control unpleasant feelings

▶ how to face and overcome your problems.

What happens?

We will work **together** with you. You have lots of useful ideas and important things to say and so we want to hear them.

We will **experiment** and test new ideas to find out what helps you. You will:

 ▶ check out the thoughts you have and find helpful ways of thinking

▶ discover ways of controlling your unpleasant feelings

▶ learn to solve and overcome your problem.

So let's have a go and see if it helps!!

What Parents Need to Know about Cognitive Behaviour Therapy (CBT)

What is CBT?

Cognitive Behaviour Therapy (CBT) is a **VERY EFFECTIVE** way of helping children to overcome their problems. It is based on the idea that how we feel and what we do are affected by what we think. CBT explores the link between:

▶ The way people think

▶ How they feel

▶ What they do.

In CBT your child will be helped to find their unhelpful ways of thinking. These ways of thinking often lead to worried, anxious, sad, angry or uncomfortable feelings. These feelings are unpleasant. We try to prevent or stop them by avoiding difficult situations or challenges. This is the **NEGATIVE TRAP**.

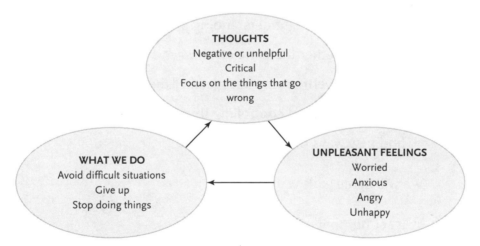

How will CBT help?

CBT will help your child to:

▶ find their negative or unhelpful ways of thinking

▶ discover the link between what they think, how they feel and what they do

▶ check and test the evidence for their negative and unhelpful thoughts

▶ find new ways to cope with their unpleasant feelings

▶ overcome their problems and do the things they would really like to do.

CBT will help your child to climb out of the negative trap to a more **POSITIVE** approach.

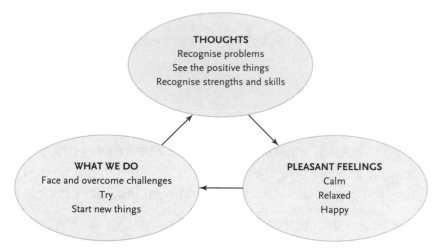

What will happen?

CBT is a fun and practical approach that helps children learn to overcome their problems. We **WILL WORK TOGETHER with you and your child to**:

▶ identify unhelpful ways of thinking

▶ develop a shared understanding of why these problems happen

▶ explore whether there are other ways of thinking about things

▶ test and experiment to see whether these are helpful

▶ learn new ways of controlling unpleasant feelings

▶ find new ways of solving problems.

We will agree with you:

▶ a set number of meetings

▶ whether we meet only with your child or whether you will join some or all of the meetings.

The last session will usually be a meeting with you and your child to review how things have changed and to agree what needs to happen next.

How can I help my child?

You can help your child by giving them your **SUPPORT**.

S – Show your child how to be successful

Children learn by watching others, especially their parents. Be a positive model for your child and show them how to approach and successfully cope with difficult situations rather than avoiding them.

U – Understand that they have a problem and need your help

Coping with worries and problems is hard work and children sometimes don't know what to do or learn unhelpful ways of coping. Although you or others might find your child's behaviour difficult, it is important to remember that they are probably not behaving like this because they are being difficult or naughty.

P – Patient approach

Change takes time – so do not expect any immediate changes. Be patient, reward success and remember that temporary setbacks are common. Encourage your child to keep trying and not to give up – they will get there!

P – Prompt them to try

Children get trapped in their old ways of thinking and behaving and will need you to remind them to use their new skills. They may also find some parts of the programme quite hard. Encouraging them to practise and reminding them to use their new skills is really important.

O – Observe what they do

Your child may have become caught in a negative trap where they find it hard to see the positive or successful things that happen. Watch what your child does and help them find the things that have gone well. Helping your child to find their successes will make them feel good about themselves, show them that they are making progress and will make them more confident to try again.

R – Reward and praise their efforts

Give your child attention for practising and using their new skills. Children often try harder if they know you are interested and will praise them. You can also use small rewards such as allowing them to stay up later, extra time on the computer, watching a DVD or having a friend for a sleepover. Rewards do not have to cost money. Agree with your child what might be a special treat.

T – Talk about what they do

Talking with your child can help them feel supported and understood. It builds self-esteem by showing them that you are interested in what they say. Talking about each session provides a way of going over the main learning points and of highlighting key messages. However, you should avoid grilling your child after each session – there are times when they may not want to talk about it.

SUPPORT your child and help them to overcome their problems

CHAPTER SIX

The process of child-focused CBT

▶ The therapeutic process of child-focused CBT

The process of undertaking CBT with children is complex and the outcome will undoubtedly be influenced by a number of factors including:

- the child's motivation and readiness to change;
- important systemic influences;
- the specific therapeutic techniques and strategies used;
- the way in which therapy is organised and structured;
- developmental considerations;
- the nature of the therapeutic relationship.

The issues of motivational interviewing and preparedness to change were discussed in Chapter 2. Once the child is prepared to engage in an active process of change and can identify possible targets, the process of CBT can begin in earnest. The Clinician needs to be cognisant of important factors within the wider system, such as carers, teachers and peers, that contribute or maintain the child's problems. The most effective way of addressing these needs to be considered and was discussed in Chapter 5.

The Clinician will have at their disposal a number of specific techniques that can be drawn upon during the course of therapy. The specific tools and interventions required will depend on the nature of the child's problems and their developmental level and will be informed by the formulation. However, it is doubtful whether the specific techniques will be effective, irrespective of how carefully they are planned and applied, if they are not delivered within the context of a warm and supportive therapeutic relationship. This was recognised by Beck (1976) who saw the therapeutic relationship as 'an obvious primary component of effective psychotherapy'.

A helpful way of conceptualising psychotherapy that acknowledges the importance of both the therapeutic relationship and the specific therapeutic techniques was suggested by Howard *et al.* (1993). The authors suggest that the development of the therapeutic relationship creates a sense of hopefulness. In turn, this is hypothesised to result in a fairly immediate reduction in symptoms with improvements in overall functioning being achieved through specific therapeutic strategies.

Despite agreement upon the importance of the Clinician/child/carer relationship, research exploring this in child psychotherapy is rare (Kazdin & Kendall 1998; Russell & Shirk 1998). Kendall & Southam-Gerow (1996) found that retrospective parental reports identified the nature of the therapeutic relationship as the most important aspect of treatment. Chu & Kendall (2004) looked at one aspect of the therapeutic relationship, namely child involvement in CBT. Child involvement, defined as the child willingly participating in therapeutic activities, engaging in self-disclosure and mentally engaging with the therapeutic process by volunteering and introducing new information into the discussion, was associated with better treatment gains. A poor therapeutic relationship has also been found to be a key reason for dropping out of therapy (Garcia & Weisz 2002).

The need to attend to the development and maintenance of a good therapeutic relationship may be particularly important with children (Shirk & Saiz 1992). Children often present at the onset of therapy as reluctant, unwilling clients with little ownership of any potential problems or the need to change. The process of engagement and developing a mutually agreed agenda for change may therefore need particular attention and take longer. Although research into the specific aspects of the therapeutic relationship is lacking, clinical experience suggests that the nature of this relationship is embedded in a number of key principles that can be captured by the acronym PRECISE summarised in Figure 6.1.

Based upon	**P**artnership working
Pitched at the	**R**ight developmental level
Promotes	**E**mpathy
Is	**C**reative
Encourages	**I**nvestigation and experimentation
Facilitates	**S**elf-discovery and efficacy
Is	**E**njoyable

Figure 6.1   The PRECISE process.

■ **Partnership working**

The therapeutic process involves the child and Clinician working together in a partnership based upon collaborative empiricism. Through this collaborative partnership the Clinician and child will detail the nature and extent of the current problems and develop a formulation. Important factors in the onset and maintenance of the problems will be identified as the child is helped to discover their dysfunctional or biased cognitions. The child is encouraged to test these cognitions by setting up experiments and collecting evidence that either supports or disproves them. In turn this leads to them discovering alternative, more balanced and helpful ways of thinking and behaving. The concept of collaborative empiricism embedded in partnership working therefore enhances engagement and active participation; the child and their parents have ownership of the resulting formulation; the intervention is jointly constructed and agreed and maximises the potential for self-discovery and change.

The process of partnership working requires:

■ the child and Clinician to form an alliance and work together;

■ a therapeutic process that is open and where both knowledge and uncertainty are shared;

■ the use of inclusive language that does not become too complex or technical for the child to access;

■ the Clinician to believe that the child is equally important as the adults and has useful information and ideas to contribute.

A collaborative relationship may feel unusual for children who may react by displaying some degree of suspicion or apprehension.

- Children are often 'sent' for therapy by others and may have no investment in developing a collaborative relationship.

- Previous experiences may lead the child to hold a set of expectations that their ideas and views may not be valued or that they will in some way be assessed as to whether their ideas are 'correct'.

- Children are used to adopting a passive relationship with adult authority figures and may expect to be told what their problems are and what they need to do to change.

In order to address these pitfalls it is essential that the nature and expectations of the collaborative partnership are made clear and explicit at the outset. The Clinician may need to differentiate themselves from other adults and to tell the child that they:

- are keen to hear the areas of change the child would like to achieve;

- will be working together to try to find out why these problems happen and to experiment to see whether they can be changed;

- do not have the solutions but instead need to learn and discover them with the child;

- want to hear the child's ideas about how change can be achieved.

Within the partnership the Clinician needs to recognise that the power differential between them and the child does exist. It is a reality that cannot be denied or completely removed. Instead it needs to be acknowledged and the Clinician should take steps to ensure that the child has opportunities to fully and actively participate in the process. This can be done in a number of different ways including:

- Ensuring that children are fully included in discussions and given opportunities to contribute their ideas.

- Emphasising that their ideas are important and useful.

- Highlighting that there are many different and helpful ways to think about problems and situations and not just one 'answer'.

- Acknowledging your limitations and admitting when you get things wrong – 'I don't think I explained that very well'.

- Explaining that when you get things wrong, you need to agree how the child can tell you this.

There are also times when the Clinician can highlight the child's superior knowledge and expertise by, for example, asking them to tell you about their interests. The child becomes the 'expert' as they educate you about their favourite music, film, hobby or sports team and learn that you listen and that they have information that you want to hear.

> ■ The Clinician and child work in an active, collaborative relationship where information is shared in an open and equal way.

■ Right developmental level

Adopting a developmental perspective requires the Clinician to consider a range of issues about the presentation and social context of the child's problems as well as the child's cognitive, linguistic, memory and perspective-taking ability. Attending to these will ensure that the Clinician is pitching CBT at the right developmental level. In considering this, the Clinician may need to address three questions.

- Is intervention required or is the child's behaviour developmentally appropriate?

■ Is the intervention compatible with the child's social, cognitive and linguistic skills?

■ Have important systemic influences been assessed and integrated into therapy?

Is the presenting behaviour a normal developmental variation or a significant deviation from this trajectory?

The first issue requires the Clinician to adopt a stance in which the child's presenting behaviours (i.e. the referral problems) are considered within a developmental framework. In essence, the Clinician needs to determine whether the child's behaviour is within expected normal variations of development or whether it represents a significant departure from the expected developmental trajectory? Behaviours that significantly deviate from the projected normal developmental process would severely compromise the child's ability to successfully meet their developmental tasks and therefore require intervention. However, many children will demonstrate temporary departures from the normal trajectory, but these do not necessarily suggest that they are presenting with problematic behaviours that require intervention (Ronen 1997). For example, Reinecke *et al.* (2003) note that young children display various fears (e.g. fear of the dark, separation) and that these are typically viewed as normal. However, if these are displayed at a later age they may indicate the existence of a significant anxiety disorder. At the later age they may adversely interfere with the child's ability to achieve the developmental tasks of separating from their parents or developing increased independence.

Has the intervention been modified so that it is compatible with the child's social, cognitive and linguistic skills?

The second issue the Clinician needs to consider is how CBT can be pitched at the right developmental level for the child to access. If CBT is pitched too high, the child will not be able to fully engage and participate in therapy. Similarly, if it is pitched too low, the child may feel patronised and become bored and disinterested. The Clinician therefore needs to consider factors in the child's development that will positively or negatively affect the success of the intervention, including the child's cognitive and linguistic abilities as well as their interests.

The cognitive capacity of the child to engage with CBT has been the subject of most attention. The influential cognitive developmental theory of Piaget (1952) suggests that children cannot begin to engage in abstract thinking until the concrete operational stage (acquired during 7–12 years of age). What is typically assumed to be meta-cognition or reflective thinking does not develop until what Piaget defined as the formal operations stage (acquired during adolescence). The implication of this model is that pre-adolescent children will be unable to engage in many of the cognitive demands of CBT and thus derive fewer benefits from this approach (Durlak *et al.* 1991).

The sequential staged model of cognitive development proposed by Piaget has been increasingly challenged. It is now recognised that children can engage in demanding cognitive tasks if careful consideration is given to the instructions the child receives (Thornton 2002). Harrington *et al.* (1998b) highlight that the cognitive demands of CBT are typically quite limited and effectively require the child to reason about concrete issues rather than engaging in highly abstract conceptual cognitive processes. The Clinician needs to be aware of and modify their intervention accordingly, but there is an emerging clinical view that children aged 7 years and above can effectively engage in child-focused CBT. Below this age there continues to be debate as highlighted by Piacentini & Bergman (2001), who suggest that regardless of Clinician accommodation, children aged 6 or less may be precluded from benefiting from many cognitive aspects of treatment. Interventions with children under the age of 7 may therefore need to pay less attention to cognitions and focus instead upon behavioural approaches (Bolton 2004). Children aged 7–11 may benefit more from the use of simple, specific and concrete cognitive techniques such as coping self-talk, while adolescents may be able to engage in more sophisticated cognitive techniques in which overarching dysfunctional cognitive assumptions and beliefs are identified and re-evaluated.

Talking therapies such as CBT rely on language as the medium through which the child conveys their inner thoughts and feelings and through which the Clinician promotes greater self-understanding and self-discovery that leads to the acquisition of more functional skills. It is therefore essential that the Clinician does not make assumptions about the child's receptive and expressive language ability. It is all too easy to assume a shared level of language when, in fact, no such understanding actually exists.

The ability of children to spontaneously volunteer information in response to open questions may also be limited. This may reflect the developing memory capacity of the child or alternatively a complex question that they are unsure how to answer. Younger children respond better to more specific and direct questions. Possible problems of recall can be addressed by providing the child with specific prompts or by providing the child with a range of options from which they can choose, e.g. 'Some children tell me they feel scared, some angry and some sad. Do you have any of these feelings?'

CBT should incorporate the child's language and use the words they use to describe their problems, thoughts and feelings. However, rather than simply reflecting back and using the child's words it is important for the Clinician to fully understand the meaning the child ascribes to their descriptors and terms. At the most basic, professional jargon and terms should be avoided. Use the child's terms (e.g. 'head talk') rather than rephrasing these within a professional ('negative automatic thoughts') context.

It is also useful to ensure that non-verbal materials are used to complement and enhance verbal discussion. In terms of preferred media the use of more visual as opposed to verbal techniques can be helpful. Visual methods provide a more permanent record of the information and help to overcome the limited verbal memory of some younger children. Thought bubbles, magazine pictures of people expressing emotions, simple three-part formulations, quizzes, drawings are all helpful ways of making some of the key tasks of CBT objective, concrete, visual and fun. Similarly, complex information such as multiple component formulations can be built up slowly by looking at connections between two elements.

It is also important to ensure that the process builds upon the child's interests and their preferred media. Some children are able verbal communicators and can join in a form of therapy that is predominantly verbal. Others prefer non-verbal methods and may feel more comfortable and able to communicate their thoughts and feelings through media such as drawings, worksheets or puppets. Computers are familiar to a number of young people and some will be motivated and readily able to design their own self-monitoring forms and diary sheets. Similarly, emailing and texting is common amongst many adolescents, so that the idea of 'downloading one's head' into a message and sending it to the Clinician may be an acceptable way of accessing a young person's cognitions.

Have important systemic influences and social contexts been considered and incorporated into the intervention?

The need to consider important systemic influences was discussed in Chapter 5. The important role of the child's parents/carers in the onset and maintenance of their child's problems was highlighted and parental psychopathology and dysfunctional cognitions that might adversely interfere with the treatment programme cannot be ignored.

The school is another important context where the active involvement of the teaching staff in the treatment programme could be very beneficial. Failure to appropriately involve teaching staff by, for example, assessing their views about the treatment programme, their commitment to supporting it and their goals can result in negative outcomes. Courtney (15) was referred to the author with problems of persistent rudeness, defiance and angry outbursts at school. He was in danger of being permanently excluded if he had another outburst and so we agreed that the immediate focus of our intervention would be to help him learn more appropriate ways of managing his angry feelings. Courtney readily participated in the intervention and he successfully implemented various anger-management strategies at school. However, I paid insufficient attention to the school context and failed to recognise that the goal of the school was not to support Courtney in the management of his temper but rather to remove him from the school. A number of teachers were frightened by his angry outbursts and, although he had never physically assaulted any of the teaching staff, some were fearful of their own safety. While Courtney did not have any other angry outbursts he was subsequently permanently suspended for persistent lateness.

> ■ CBT needs to be adapted to the child's developmental level by using more visual techniques that are tailored towards the child's interests and built around their preferred media.

■ Empathy

The non-specific factors of therapy are very important and one of the key skills in developing an effective therapeutic partnership is that of empathy. Empathy means *really understanding* what the child is thinking, how they feel and the meaning they ascribe to events. The Clinician needs to view the world through the child's eyes and to understand their beliefs, assumptions and attributions and their ambivalence about change. The Clinician therefore signals empathy by adopting a warm, caring and respectful approach. It is, however, important to strike the right balance and ensure that the Clinician does not appear patronising.

Empathy is expressed through curiosity, interest, genuineness and acceptance, characteristics that signal to the child that the Clinician is keen to hear what they have to say. This is conveyed through a number of core counselling skills.

- Good listening skills. The Clinician needs to maintain eye contact with the child, to nod and encourage the child to speak, thereby sending the message that the Clinician is interested, that the Clinician wants to hear what the child has to say and that the child has something important to contribute.

- Summaries. These provide a useful way of showing the child that you have heard what they have said and provide an opportunity to check your understanding. They also allow the Clinician to identify and highlight important parts of the discussion and to summarise key points and issues.

- Reflections. These help to focus the child's attention upon what they have said and to explore patterns or connections between different events, thoughts and feelings. They also provide opportunities to acknowledge how the child may, for example, have felt when they experienced certain types of thoughts or other events.

- Validation. Comments that serve to validate the child's experiences are important ways of demonstrating empathy. A simple statement such as 'It sounds as if you were really frightened', can be very powerful. It serves to highlight the importance the child has attributed to their experience and acknowledges that this has been recognised by the Clinician.

> ■ The Clinician's interest and curiosity promotes empathy and encourages the child to vocalise their thoughts, assumptions and beliefs about their world.

■ Creativity

The Clinician needs to be creative and flexible as they explore how the concepts of CBT can be conveyed to the child in a way that matches the child's interests and experiences. Clinicians need to adopt an open approach in which therapy is viewed as a unique process in which different methods and media are matched to the skills and interests of the child. This is in contrast to therapy undertaken with adults where the standard medium is verbal. Alternative, non-verbal methods are typically used with adults when therapy becomes stuck or if things go wrong. This is in contrast to therapy with children where creativity and the use of a range of different media is standard practice.

Creativity involves using a variety of techniques and methods to engage with the child and help them secure their therapeutic goals. This will involve the use of a wide range of media such as computers, pictures, games, quizzes, puppets and stories that will help to maintain their interest. The choice of materials will depend upon the interests of the child. Many children are, for example, unwilling to keep self-monitoring records but may become more motivated if asked to design their own form on their computer which they can keep and print out for the next appointment. Similarly the identification of important thoughts that accompany hot situations (i.e. when a child notices a strong emotional reaction) can be captured by asking the child to download their heads into a tape recorder or into an email message.

Children may be unable to volunteer their thoughts or feelings when directly asked but often can convey these through thought bubbles or play. Similarly, the situation can be turned into a game in which the child is asked to guess what someone else might think or feel in their worrying situation. A sorting game can be used to help children distinguish between thoughts, actions and feelings, and unfinished sentences as a way of eliciting thoughts related to specific situations or feelings.

Black and white boards are very useful, providing a way of visually capturing and highlighting information. Important thoughts can be captured and the visual link between events, thoughts and feelings can be emphasised.

A key challenge for the Clinician is how to make some of the ideas of CBT concrete and understandable for the child. Abstract concepts and complicated processes need to be made simple and translated into concrete steps and metaphors to which the child can relate. The concept of challenging distorted thoughts can be broken down into a series of simple steps that take the child through the process (TGFG, page 109). The idea of negative automatic thoughts can be highlighted by asking the child to participate in a game such as using their non-preferred hand to draw a house or to write their name. Once the task is completed the child is asked what thoughts went racing through their head as they undertook this task.

The idea of selective attention can be highlighted by the idea of watching a film. A number of things are noticed first time around but if the film is watched again, then new information is seen. Similarly, the concept of negative automatic thoughts can be explained to children interested in computers by using the metaphor of computer spam. Turning on the PC and connecting to the internet (i.e. the child's brain) results in computer spam suddenly appearing to advertise various products. The spam is not asked for (i.e. is automatic), is hard to block (i.e. you can't turn them off), most of it is unrecognised (i.e. you simply delete without reading) but some messages are read (selectively attended to). This metaphor conveys to the child in a concrete and understandable way a number of the core features of automatic thoughts.

Finally, the Clinician should be aware of the child's interests and how these can be built upon and incorporated into any intervention. Books and films such as Harry Potter and *The Lord of the Rings* provide many ideas that can be developed and used. For example, in *The Prisoner of Azkaban*, Harry Potter learns to beat his fears by thinking about them in a humorous way. The idea of changing an unpleasant emotion such as anxiety or anger to one that is more pleasant and comfortable is a simple technique that can be used with children.

Creativity is concerned with finding ways of effectively communicating with the child so that concepts or issues can be explained in an understandable and enjoyable way. It is important that Clinicians maintain their therapeutic focus and do not become so enthusiastic that they lose sight of their purpose. The Clinician also needs to feel comfortable with the idea of creativity. This will involve the Clinician having to think on the spot and some people may not feel comfortable or confident with this way of working. At these times it may be useful to construe this as an exercise in which the Clinician is checking a number of ways in which the concept can be explained, thereby avoiding the implicit need to get it right. Approaching the process in this way also means that some ideas will work and others will not. This is not a sign of therapeutic failure, but rather part of the inevitable matching of the therapeutic process with the child that is an intrinsic part of CBT. This is not the sole responsibility of the Clinician but one that is undertaken in partnership with the child where they discover the most effective way of communication.

> ■ The Clinician's creativity adapts and tailors the concepts of CBT to the child's interests.

■ Investigation

The concept of guided discovery and investigation is a key feature of CBT. It is based upon the premise that thoughts and behaviour will be more readily changed if the rationale for change comes from their own insights. In essence, the child is encouraged to test out and experiment with new skills and ways of thinking and to check what happens. A number of concepts have been used to capture this investigative process with children and include the Private I (Friedberg & McClure 2002), the Social Detective (Spence 1995) and Thought Tracker (Stallard 2002a). The Social Detective, for example, teaches a three-stage process for social problem solving in which the child detects, investigates and then solves.

The therapeutic relationship needs to provide the child with a safe place that enables them to explore alternative ways of behaving and thinking. This investigative process is particularly important, with behavioural experiments proving a very powerful way for children to directly test their beliefs and assumptions. The investigative process needs to be an open process of curiosity and, as such, it is important for the Clinician to suspend judgement and their own preconceived ideas. Similarly, experiments are not undertaken to simply prove the child wrong, but instead to help the child test the validity of their cognitions and to use this information to help them discover a new or different meaning. Indeed, there will be some times when an experiment will confirm the child's predictions and this is important information for the Clinician to discover.

Adopting an open 'Shall we try to see what happens?' conveys to the child a number of important messages.

- ■ It builds upon the collaborative process of working in partnership and learning together.
- ■ It conveys the sense of inquisitiveness and openness.
- ■ It highlights that there are often many possible solutions or ways of thinking about events, thereby challenging the dichotomous thinking of many children.
- ■ It provides an experimental framework that can be used with other problems.
- ■ It encourages learning from others. 'You told me that Mike never has any problems like this, so what does he do in this situation?'

> ■ The child is encouraged to be an active investigator who tries out and evaluates ideas and new skills.

■ Self-discovery and self-efficacy

The concept of self-efficacy highlights the positive, empowering aspect of CBT. The aim of the approach is to help the child find and build upon their strengths and skills. Maintaining this positive and enabling focus is important, since there is a danger within any therapy, but particularly within one that is concerned with identifying dysfunctional cognitive process, that the model can become deficit-driven. While dysfunctional processes need to be addressed, the child's skills and strengths need to be highlighted and, where possible, built upon and used to promote more adaptive and functional processes.

Children often overlook their strengths and may appear tentative when some of their skills are reflected back. On some occasions this may be due to a lack of confidence on the part of the child, thinking that they are unable to help themselves or fearing that they have not found the 'right' answer. At these times it can be helpful to highlight that there are no right answers but instead one is hoping to identify a range of ideas that may help on some occasions, but at other times may not.

Children can be helped to discover their strengths by reflecting upon their past experiences.

- What did you do that helped you to cope with that situation?
- What sort of things have you found helpful?
- There are times when it hasn't been too bad. What did you do differently that helped?

Similarly for those children who find it very difficult to acknowledge any of their strengths and successes, positive diaries can be particularly helpful. These encourage children to actively seek and find their strengths and skills and the good things that happen that they often overlook. The positive focus upon self-efficacy promotes within the child the idea of mastery. With this comes increased motivation and a belief within the child that they do have positive skills that they can use to effect change.

Each day the child is asked to record two or three positives, with the growing list providing a useful visual reminder that the child does have strengths and can be successful. However, some children may be fixed in their negative cognitive style and struggle to find anything positive. In these situations the help of a third party is required to provide an objective view that can challenge the child's distorted perception.

> ■ Self-efficacy is promoted by helping the child to identify their own ideas and build upon their skills.

■ Enjoyable

Traditional therapy can at times feel quite dull and boring. Given the engagement issues outlined earlier, it is important to ensure that child-focused CBT is enjoyable and continues to capture the child's interest and maintain their motivation.

The process of CBT with children can be less didactic than with adults, resulting in the Clinician adopting a more active role within sessions. The Clinician therefore needs to ensure that the child remains engaged and that they continue to participate. Paying attention to a number of variables may help to ensure that the process is positive and fun.

- Humour can be used within the therapeutic relationship. For example, one Clinician rushed to get their camera when a child described themselves as 'always getting things wrong'. The Clinician returned saying that they had never ever met anyone before who 'always' got things wrong and so wanted to take a picture. This swift intervention helped the child to see in a humorous way the cognitive distortion they made.

- Using a variety of materials can be a helpful way of maintaining the child's interest and creating a sense of fun. A session looking at the link between thoughts and feelings could start with a brief verbal update. This could be followed by completing a worksheet and then a game in which the child sorted thought, feeling and behaviour cards into separate piles.

- Ensure that sessions are not too long. For many children a 50–60-minute session is too long and may result in them becoming bored or losing interest. At these times make the sessions shorter.

- If possible make the session more active by moving around the room. Do some work on a board, sit and draw, move to a more comfortable area to talk.

- Negotiate tasks. During each session there may be a number of different things you want to do or areas you would like to cover. Make these explicit and give the child some choice about the order in which they are undertaken.

> - Make the therapeutic process fun and enjoyable and use a variety of materials to maintain the child's interest.

▶ PRECISE in practice

■ Ella's obsessional thoughts

Ella was a 7-year-old girl referred with OCD. Ella had many obsessive thoughts related to the safety of her family and engaged in a range of compulsive safety-checking behaviours. Before she went to bed each night she would check that the windows in their flat were shut and that the doors were locked. She would check that all the electrical appliances were unplugged and that the cooker was turned off. Once in bed Ella would continue to have these obsessive thoughts and it would take her approximately 2 hours before she could fall asleep. Ella would typically wake two or three times each night and on each occasion she would go around the house and engage in her compulsive safety-checking behaviour.

Ella was engaged in a course of CBT to address these problems, but during one meeting she was particularly troubled by her obsessive thoughts and wanted to stop them. When asked what Ella would like to do with her thoughts at bedtime she replied, 'I'd like to lock them away so they can't get at me'. This was discussed in more detail and Ella's idea of how things could be safely locked away developed into a prison. Ella saw a prison as a place where bad people go and are kept locked up so that they can't get out. The idea of locking her bad (i.e. worrying) thoughts somewhere safe so that they couldn't get out seemed a useful metaphor. As we talked, Ella started to develop an image of herself writing her worrying thoughts across the chest of a prisoner and locking them away in a cell each night. Ella was helped to describe this image in detail and could see herself writing her worries and then locking them away so that they could not trouble her. Ella became quite excited by this idea and was keen to try it at home.

This brief summary highlights the key aspects of the process of undertaking CBT with children. The Clinician worked in *partnership* with Ella and helped her to voice her ideas. Ella was helped to create a *developmentally appropriate* concrete metaphor of locking her worries away somewhere safe so that they couldn't trouble her. The Clinician conveyed *empathy* by really listening to what Ella had to say and by reflecting back and highlighting what she had said. The idea for helping Ella to control her thoughts was *creative* and encouraged Ella to *investigate* whether change was possible and whether her idea could help. The process was empowering for Ella and by building upon her suggestions promoted the concept of *self-efficacy* highlighting that she had useful ideas that could help with her problems. Finally, the process was *enjoyable* and engaging for Ella who was highly motivated to try her ideas at night-time.

■ Joshua's negative thinking

Joshua was a 9-year-old boy referred by his GP with low mood, panic attacks and generalised anxiety, problems that were particularly noticeable at school. During the assessment it became clear that Joshua had a number of dysfunctional cognitions. Joshua misinterpreted ambiguous events as threatening, expected bad things to happen, was biased towards focusing upon negative events and failed to recognise his successes. A major aim was to help Joshua recognise his negative bias and to check to see whether there was information that he was overlooking.

Joshua was a keen Harry Potter fan. He had read the books many times and was very interested by the idea of magic. During one session we explored some of the ideas from the books that could be used to help Joshua test his thoughts and check whether he was seeing the whole picture or just noticing the negative things. Joshua talked about the mirror of *Erised*, in which Harry Potter could look and see everything he ever desired. We explored and developed this idea so that Joshua could look into a mirror and find the positive things that he overlooked. Joshua became very interested by this idea and went home and made his own mirror. Upon returning home from school he would tell his mother what had happened and would then be encouraged to look into his mirror and 'take another look'. This time Joshua would find the positive things he had overlooked. This countered his initial negative cognitions and provided a more balanced view of events. Each day Joshua would use his mirror to check out what had happened. He began to recognise his negative biases and started to challenge his thoughts and develop a more balanced way of thinking.

Once again the Clinician worked in *partnership* with Joshua and helped him to express his ideas. The process of thought testing was undertaken in a *developmentally appropriate* way that made the idea of 'looking again' concrete by the use of a magic mirror. *Empathy* was used to encourage Joshua to express his ideas and to really understand his interest in Harry Potter. The intervention was imaginative and *creative* and Joshua was motivated to *investigate* whether he was overlooking important information. The idea for the mirror came from Joshua and so built upon the idea of *self-efficacy*. The intervention was both effective and *enjoyable* and provided Joshua and his mother with a very practical way of challenging Joshua's biased thinking.

■ Adam's formulation

Adam was 9 and was referred by his GP because of anxiety and panic attacks at school. These occurred at lunchtime and resulted in Adam refusing to eat or drink throughout the school day.

During the assessment interview it emerged that Adam was very concerned about his appearance. He wore designer clothes, highlights in his hair and took a great deal of care over his appearance. He commented that when he sat at the table at lunchtime he often thought the other children stared at him. When asked why they were looking at him Adam commented that they probably thought 'I looked ugly or that there was something wrong with me'. Adam reported a number of anxiety symptoms at lunchtime, particularly a dry throat, racing heart, shortness of breath and sweating. When Adam noticed these he felt unable to eat his lunch and wanted to leave the dinner hall.

The assessment continued during the second meeting and towards the end the Clinician pieced together the following formulation to describe Adam's problems.

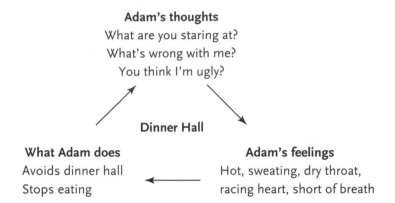

Adam's thoughts
What are you staring at?
What's wrong with me?
You think I'm ugly?

Dinner Hall

What Adam does
Avoids dinner hall
Stops eating

Adam's feelings
Hot, sweating, dry throat,
racing heart, short of breath

Adam listened to this explanation with interest but then commented 'it wasn't right' and produced the following alternative formulation:

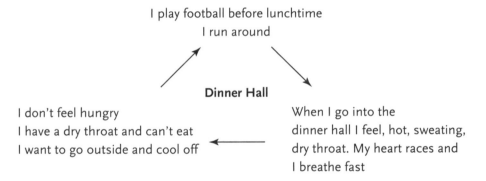

I play football before lunchtime
I run around

Dinner Hall

I don't feel hungry
I have a dry throat and can't eat
I want to go outside and cool off

When I go into the
dinner hall I feel, hot, sweating,
dry throat. My heart races and
I breathe fast

Adam's explanation made a great deal of sense. While he did not make any reference to his cognitions he did manage to integrate what was happening with his feelings and subsequent behaviour. In terms of the process, Adam was clearly feeling comfortable and able to challenge the explanation provided by the Clinician and to offer his own ideas. It was important to acknowledge Adam's contribution and to facilitate a process of guided discovery where the two alternatives could be investigated.

The need to maintain this enabling and objective focus became particularly important as Adam's mother, who was present during this session, voiced her support for the Clinician's explanation. It could have been very easy for the process of collaboration to shift towards that of a partnership of the adults who, with their superior verbal skills, could have argued and in effect imposed their explanation upon Adam. Instead, both explanations were highlighted as equally important and we discussed whether an experiment could be devised to check which provided the best explanation.

Adam agreed to monitor what happened on the next three wet playtimes. The children were not allowed outside when it rained and so Adam could not play football. If Adam's explanation was right, then if he were unable to play football he would not feel hot and would be able to eat his lunch. If he was still unable to eat his lunch, then there must be another explanation. The experiment showed that even though Adam had played football he had still not eaten his lunch. Adam was now prepared to consider an alternative explanation.

Once again this example serves to highlight a number of key aspects of the therapeutic process. The primary therapeutic *partnership* continued to be with Adam. The formulation was simple and pitched at the *right developmental* level for Adam to access. The Clinician adopted an *empathic* approach that clearly heard and recognised Adam's understanding of events. The proposal to test the different views was *creative* and encouraged the use of an *investigative* process. The experiment promoted *self-discovery* and, above all, was *enjoyable*.

The PRECISE process involves:

- Developing an open therapeutic PARTNERSHIP with the child.
- Ensuring that interventions and concepts are pitched at the RIGHT DEVELOPMENTAL level.
- Using good listening skills and summaries to convey EMPATHY and interest.
- Being CREATIVE and building interventions around the ideas and interests of the child.
- Promoting objectivity by facilitating an INVESTIGATIVE approach.
- Building upon the child's strengths and developing the concept of SELF-EFFICACY.
- Making therapy ENJOYABLE will increase and maintain the child's motivation.

Adapting CBT for children

▶ The cognitive capacity debate

There has been much debate about the age at which children are able to participate in CBT. Some have suggested that the optimal benefits of CBT with children cannot be achieved until the child is at least 12 years of age (Durlak *et al.* 1991, 2001). The implication of this suggestion is that the necessary cognitive skills are underdeveloped or absent in younger children resulting in them not possessing the necessary conceptual platform to engage in CBT (Shirk 2001). Others suggest that the issue is not about whether young children possess the necessary cognitive or conceptual skills but instead whether CBT has been modified and provided in a developmentally appropriate way for the child to access (Friedberg *et al.* 2000; Ronen 1997; Stallard 2002b). This perspective suggests that children aged 7 and over can benefit from CBT if the techniques are appropriately adapted.

■ What are the cognitive demands of CBT?

In considering this question it may be helpful to think about the cognitive demands of CBT rather than the child's chronological age or level of cognitive development. In order to participate in CBT children must be able to undertake a number of core tasks (Shirk 2001). They need to be able to

- monitor affective states;
- reflect on automatic thoughts;
- distinguish between and understand the link between thoughts and feelings;
- engage in thought appraisal and cognitive restructuring.

Each of these core tasks poses significant challenges, particularly for younger children. Children may have difficulty distinguishing different emotional states (Piacentini & Bergman 2001); the capacity for metacognition is evolving during childhood and may not be sufficiently developed in young children (Durlak *et al.* 2001; Shirk & Russell 1996); children may find it difficult to attribute emotions and behaviour to internal cognitive processes rather than external events (Shirk 2001); children tend to use problem-specific strategies to cope with difficulties rather than engaging in a more general process of cognitive restructuring (Vernberg & Johnston 2001). Observations such as these would suggest that young children may not be developmentally able to fully engage in child-focused CBT.

However, the question arises as to whether the above skills are a prerequisite for CBT or whether they can be addressed and taught as part of the intervention. Children can, for example, be taught to distinguish different emotional states by the use of feeling worksheets in which they are helped to attend to facial expression, body posture and behaviour (Stallard 2002a). Similarly their awareness of emotional states can be increased by the use of emotional dictionaries made from newspaper photographs or games such as emotional charades in which they have to act out various emotions (Friedberg & McClure 2002). In terms of accessing thoughts children are able to verbalise their thoughts, either indirectly through play and conversation or more directly through the use of exercises or thought bubbles. Children as young as 3 and 4 can, with some preliminary training, understand that thought bubbles represent what a person may think (Wellman *et al.* 1996). Similarly, studies have highlighted how children under the age of 7 can distinguish between thoughts, feelings and actions and can acknowledge that thoughts are subjective and thus that two people can have different thoughts about the same event (Quakley *et al.* 2004; Wellman *et al.* 1996). In terms of self-awareness Flavell *et al.* (2001) suggest that children can recognise their own inner speech by approximately 6 years of age. Thus the concept of talking to oneself and the use of positive self-talk that forms a key part of many interventions is a method that is both accessible and familiar to young children. Finally, in terms of cognitive restructuring, CBT with younger children may require a more problem-specific approach since they may be unable to recognise overarching rules or generalise their strategies to other situations (Stallard 2004). The focus upon specific problems is not uncommon in child-focused CBT. Indeed the problem-based, present-time focus is a factor that makes this form of intervention attractive to children.

These observations suggest that young children do have the ability to engage in many of the tasks required in CBT. Their perceived lack of ability may reflect the fact that the Clinician has not provided the child with enough information or been sufficiently clear about what they are expected to do (Grave & Blissett 2004; Siegal 1997). Given clear and simple instructions and using familiar activities and events from the child's everyday life will increase the likelihood that younger children can actively engage with, and successfully participate in, CBT.

> ■ Younger children can engage with many of the core demands of CBT if the methods are simplified, made concrete and matched to the child's development.

■ A pragmatic alternative

Undoubtedly the academic and theoretical debate regarding the cognitive capacity of children to engage in CBT will continue. From a clinical perspective Bolton (2004) provides a pragmatic solution to the question of whether the child's cognitions play an important role in the child's problems and thus whether they need to be addressed. Bolton (2004) suggests that the key task during assessment is to identify 'what kinds and contents of appraisals are in practice at work in the generation and/or maintenance of the problems presented by the particular child'.

Therefore, regardless of the child's age or level of cognitive development, if dysfunctional cognitions or processes are present, then they need to be addressed during the course of therapy. If the hypothesised cognitive distortions or deficits are not present, then they do not need to be a specific or direct target of therapy. The issue of whether or not the child possesses the necessary cognitive skills to engage in CBT therefore becomes less important. While providing a practical and potentially useful solution to a complex problem it nonetheless highlights the need to ensure that a comprehensive assessment is undertaken in a developmentally appropriate and sensitive way. Without a thorough assessment it is not possible to confirm or discount the presence or potential role of maladaptive cognitions or processes. This highlights the need for Clinicians to use a range of developmentally appropriate verbal and non-verbal methods during the assessment process.

> - Clinically, if dysfunctional cognitive processes are evident, then they need to be addressed during the intervention.

▶ Adapting CBT for use with children

There is widespread acceptance amongst practitioners of child-focused CBT that the predominant verbal method of therapy developed for work with adults needs to be creatively adapted and modified for use with children (Friedberg *et al.* 2000; Ronen 1997; Shirk 2001). Ronen (1997) emphasises the need for Clinicians to carefully consider how cognitive therapy can best be applied to children at different levels of development. Friedberg *et al.* (2000) note that CBT can be developmentally insensitive and, unless suitably modified, may exceed the child's capacity. This view is shared by Reinecke *et al.* (2003) who note that children may lack the linguistic, social or cognitive sophistication to benefit from a predominantly verbal mode of CBT.

In terms of process, as highlighted in the preceding chapter, there is a need to ensure that CBT is entertaining and not dull (Stark *et al.* 1996). Friedberg & McClure (2002) note that the traditional therapeutic process of sitting in a chair and talking with a Clinician can feel uncomfortable and alien to many children. There is therefore a need to explicitly clarify the nature and expectations of the therapeutic process. This is often less didactic than that with adults, resulting in the Clinician adopting a more active role. With reticent or unforthcoming children the Clinician may adopt a rhetorical approach in which they muse aloud a range of possibilities for the child to select. Finally, Bailey (2001) suggests that attention needs to be paid to the pacing of treatment sessions and that their length may need to be shortened so that they do not exceed the child's attention span.

> - There is a need to match the methods, style and process of therapy to the child's developmental level.

There are a variety of ways in which the ideas and methods of CBT can be conveyed in more developmentally appropriate ways.

■ Games

Games are familiar activities for young children and provide the Clinician with a useful method of communication. Games can be used, for example, to distinguish between thoughts and feelings or to highlight the connections between various aspects of the cognitive model. Friedberg *et al.* (2000) describe a card-sorting game that helps children differentiate between thoughts, feelings and situations. During assessment the Clinician notes the thoughts, feelings or situations that are important for the child and their current problems and writes these on to flashcards. The child is invited to participate in a game in which they have to sort them into categories (e.g. thoughts, feelings and situations) as quickly as possible. This game is psychoeducational and the child can be helped to examine the links between the different piles.

Friedberg & McClure (2002) suggest a game called 'Thoughts–feelings hoops' as a way of introducing children to self-monitoring skills. The child is asked to throw a ball or crumpled piece of paper through a basketball hoop or into a wastepaper basket. As they do so, the child has to share their thoughts or feelings as they take each shot. The game can be developed. The Clinician can introduce pressure (e.g. 'You've really got to score this time'); used to access and test the child's predictions about whether or not they will score ('I am not feeling very confident about this') or to challenge some of the child's negative attributions about themselves (e.g. 'I never get this right').

Barrett *et al.* (2000b) use a game to help children learn the steps involved in problem solving. Children are presented with a set of materials, which they use to get a balloon from one side of a room to another as quickly as possible without touching it with their hands or feet. The children are taken through a six-stage approach in which they learn to define the problem; identify potential solutions; consider the potential consequences of each solution; use this information to select the best solution; test it and then evaluate it. This provides the children with a fun and concrete exercise that helps them understand the steps involved in problem solving.

Finally, Ronen (1992) described how she used a game of soldiers with a 6-year-old boy with encopresis to explain the concepts of automatic thoughts (i.e. doing something without thinking about it) and mediated thoughts (i.e. a signal sent to the body from the brain). The objective was to help the child understand that his soiling was a behaviour directed by his brain and therefore his responsibility rather than 'sickness', 'bad luck' or something that happened 'against his wishes'. During the game the concept was explained as a commander (brain) who sent orders (mediated thought) to his soldiers (child's body).

Finally, quizzes are fun and useful ways of working with children and provide a way of assessing what the child has learned. 'What are the thinking errors?' included at the end of this chapter is an example of a short quiz that can be used with children to identify some of the common negative cognitive biases.

> ■ Games are familiar to children and provide an entertaining and developmentally appropriate way of communicating the concepts and strategies of CBT.

■ Puppets

Puppets can be an engaging and effective way of communicating, particularly with younger children. They can be used to:

- facilitate discussion as part of the assessment process;
- model alternative ways the child might cope with difficult situations; or
- engage the child in rehearsal and practice of new skills.

In terms of assessment young children may find it difficult to talk with a Clinician about their own problems but may feel more relaxed and comfortable talking with, or through, a puppet. Knell & Ruma (2003), for example, note that young children who have been sexually abused find it difficult to talk about their own abuse. Similarly Kane & Kendall (1989) note that young children may find it difficult to describe their own cognitions but are often able to describe what someone else in the same situation may be thinking. In both these situations puppets can provide a useful way of helping the child to feel relaxed and provide a developmentally appropriate way of facilitating a discussion that can help to clarify what happened or identify what the child may be thinking.

Knell & Ruma (2003) highlight how the Clinician can use puppets to structure a play or discussion around the issues relevant to the child. The Clinician uses the puppet to establish a rapport with the child and then asks the child to tell the puppet what happened. Alternatively the puppet can pretend to have experienced a similar situation to the child and can engage the child in attempting to guess what they might be thinking or how they are feeling about the event.

Secondly, puppets can be used to highlight dysfunctional cognitive processes or emotions and to coach and model more adaptive coping skills. The puppet pretends to be the child and engages the Clinician in a discussion about the child's problems. The puppet verbalises potentially important negative cognitions, which the Clinician highlights. The Clinician then coaxes the puppet through their problems and models more functional cognitive processes and alternative more helpful skills. This provides an indirect and uncritical way of highlighting to the child their unhelpful cognitions or behaviours which helps them to consider alternative, more helpful strategies.

Finally, as identified by Friedberg & McClure (2002), puppets can be used to engage children in the process of Socratic questioning and self-instructional techniques. They report a dialogue in which the Clinician and child both used puppets to act out a situation in which one of the puppets is helped to control their angry feelings by using helpful cognitive strategies, e.g. 'Turn down the heat on your angry stove.' This scenario provided an entertaining way of rehearsing and modelling the use of positive self-talk.

While puppets can provide a useful method of communication the Clinician needs to ensure that their use remains simple and clear. Children may become confused if they are asked to use the puppet to represent themselves (Salmon & Bryant 2002). It is therefore important that puppets are used as either a surrogate Clinician or as a model in which the child's dysfunctional processes are highlighted and alternative coping skills demonstrated.

> ■ Puppets provide a way of clarifying behaviour, assessing cognitions, modelling new skills and practising more functional ways of coping with problems.

■ Story telling

Story telling is a familiar method of communication for children. It provides a developmentally appropriate medium that children can use to describe their experiences, thoughts and feelings (Brandell 1984; Gardner 1971). Story telling therefore can:

- provide an insight into the child's inner world;
- provide a way of externalising and accessing the child's cognitions;
- provide an opportunity to indirectly challenge the child's cognitions and cognitive processes in an uncritical way;
- introduce the child to positive and more functional coping and cognitive skills;
- be used to model success;
- help the child develop more functional assumptions and beliefs.

Children are familiar with the concept of stories. As they grow up they develop their own life story, the narrative they use to describe and make sense of their past experiences. This narrative provides the basic framework they use for filtering information in new situations and for making predictions about future events.

Story telling in CBT can be used for assessment or as a therapeutic method. In terms of assessment, stories can be used to identify the child's feelings, behaviours, automatic thoughts, beliefs and assumptions. Therapeutically they can help the child to consider new information or alternative views and perspectives. The new story is then integrated into the child's cognitive framework, thereby helping the child to construct a new narrative about themselves, their performance and their world.

■ **Assessment**

Stories can take a semi-structured form which the child's problems are directly focused upon or a more open format in which the child chooses the content and creates a story of their choice.

Guided assessment stories

Semi-structured stories are created jointly with the Clinician and provide opportunities to ask questions that directly assess what the child might think, feel or behave. For example Zara, an unhappy child who was bullied at school, was invited to tell a story about a little bear who was scared to go to school. The story started like this:

PS:	Shall we tell a story about a little bear who had just moved to a new school?
ZARA:	OK.
PS:	What would you like to call the bear?
ZARA:	Little Brownie.
PS:	So where does Little Brownie live and what is she like?
ZARA:	Little Brownie lives in a bush at the bottom of a small tree. She lives with her mum and brother. Little Brownie isn't very good at sports and games and doesn't talk much with the other bears.
PS:	Does Little Brownie have any friends?
ZARA:	No, she's new to the area and so she hasn't made any friends yet?
PS:	So does Little Brownie go to school?
ZARA:	Yes, and today is her first day.
PS:	Wow, her first day, I wonder what will happen?
ZARA:	Well, Little Brownie will be taken to school by her mummy. As she gets to the school gates she will get really scared. She will start to cry and will want to stay with her mummy. She won't want to go into school.
PS:	Little Brownie sounds really scared. I wonder what she is scared about?
ZARA:	She doesn't know anyone at school and she isn't very good at making friends.
PS:	So what does Little Brownie think will happen if she goes into school?
ZARA:	Oh, the usual stuff.
PS:	The usual stuff?
ZARA:	Yes, the other bears will want to know where she moved from, why she hasn't got a daddy and will laugh at her because she talks with such a quiet voice.

The story started to highlight the importance of some of Zara's past experiences and her current worries. Zara's father was a drug addict who regularly broke into houses in the local neighbourhood and terrorised her mother for money to fund his addiction. This resulted in the family frequently having to move house and Zara having to settle into a number of schools. On each occasion she would be asked by the other children about her family and father, questions Zara found very difficult to answer. She became increasingly reluctant to attend school and became upset each morning when she had to leave her mother.

Open assessment stories

As an alternative to the semi-structured guided approach, story telling can be used in a more open way. The child could be invited to choose some toys, soft animals, dolls or puppets and to use them to make a story. The child is asked to make a new story that they have never heard before with a start, middle and an end. The story has to have a moral and they are instructed that some of the things that happen in their story might also have happened to them. The child decides upon the content of the story while the Clinician facilitates its construction. Clinician-initiated questions are therefore designed to help the child construct their story and can be general prompts (e.g. 'What happened next?'), clarification of detail (e.g. 'And what was she called?'), reflections (e.g. 'It sounds as if she was very scared') or summaries (e.g. 'So she has now managed to climb the mountain, find the cave and get past the three dragons'). During the story the Clinician needs to pay particular attention to the content:

- Where the story is set, e.g. dark and scary place where the child is on their own, or a more friendly place with others.
- Dominant feelings, e.g. anger, fear, unhappiness.
- Key themes, e.g. failure, being victimised, left on their own.
- The nature of important relationships, e.g. parents being unable to look after them.
- Important assumptions, beliefs or cognitive biases, e.g. 'No matter what you do you always get things wrong.'

Therapeutic stories

Story telling can also be used as a therapeutic technique. This involves the Clinician telling a story that will help the child consider and assimilate new information into their own life narrative. After the child has created their story the Clinician tells another similar story in which there is an alternative more helpful solution or where more positive coping skills can be demonstrated. The story therefore provides the means through which young children engage in the process of inductive reasoning in which they are helped to consider new or overlooked information. This reconstruction of the child's story helps the child to develop a new, more balanced and functional narrative of themselves, their performance and their future.

An effective therapeutic story needs to complement the child's narrative by correcting any factual inaccuracies or causal attributions. The story introduces new information or useful skills, which can be assimilated into the child's life narrative to promote more balanced and functional cognitions. In order to achieve this the child must be able to relate to the characters in the story and see their problems, cognitions, feelings and behaviours as similar to their own. The means by which the Clinician facilitates change is often by the use of metaphor. This provides the link between old and new knowledge by offering a different perception or way of coping.

Toots the tortoise

After Zara had created her story about Little Brownie, the Clinician provided another story. The main character in this story was Toots, a tortoise who liked to go for long walks. One day she walked too far and found herself in a new field that was full of rabbits. Toots looked very different from all the other rabbits. They crowded around to see the new animal and all started talking at once. 'Where are you from?' asked the first rabbit. 'What is your name?' asked the second. 'What have you got on your back?' asked a big scary-looking rabbit, while another asked, 'Where are your mummy and daddy?' Toots didn't like all these questions.

The rabbits were only being friendly and wanted to get to know the new animal, but Toots found herself feeling very frightened. She pulled her head into her shell. It was dark inside her shell but she felt safe. She couldn't see the rabbits or hear their questions any more, so she stayed inside her shell and fell asleep. When she woke she put her head outside her shell. The rabbits had gone and it was quiet. Suddenly one of the rabbits bounced up and sat beside her. 'Hello,' he said. 'Hello,' said Toots with a quiet little voice. 'My name is Springer,' said the rabbit. 'My name is Toots,' she said with a slightly louder voice. Soon they were talking and laughing together. 'I am pleased that you came out of your shell again,' said Springer. 'If you stayed inside your shell, we wouldn't have been able to talk and become friends'. Toots was pleased to be Springer's friend and noticed that the frightened feeling in her tummy had gone.

In this story Toots was a similar character to Zara. They both found themselves in a new situation and became scared by all the questions they were asked. Both coped by doing something that made them feel safe; Toots by pulling her head into her shell, Zara by refusing to leave her mum and go into school. While this made them feel better, it didn't help them overcome their problems and make new friends. As Toots found out, it was only once she faced her fear by coming out of her shell that she realised that the rabbits were just being friendly.

Storybooks

There are a number of useful storybooks that can be used as an adjunct to CBT. These help children understand their problems and symptoms and highlight some of the ways they can learn to overcome them. Clinicians will develop their own library of helpful books over time, but the following are examples of useful and enjoyable books. *The Huge Bag of Worries* (Virginia Ironside 2003) is a story for children under the age of 11 that helps them to recognise that worries grow and grow unless they are confronted. *The School Wobblies* (Chris Wever 1999) has a number of engaging cartoons that will appeal to adolescents. It describes the sort of worries children have that prevent them from going to school and some of the tricks that can be used to beat them. *The Secret Problem*, also by Chris Wever (2000), is presented in a similar style. It focuses upon OCD and shows how compulsive behaviours can be chased away. Finally, *The Panic Book* (Neil Phillips 1999) uses fun cartoons and words to describe panic disorders and how worrying situations need to be challenged and faced rather than avoided.

> ■ Stories can be used to identify important cognitions, feelings and behaviours or therapeutically as a way of helping the child attend to new information or helpful skills.

▶ Visualisation

Young children have very good imaginations and are often able to take part in methods that involve visualisation. This involves creating a detailed image that can be used as part of the assessment or therapeutic process.

■ Assessment

As a method of assessment, visualisation can be used to identify possible feelings and cognitions. Important or high-profile sporting events can provide the basis of creating readily familiar images to use with children.

- A child could, for example, be asked to create an image of a penalty shoot-out in a major football competition. The child could be asked to name their favourite footballer and to then imagine them standing in front of the goal facing the goalkeeper. This is the final penalty that will decide whether they win or lose the match. The ball is on the penalty spot and the footballer looks at the goal. The child is then asked to describe what the footballer may be feeling or thinking as they run forwards to take the penalty. The image can continue with the child being asked to consider what the footballer might think and feel after scoring or missing the goal.
- The Olympic or Commonwealth Games provides another possible source of familiar images that can be used to highlight different feelings (e.g. before the event and after) and possible unhelpful or helpful thoughts.

If the child finds it difficult to create their own image, the Clinician can collect pictures from newspapers, which can be used as a library of visual prompts to engage in this discussion.

Coping imagery

Visualisation and imagery can also be used therapeutically as a method of combating unpleasant and unhelpful emotions or to reappraise cognitions. In the previous chapter an example was described of a young boy who visualised a magical mirror that helped him counter his biased negative cognitive processes and promoted more balanced thinking. While imagery can be used as a way of helping children to challenge distorted cognitions, it is more often used as away of promoting control over unpleasant emotions such as anger or anxiety.

Changing the emotional content of problematic situations

Emotive imagery was described by Lazarus & Abramovitz (1962) as 'those classes of imagery, which are assumed to arouse feelings of self-assertion, pride, affection, mirth and similar anxiety-inhibiting responses'. Emotive imagery is used as part of systematic desensitisation. The child develops adaptive imagery that allows them to confront and overcome their problems. The resulting image provides the child with a method of countering any unpleasant emotions or a way of changing the emotional content of problematic situations.

In their original paper Lazarus & Abramovitz (1962) describe the process as involving the following steps:

- The child's fears are assessed and a fear hierarchy developed.
- The child's hero-images are identified.
- The child is then asked to imagine a story based around their problems in which their hero is introduced as a coping model.
- The story should arouse a pleasant emotional response in the child.
- Starting with the least anxiety-provoking, the child's fears are introduced into the image as the process of systematic desensitisation occurs.

In one case study a child with a fear of the dark was helped by his comic super-heroes. The child was asked to imagine that he was a special agent working for Superman and Captain Silver. The child was told that he was on a secret mission so that when he received a message from the super-heroes he had to go somewhere on his own. The child received various messages and imagined himself starting in a dimly lit lounge until he was able to imagine himself, with no discomfort, waiting in the dark bathroom on his own for the next message from Superman.

Emotive imagery can also be used to replace anger with laughter. This concept may be familiar to a number of children who have read the stories by J.K. Rowling about the boy wizard Harry Potter. In the third book, Harry is taught how to overcome his biggest fears (e.g. Boggarts) by laughter. The frightening image is therefore changed to one that is humorous. A frightening image of a spider can be transformed if it is visualised wearing a ballet dancing tutu, big boots and a silly hat.

Calming imagery

Relaxing imagery is a helpful way for children to control anxious or unpleasant feelings. The process requires the child to imagine and describe their restful, calming or happy place. The image is created in the present time and described in the first person. This can be either a real or imaginary place but somewhere the child feels pleasant and safe. The child is asked to either draw this or to describe it in detail to the Clinician. The role of the Clinician is to help the child create a vivid and powerful image by making it as detailed and as real as possible. The Clinician prompts the child to attend to colours, shapes, textures, smells and sounds, thereby creating a multi-sensory image. Once developed and practised, the image can be used to counter and control any anxious or uncomfortable feelings.

Aisha's calming image

Aisha's restful image was a café her mother's friend ran in a little seaside town.

- Aisha was first helped to describe the image in as much detail as possible.
  — 'The café is in a little courtyard behind the shops. There are three tables outside where people can sit. As you walk into the café, there are five more tables and then a counter where you can buy all sorts of drinks and cakes.'
- Aisha was given a number of prompts that helped her describe the inside of the café in more detail.
  — 'Is there anything on the tables?' – 'Yes, on each table is a red and white checked tablecloth. There is a white sugar bowl and a red flower in a vase.'
  — 'Are there any windows or curtains?' – 'Yes, the whole of the front of the café is glass so you can look out. At each window are red and white checked curtains.'
  — 'What sort of cakes can you buy?' – 'You can buy homemade scones, fruitcake, carrot cake and a wonderful chocolate fudge cake.'
  — 'Are these whole cakes or slices?' – 'The cakes are already cut into thick slices.'
  — 'What is your favourite?' – 'The chocolate cake.'
  — 'And what does that look like?' – 'It is a lovely dark colour with soft chocolate fudge oozing out of the middle. It is soft, squidgy and tastes wonderful.'
- Aisha was then prompted to listen for any sounds.
  — 'There is a stream outside and you can hear the water rushing past. Inside people are talking and there is music playing in the background.'
- Aisha was prompted for any smells.
  — 'The whole place smells of freshly ground coffee.'

The development of the image continued until it was created in sufficient detail to enable Aisha to feel relaxed and safe. The creation of the image was practised on a number of occasions with the Clinician and was then used by Aisha when she felt anxious and needed to relax.

Anthony's humorous image

Anthony was 15 and was often in trouble at school and was now in danger of being excluded. He was rude, would argue with the teachers and when he was corrected become angry, throwing his bag and books around the classroom, kicking over desks and running out of the class. All of the major incidents occurred with one teacher. Anthony didn't like this teacher who, he felt, unfairly picked on him. He entered these lessons expecting an argument and so was determined to have the first and last word. Anthony recognised that this wasn't helpful and was interested in exploring whether imagery could help him to remain calm.

During the assessment Anthony mentioned that he had recently seen this teacher in a school pantomime dressed as an elf. He clearly found this image very funny and was able to describe how his teacher was dressed in detail. We decided to experiment to see whether Anthony could use this image as a way of remaining calm so that he replaced his anger with humour. Anthony practised initiating the image with the Clinician and rehearsed how he could use it to calm and be successful. Anthony then conjured up the image as he walked into the classroom with this teacher or when he felt himself becoming angry. The humorous image provided a useful way of helping Anthony to remain calm. It was difficult for Anthony to become wound up or take what he perceived to be his teacher's critical comments seriously when he looked so ridiculous.

> ■ Coping imagery can be used in CBT for assessment and to counter unpleasant or dysfunctional emotions.

■ Non-verbal methods

The attention span, memory and linguistic ability of children are developing throughout childhood. In order to counter any possible limitations arising from poor or underdeveloped skills in these areas, CBT with children involves the use of many visual techniques. These are especially helpful since they:

- ■ enhance understanding by providing important information through different mediums;
- ■ are attractive and engaging and so help to maintain the child's attention and interest;
- ■ provide the child and their carers with a permanent record of important information or tasks;
- ■ link different sessions and tasks together in a coherent and understandable way;
- ■ provide a way of reviewing progress;
- ■ facilitate the sharing of key information with those who were unable to attend therapy sessions.

There are many ways in which CBT can be visually adapted for use with children and a number of ideas and worksheets are presented in *Think Good – Feel Good* (Stallard 2002a). Briefly, visual methods can be used for assessment, as a way of quantification and therapeutically to help reassess assumptions and cognitions about events. A range of materials are useful including black/white boards, flip charts, paper and pencils and colourful worksheets

Assessment

Cartoons and thought bubbles can be used as an entertaining and fun way of assessing specific cognitions and cognitive processes. A range of general worksheets can be prepared and used to:

- ■ introduce the child to the idea of describing their thoughts;

- identify common thoughts about themselves, their performance and their future;
- highlight how there are different ways of thinking about the same event;
- emphasise how different thoughts are associated with different feelings.

Children aged 7 can readily understand that a thought bubble represents what a person is thinking. The worksheet at the end of this chapter, 'Sharing our Thoughts', provides a simple way of exploring whether the child understands the idea that people have thoughts about events and that thought bubbles are a way of communicating these. Once understood, the idea of a thought bubble can then be applied to the child's current problem situations and provides a means through which their thoughts can be communicated.

Visual methods can be used in many ways and some examples of worksheets are included in this book. These include worksheets that help to identify important physiological changes associated with feelings ('When I Feel Worried'), possible reasons to change ('The Scales of Change') and important attributions ('Responsibility Pies'), and to visually highlight the steps that would need to be in place before the child's cognitions occur ('The Chain of Events').

Psychoeducation

Visual methods are also very useful ways of psychoeducation. In addition to helping the child understand the links between the various components of the CBT cycle, visual summaries powerfully and graphically describe differences between functional and dysfunctional ways of coping.

Gail's negative thoughts

Gail was the single parent of a 4-year-old who was presenting with defiant and challenging behaviour. During sessions Gail volunteered a number of negative thoughts and statements that were captured by the Clinician. These were then reflected back to Gail by writing them up on a blackboard with arrows leading into a blank box in the middle. This resulted in a discussion about the possible overarching core belief that was fuelling these thoughts and led to the identification of Gail's belief that she was a bad mother. This visual representation, summarised in Figure 7.1, provided a very powerful and useful way of helping Gail to verbalise her fear.

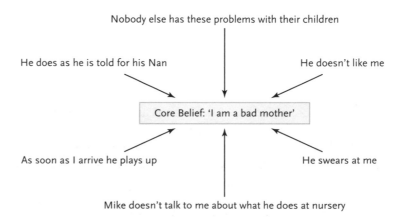

Figure 7.1   Gail's thoughts and her core belief.

Becky's habits

Becky was 12 and had a number of compulsive behaviours. Many of these were related to the order in which she had to do things and the fact that she had to do them a fixed number of times. This became particularly difficult first thing in the morning when Becky had to get herself ready for school. However, there had been a couple of recent occasions when Becky had resisted her obsessional thoughts and had not engaged in her compulsive rituals. The functional and dysfunctional cycles were mapped during a session and provided a powerful visual comparison that highlighted how Becky tumbled from one habit to another (Figure 7.2).

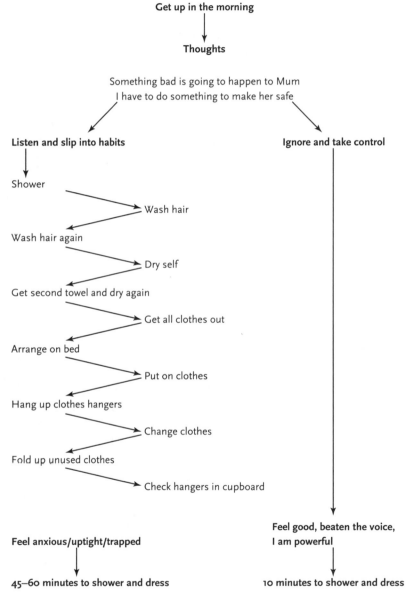

Figure 7.2 Becky's habits.

Quantification

A core feature of CBT is quantification, in which the child is helped to rate various aspects of their behaviour, the strength of their feelings or beliefs in their assumptions. Quantification is important since it:

- provides an objective way of rating internal cognitive processes and emotions;
- challenges the dichotomous thinking of adolescents by highlighting the graduations between two anchor points;
- highlights change within session (e.g. during exposure);
- demonstrates the potential effectiveness of specific techniques (e.g. relaxation);
- highlights longer-term progress.

The Clinician can devise simple and colourful visual analogue rating scales which can be used to assess the strength of their feelings (e.g. feeing thermometer) or the degree to which they believe in their thoughts (e.g. thought thermometer). Alternatively pie charts can be used as a way of visually quantifying the specific contribution of various factors.

Theo's washing

Theo had many compulsive behaviours and engaged in regular hand-washing in which he felt a need to wash his hands four times before he felt his hands were clean. The pie chart of Figure 7.3 was constructed with Theo to quantify how much he felt each of the four washes contributed to his hands becoming clean. This pie chart proved a simple visual way of demonstrating to Theo that, while the first two washes were clearly important, the fourth wash resulted in very little added cleanliness. This enabled Theo to experiment with setting some boundaries around his hand-washing by limiting himself to three washes and eliminating the fourth.

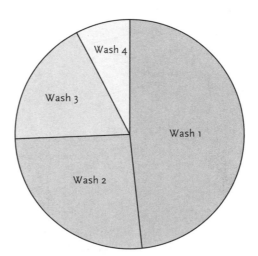

Figure 7.3   Theo's washing.

Therapeutically to reassess attributions

A variation of the pie chart is the 'responsibility pie' where children are helped to identify all the factors that might have contributed to a particular event and then to consider how much each contributed to the overall outcome. If a factor is considered to have a major effect upon the overall outcome, then it is assigned a large slice of the pie, whereas more minor factors will have smaller slices.

Joshua's accident

Joshua was recently involved in a car accident and drew the responsibility pie of Figure 7.4 for what had happened. The pie clearly highlighted how Joshua saw himself as the major reason for the accident. From Joshua's perspective he thought that the accident would have been unlikely if he was ready for school on time and hadn't been arguing with mum.

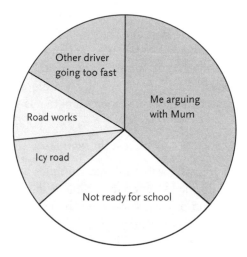

Figure 7.4 Joshua's responsibility pie for the car crash.

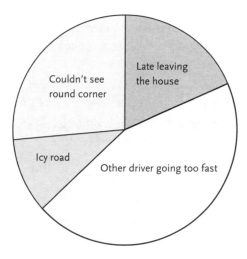

Figure 7.5 Joshua's mother's responsibility pie.

Once Joshua's attributions about the accident had been identified, it was possible to compare his understanding with that of his mother who was driving (see Figure 7.5). Joshua's mother attributed the accident to the other driver going too fast round a corner on an icy road. Although she also recognised that she was late leaving the house, the discussion revealed that this was not because of her son. Joshua's mother was late because she was collecting the washing so that she could set the washing machine running before they left. This provided an objective way of testing Joshua's attributions and of helping him reappraise his understanding and to reduce his personal responsibility for the accident.

> ■ Visual techniques provide a powerful adjunct to CBT.

■ Externalisation

Young children find it helpful if abstract concepts are externalised and made concrete. This can be done by asking the child to draw a picture of their problem. This helps to identify the problem as something separate from the child and can help to form an alliance between the child and their family in joining together to fight and overcome it. Responsibility for the problematic behaviour is therefore removed from the child and the effect of this is to challenge any parental cognitions that the child is being wilful, naughty or to blame for their behaviour. This technique is used in the programme with children, 'How I ran OCD off my land'. The child is asked to draw a picture of their OCD and to then give it a nasty name. This name can then be used during therapy thereby emphasising that the child and the problem are separate. This may also facilitate a more open discussion where the child may feel less embarrassed talking about a problem that is separate from themselves.

■ Find concrete ways to test the worry real

When using CBT with children, complex abstract concepts and strategies need to be simplified and made concrete. Problem-solving techniques should be based around real examples and problems from the child's everyday life rather than dealing with hypothetical situations or events (Chang 1999). The Clinician needs to creatively find objective external ways of evaluating the child's internal cognitive processes. A boy of 8, for example, developed a fear of eating meat, fearing that the meat would not be cooked and that he would become infected with germs. His mother worked in the catering trade and was able to help her son understand that when cooked meat reached a certain temperature any germs and bacteria were destroyed. The use of a meat thermometer provided the boy with a simple, objective way of checking that his meat was cooked thereby challenging his dysfunctional cognitions that the meat was infected.

- Children can be helped to externalise their problems through drawing.
- Concrete and objective methods are helpful ways of challenging abstract fears.

The Thought Tracker Quiz

What are the thinking errors?

We need to get better at spotting the sort of thinking errors we make.

▶ **NEGATIVE GLASSES** – only let you see the negative things

▶ **POSITIVE DOESN'T COUNT** – you rubbish the good things that happen

▶ **BLOWING THINGS UP** – negative things become bigger than they really are

▶ **MIND READERS and FORTUNE TELLERS** – expect things to go wrong

Look at these thoughts and see if you can find the thinking error.

'People are *always* unkind to me.'

The thinking error is:

Luke went on a school trip to a great theme park. When asked if he had a good day Luke said, 'No, I didn't like my sandwiches.'

The thinking error is:

'My friends will think I look really stupid in these trainers.'

The thinking error is:

Amy played her flute brilliantly in the school concert. When her teacher said how well she had done Amy thought, 'That was just lucky, I don't usually play that well.'

The thinking error is:

Responsibility Pies

The Responsibility Pie helps you to see all the things that might have caused something to happen and how much each was responsible.

▶ **Write down what happened**

▶ **Now write down all the things that you think might have caused this**

▶ **Now divide up the pie**. If you think something played a big part, it would have a big slice of the pie. If it you think it played a small part, it would have a small slice of the pie.

When I Feel Worried

These are some of the changes that people notice when they feel worried, stressed, anxious or frightened. Circle any of the changes you notice when you get worried or stressed.

Light headed/feel faint

Red face/feel hot

Headache

Dry mouth

Blurred eyesight

Lump in throat

Shaky voice

Butterflies in tummy

Heart beats faster

Sweaty hands

Difficulty breathing

Jelly legs

Want to go to the toilet

Do you notice any other changes?

▪

▪

Which signals do you notice most?

▪

▪

When I Feel Angry

These are some of the changes that people notice when they get angry or uptight. Circle any of the changes you notice when you get angry.

Can't think clearly   Mind goes blank

Feel hot   Voice gets louder

Angry face   Swear

Clench teeth   Threaten people

Make fists   Hit people

Shake   Throw or break things

Feel tense/uptight   Shove or push people

Sweat   Argue

Do you notice any other changes?
-
-

Which changes do you notice most?
-
-

When I Feel Sad

These are some of the changes that people notice when they feel sad or unhappy. Circle any of the changes you notice when you get sad.

Can't think clearly

Can't concentrate

Not interested in doing anything

Can't stop crying

Don't go out so often

Tearful for no reason

Don't feel like eating

Sensitive and easily upset

Hard to get off to sleep

Feel tired

Waking up early

No energy

Can't stop eating

Feel sick

Do you notice any other changes?

■

■

Which changes do you notice most?

■

■

THINK GOOD – FEEL GOOD

Sharing our Thoughts

We often keep our thoughts locked up inside our heads.
We can hear them but we may not tell other people what
we are thinking. We can use **thought bubbles** like these to show our thoughts

In this picture below, the mouse is thinking, 'It must be dinner time'

It must be
dinner time

The cat is thinking, 'I will climb that tree'

I will climb that tree

What do you think this person may be thinking?

What do you think this person may be thinking?

CHAPTER EIGHT

Core components of CBT programmes for internalising problems

CBT is used as a generic term to describe a 'diverse collection of complex and subtle interventions' (Compton *et al.* 2004). Although the authors note differences between individual programmes they also observe that CBT interventions tend to share five core characteristics:

- A commitment to evidence-based treatment and a scientific/evaluative approach to individual case work.
- A functional analysis of the presenting problem to determine important factors associated with onset and maintenance.
- An emphasis upon psychoeducation.
- Interventions specifically tailored to address the presenting problems.
- A focus upon relapse prevention and generalisation of new skills.

While there may be a number of overarching similarities in terms of philosophy and process the fact remains that the specific content and emphasis of individual programmes varies considerably. This variability is undoubtedly fuelled by the large number of specific techniques and strategies that are available to the Clinician. These can be used in various combinations to address particular difficulties in each of the cognitive, emotional or behavioural domains. These techniques form the 'Clinician's toolbox' and are summarised in Figure 8.1.

▶ What is the balance between cognitive and behavioural strategies?

The specific strategies that will be used in any intervention should be determined on the basis of the case formulation. However, a constant dilemma facing the Clinician is the therapeutic focus and balance within the treatment programme between cognitive and behavioural strategies. As mentioned previously, cognitive and behavioural techniques are combined in numerous permutations and sequences but are still classified under the general umbrella term of CBT (Durlak *et al.* 1991; Graham 1998; Ronen 1997).

Shirk (2001) highlights that child cognitive therapy is 'inherently integrative with an equal emphasis on cognitive, behavioural and interpersonal factors'. However, the direct focus within many treatment programmes upon the cognitions that are assumed to underpin specific child problems is often extremely limited (Stallard 2002a). This raises a theoretical issue of how much of a cognitive focus is required before a behavioural intervention constitutes CBT. Whatever the specific balance, Reinecke *et al.* (2003) note that 'clinical work with children and adolescents requires that we attend to how these cognitive contents and processes develop, the social contexts in which they function and their implications for functioning'.

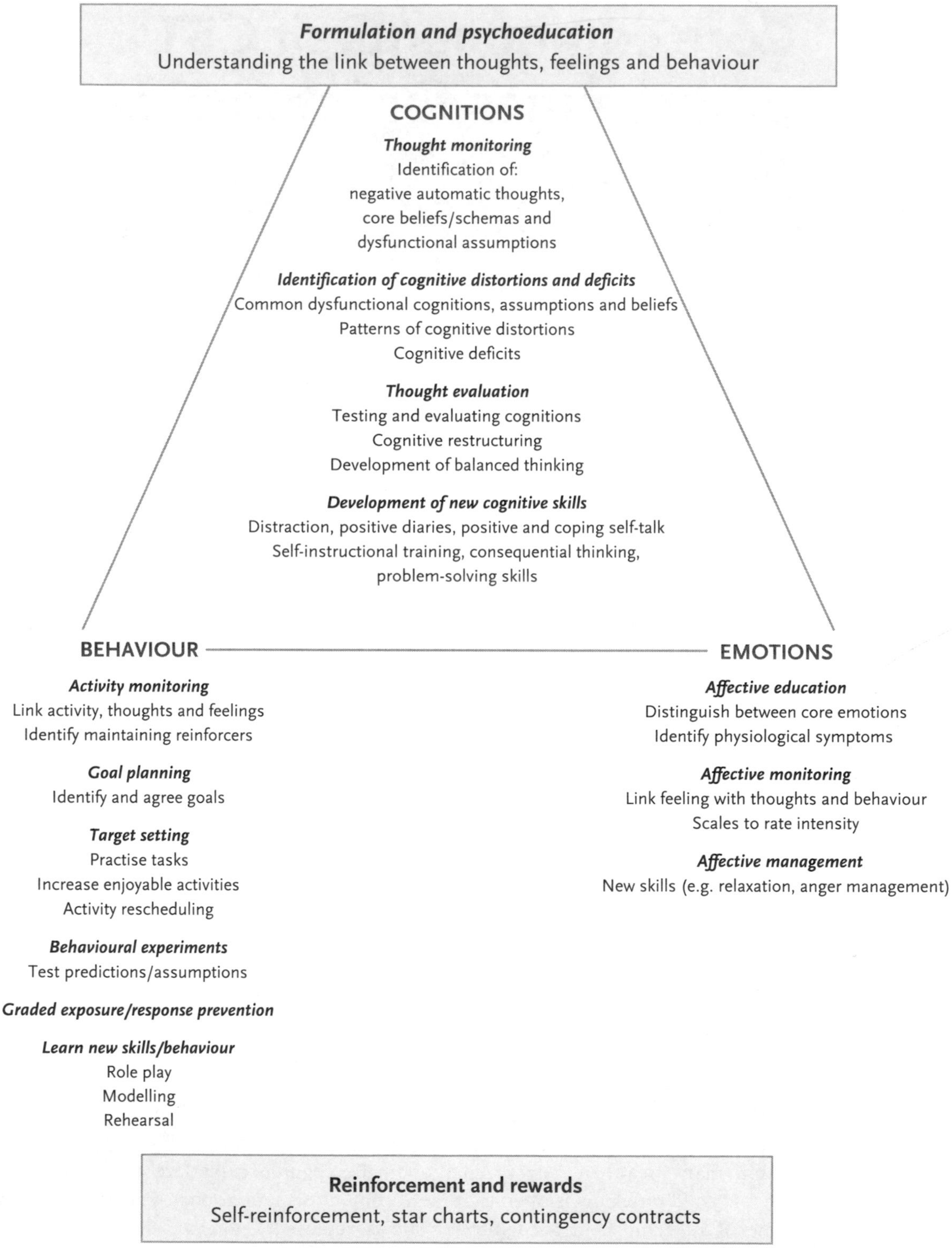

Formulation and psychoeducation
Understanding the link between thoughts, feelings and behaviour

COGNITIONS

Thought monitoring
Identification of:
negative automatic thoughts,
core beliefs/schemas and
dysfunctional assumptions

Identification of cognitive distortions and deficits
Common dysfunctional cognitions, assumptions and beliefs
Patterns of cognitive distortions
Cognitive deficits

Thought evaluation
Testing and evaluating cognitions
Cognitive restructuring
Development of balanced thinking

Development of new cognitive skills
Distraction, positive diaries, positive and coping self-talk
Self-instructional training, consequential thinking,
problem-solving skills

BEHAVIOUR ——————————————— EMOTIONS

Activity monitoring
Link activity, thoughts and feelings
Identify maintaining reinforcers

Goal planning
Identify and agree goals

Target setting
Practise tasks
Increase enjoyable activities
Activity rescheduling

Behavioural experiments
Test predictions/assumptions

Graded exposure/response prevention

Learn new skills/behaviour
Role play
Modelling
Rehearsal

Affective education
Distinguish between core emotions
Identify physiological symptoms

Affective monitoring
Link feeling with thoughts and behaviour
Scales to rate intensity

Affective management
New skills (e.g. relaxation, anger management)

Reinforcement and rewards
Self-reinforcement, star charts, contingency contracts

Figure 8.1 The Clinician's toolbox.
Source: From Stallard (2002). *Think Good – Feel Good*. © John Wiley & Sons, Ltd. Reproduced with permission.

- Potentially important cognitions and processes need to be assessed.
- The balance between and emphasis upon the cognitive and behavioural components will vary.

▶ Do we need to directly focus upon dysfunctional cognitions and processes?

While the balance between, and use of, cognitive and behavioural strategies poses an intriguing question, a more practical issue for the Clinician is whether the child's cognitions need to be directly addressed in order to facilitate change. It is clear that cognitive change occurs indirectly through behavioural techniques such as exposure and response prevention. Indeed, in vivo exposure has been identified as the most beneficial intervention for children under the age of 11 with specific phobias (British Psychological Society 2002). Similarly, behavioural experiments are powerful ways of undertaking cognitive restructuring and provide children with objective ways of testing and reappraising their predictions and assumptions. The important contribution of behavioural techniques to CBT is indisputable and in some instances the mechanism for change may be behavioural rather than cognitive (Quakley *et al.* 2004). The issue the Clinician needs to consider is whether CBT can be further enhanced by paying direct attention to the specific cognitions that underlie the child's problems.

- Cognitive change can occur indirectly through behavioural strategies and experiments.
- It is unclear whether change may be enhanced by directly focusing upon key cognitions and cognitive processes.

▶ What cognitions or cognitive processes might be important?

The different levels of cognitions and important cognitive processes are summarised in Chapter 3 on developing formulations. Cognitions tend to focus around the cognitive triad, namely thoughts about the self, the world and the future (Beck 1976). Core beliefs and schemas are the deepest and least immediately accessible level of cognitions and are characterised by short, absolute, general statements (e.g. 'I am a failure'). These are operationalised by assumptions ('No matter how hard I work I will still fail') that are activated by triggering events (school examinations) resulting in the generation of automatic thoughts ('I can't do this work') and, in turn, these effect behaviour (don't do any exam revision).

Clinical experience suggests that direct work with schemas or core beliefs is limited in child-focused CBT. In some respects this is not surprising. Given the dynamic nature of the cognitive development of children comparatively little is known about when core beliefs or schemas become established, enduring or dysfunctional, thereby constituting a significant abnormal variation from a normal developmental trajectory. In terms of process, given the dynamic and emerging nature of schemas and core beliefs and the importance of early experiences, the question arises as to whether the child or their carers should be the main target of schema-based interventions. At this stage while core beliefs and schemas are more malleable, modifying the child's experiences and environment (i.e. the assumed significant influences upon their development) may be more effective than direct work with the child. Unfortunately, comparatively little is known about when or how to intervene at this level.

In terms of other cognitions, the Clinician is interested in identifying any dysfunctional biases or deficits that are associated with the onset and maintenance of the child's problems.

A number of common biases have been identified in work with adults including selective abstraction, personalisation, catastrophising, dichotomous thinking, arbitrary inferences, etc. Once again clinical experience suggests that these need to be simplified for use with children who are often less interested in the subtle definitional differences. Using metaphors, such as looking through negative glasses (selective abstraction), blowing things up (catastrophising), using dustbin labels (personalisation), crystal-ball gazing (predicting failure), can help children understand the type of biases they make.

Finally, the attributions the child attributes to the events that occur are important and may be subject to some of the distortions highlighted above. Attributions tend to be bipolar and revolve around the dimensions of:

- internal (responsible for the things that happen) versus external ('I am a victim and have no control over what happens');
- specific (related to a particular event) versus global (applied to many different events and situations);
- stable (persist over time) versus unstable (vary depending upon events).

▶ Does cognitive change result in problem improvement?

The cognitive model predicts that reductions in psychological problems should be associated with changes in cognitions (Durlak *et al.* 1991). However, in their meta-review Durlak *et al.* (1991) failed to find a significant association between cognitive change and outcome. However, comparatively few studies include cognitive measures that are tailored towards assessing the specific assumptions, beliefs or cognitive processes that child-focused CBT is designed to address. The lack of the positive relationship found by Durlak *et al.* (1991) may therefore be due to the inadequacy of appropriate assessments. Alternatively, if insufficient attention is paid to specifically and directly addressing the important cognitions and processes that underpin the child's problems, then it is questionable how much cognitive change will occur. At present there is insufficient research to determine whether, as the cognitive model would predict, cognitive changes are associated with improvements in psychological functioning (Durlak *et al.* 2001).

> ▪ Comparatively little attention has been paid to assessing the assumed relationship between cognitive change and problem improvement.

▶ Is CBT effective?

A number of RCTs have now been reported that have explored the effects of CBT with children. The results of these trials are generally positive and suggest that CBT is effective in the treatment of a range of problems, particularly internalising disorders. These include generalised anxiety (Kendall 1994; Kendall *et al.* 1997), depression (Clarke *et al.* 1999; Harrington *et al.* 1998a), OCD (Barrett *et al.* 2004), post-traumatic symptoms resulting from sexual abuse (Cohen *et al.* 2004), social phobia (Spence *et al.* 2000), phobias (Silverman *et al.* 1999a), abdominal pain (Sanders *et al.* 1994) and chronic fatigue syndrome (Stulemeijer *et al.* 2005).

In considering these findings it is important to note that the effects are sometimes modest and, when compared with other active interventions, do not necessarily suggest the superiority of CBT. Sample sizes are often small and cohorts, particularly in earlier studies, consisted of volunteers with less severe problems, thereby limiting the generalisation of findings to the more complex and multiple problems referred to clinical services. Finally, while there are some notable exceptions (Barrett *et al.* 2001) there is an absence of long-term follow-up data detailing the maintenance of improvements over time.

> - There are a growing number of RCTs to demonstrate that CBT results in a number of positive changes with a range of different problems.
> - The superiority of CBT over other active interventions has not yet been consistently demonstrated.

▶ What are the effective components of CBT interventions?

Neither the most effective mix of cognitive, behavioural or familial treatment strategies nor the relative contributions of specific treatment components to the overall success of CBT programmes are known (Barrett *et al.* 1996b; Silverman *et al.* 1999b). In one of the few studies that have examined this issue Kendall *et al.* (1997) found that the cognitive element of the treatment programme was not effective in bringing about change in anxious children without behavioural exposure.

The sequencing of the specific treatment components is also important since Kazdin & Weisz (1998) highlight that many children drop out of treatment before the programme has been completed. The potential difficulty this creates is exemplified in the study by Feehan & Vostanis (1996). The authors note that only half of the children in their study actually attended the main cognitive sessions focusing upon cognitive restructuring. If the cognitive component is a key aspect of the programme, then the effectiveness of the intervention will be reduced if children do not attend these important sessions. This raises the question of whether the key components of the intervention should be scheduled into the early stages of the programme. Unfortunately the argument becomes circular since there is little information currently available assessing the relative importance and contribution of the specific components. Further studies are required to determine the effective ingredients of treatment programmes and to explore the optimum timing and sequencing of the individual components.

> - The relative importance and particular contribution of the specific components of child-focused CBT, their mix or sequencing has not yet been determined.

▶ Where is it best to start?

After agreeing the formulation the first task is that of psychoeducation in which the child and their family are educated into the cognitive model and the process of CBT. Once undertaken the Clinician is faced with a choice as to which domain will be the initial major focus of the intervention. Unfortunately there is no research available to inform the Clinician as to whether it is initially better to focus upon the cognitive, emotional or behavioural domain. However, an analysis of the sequencing of effective standardised treatment programmes suggests a similar pattern with an initial focus upon the emotional domain to develop emotional awareness and effective emotional management skills. The focus typically shifts to the cognitive domain as the child identifies the maladaptive cognitions and processes that are associated with their emotions. Maladaptive cognitions are challenged and replaced with alternative more functional and balanced cognitions. The newly acquired emotional and cognitive skills are then practised as the focus shifts to the behavioural domain. The child then learns any new behavioural skills that may be required as they systematically confront any avoided situations and learn to overcome their problems.

> ■ Programmes typically start with psychoeducation and then focus upon the emotional domain. A cognitive focus typically follows before moving into the behavioural domain.

▶ How many treatment sessions are needed?

While there are exceptions the majority of standardised treatment programmes typically consist of 12–16 sessions. However, Clinicians working with individual children often report that significant change can be achieved with fewer sessions. This typically depends upon the aim and focus of the intervention, which can broadly be categorised into three different levels.

Level 1 interventions are the most limited and typically require up to four sessions. The predominant focus is upon assessment and psychoeducation in which the child and their family develop a clear CBT formulation that explains the onset and/or maintenance of the child's difficulties. Formulations are powerful and serve to raise general awareness of the existence of negative cognitions and the possible effects these have upon emotions and behaviour. For a number of children and families the development of such an understanding may be all they require. This can enable and empower the child and their family to explore ways in which this negative cycle can be changed.

Level 2 interventions build upon this work and identify in more detail the specific cognitions and emotional reactions that are important for the child. This typically involves an additional 4–6 sessions and aims to help the child and their parents identify the negative and unhelpful thoughts they have in specific problem situations and to explore the effects of these. The child will be helped to identify and control their unpleasant emotions and to systematically confront and cope with stressful or difficult situations. General treatment techniques that are helpful such as positive self-talk, positive diaries and relaxation techniques are often incorporated into the intervention. Emphasis is placed upon understanding the features of negative automatic thoughts and behavioural experiments are used to identify and test the child's predictions. This facilitates the development of alternative more functional and balanced cognitions that are helpful in future situations.

The next stage of intervention, Level 3, typically involves an additional 4–8 sessions and aims to help the child extrapolate from specific problems and situations in order to identify common cognitive patterns and behaviours that pervade a number of situations and events. Greater emphasis is placed upon understanding and identifying the different types of cognitive distortions and the possible schemas or core beliefs that underlie them. Interventions at this level are designed to identify, detect and challenge the cognitive biases that cross a number of situations and to build alternative, more balanced and helpful schemas. Finally attention is paid to relapse prevention and in preparing the child for possible problems and how they can be addressed.

> ■ Level 1 interventions provide psychoeducation and focus upon the development of a cognitive formulation.
>
> ■ Level 2 interventions aim to develop general cognitive and emotional skills that are helpful in particular situations.
>
> ■ Level 3 interventions identify and challenge common dysfunctional cognitions and processes that effect a number of aspects of the child's life.

▶ What about home-based assignments?

Treatment sessions can usefully be complemented by home-based assignments in which monitoring, behavioural experimentation or skills-based tasks can be practised. These provide opportunities for information from real-life situations to be brought into treatment sessions and to promote guided discovery, self-efficacy and the practice of new skills in the child's everyday environment.

While undoubtedly important, home-based assignments are not always essential. During the initial stages the Clinician is concerned with maximising the child's engagement in therapy and increasing their motivation to change. Additional demands that might be perceived negatively need to be minimised while this relationship is developing. It is also during the early stages of therapy that the main home-based task focuses upon self-monitoring. An understanding of key cognitions, emotions and behaviour can be achieved by simply talking through in detail during treatment session any difficulties that might have arisen. However, home-based assignments become more important during the latter stages of treatment when they involve skills practice or exposure, tasks that are essential in demonstrating to the child that they can master and overcome their problems.

Terminology is important and home-based assignments should not be described as 'homework', a term that has negative connotations for many children. Homework typically implies that the child is given 'work', that it will be marked and that there is a 'right' answer, all issues that run counter to the open and collaborative process of CBT. At other times, irrespective of terminology children may find home-based assignments difficult, boring or hard to schedule into their everyday life, or may simply have forgotten about them. It is therefore not uncommon to find that they have not been completed. This can place the child in the difficult situation of having to face the Clinician during their next clinical session to explain their 'failure'.

This negative situation needs to be avoided and can be circumvented by an open and honest discussion. The child's reluctance needs to be openly discussed as a possibility and agreement sought as to whether out-of-session assignments can realistically be undertaken. The child's motivation may be increased by making the task more attractive or by using different media. While some young people prefer paper and pencil diaries and records, monitoring can also be undertaken on self-designed computer records or by email. Similarly, behavioural experiments are more likely to be undertaken if planned in detail with dates, times and places being specified and agreed. In all instances it is important to openly discuss the potential benefits and difficulties of home-based assignments and to realistically and openly agree what can or cannot be achieved.

> ■ Home-based assignments are not essential during the assessment stage but are important in facilitating the use and transfer of skills to the child's everyday environment.

▶ What are the core components of standardised CBT programmes?

There is growing evidence from RCTs to highlight the combinations of techniques and strategies that have been found helpful in the treatment of particular childhood problems. These trials have typically involved standardised treatment packages and thus the relevancy and importance of each component for individual children will vary. Most have compared CBT with waiting list control groups rather than alternative treatments. In terms of age, most trials have been undertaken with children aged 7–16 years, thereby raising questions about their applicability to younger children and possible developmental variations within this age range. The ways in which the programmes have been adapted for use by children at each end of these wide age bands are rarely described. In terms of size most studies are small and lack sufficient power to detect small but important differences. The considerable variability in what is described as CBT and the heterogeneity of samples between children, the presentation of problems, age and development is often overlooked. Finally, a number of studies have been undertaken with children recruited via media adverts, thereby raising the question of whether these programmes would be as effective with the multi-problem children seen by specialist child mental health teams. Recognising these caveats the following core components have been included in randomised trials assessing the effectiveness of CBT in the treatment of generalised anxiety disorders, OCD, depression, and PTSD.

■ Generalised anxiety

Effectiveness

A number of RCTs using CBT with anxious children have now been reported (Compton *et al.* 2004) leading to the conclusion that CBT is 'probably efficacious' in the treatment of childhood anxiety (Chambless & Ollendick 2001). Many of these studies are based upon variants of the 16-session Coping Cat programme that was developed by Phillip Kendall (1994). The first eight sessions of the programme are concerned with education and skill acquisition with the remaining eight focusing upon exposure-based practice. Variants of the programme have compared group or individual administration (Flannery-Schroeder & Kendall 2000; Kendall *et al.* 1997), parental involvement (Barrett 1998; Barrett *et al.* 1996b), effects of parental mental illness (Cobham *et al.* 1998) and whether the programme can be adapted and used as a universal preventative intervention (Barrett & Turner 2001). In all instances CBT has resulted in significant post-treatment gains and a recently published six-year follow-up study suggests that these gains are maintained (Barrett *et al.* 2001).

Rationale informing the treatment programme

The underlying model is based upon a premise that anxiety is a conditioned response (Compton *et al.* 2004). When an individual confronts an anxiety-arousing situation there is an increase in unpleasant feelings (increased heart rate, shortness of breath, sweating) and cognitions ('I won't be able to cope'). In terms of key cognitions a number of studies have highlighted how anxious children have a cognitive bias towards threat. Ambiguous situations are more likely to be perceived as threatening by clinically anxious children (Barrett *et al.* 1996b; Bogels & Zigterman 2000). For anxious children, these unpleasant feelings are minimised by removing or escaping from the threatening situations. This brings immediate emotional relief and the child learns to cope with and reduce their anxious feelings by avoiding anxiety-provoking situations.

The increased awareness of the role of parents in the onset and maintenance of their child's anxiety has resulted in many child-focused CBT programmes including a parental component. The child's bias towards threatening cognitions and their avoidant behaviour may be encouraged, reinforced and modelled by their parents (Barrett *et al.* 1996a). Parents of anxious children are more likely to be protective and over-involved. This conveys a sense of continual danger to the child with their parent's over-involvement limiting their chances of developing appropriate coping mechanisms or acquiring helpful problem-solving skills (Krohnc & Hock 1991; Rapee 1997).

Core components of treatment programmes for anxiety disorders

Psychoeducation in the cognitive model and the theoretical rational underlying the use of CBT in the treatment of childhood anxiety are undertaken early in the programme. The intervention then typically shifts into the emotional domain and helps the child to identify the specific physiological cues their body uses to signal feelings of anxiety. To counter these unpleasant feelings the child is taught relaxation skills and is encouraged to practise these when they become aware of anxious feelings. Important cognitions associated with these anxious feelings are then identified. These beliefs, assumptions and automatic thoughts are often referred to as the child's self-talk. Children are helped to identify their anxiety-generating cognitions and to replace these with anxiety-reducing cognitions (positive self-talk). The emotional and cognitive elements facilitate self-awareness and evaluation. Children are encouraged to develop self-reinforcement skills and to praise attempts to use coping self-talk and relaxation strategies. Once these positive coping skills have been mastered, the child is encouraged to identify their feared situations or events and to arrange these in a hierarchy of fearfulness. Fearful events are treated as problems that need to be solved and so, starting with the least fearful, the child is exposed to each in turn. They are encouraged to use their new emotional and cognitive strategies as they face and confront their fears and learn to overcome their anxieties.

A number of programmes have augmented child-focused sessions with parent sessions (Barrett *et al.* 1996a). Parents are encouraged to identify and confront their own anxious behaviour; to reduce overprotective and dependent behaviour; to encourage, notice and praise courageous child behaviour; and to learn new skills to solve problem situations.

Interventions for children with anxiety disorders typically involve:

- psychoeducation
- emotional identification
- relaxation training
- identifying anxiety-increasing cognitions and replacing these with anxiety-reducing cognitions
- positive praise and reinforcement
- development of a fear hierarchy
- systematic desensitisation via exposure.

Important cognitions

Children with anxiety disorders tend to have more expectations that negative events will occur, make more negative evaluations about their performance, are biased towards possible threat-related cues and perceive themselves as being unable to cope with any frightening events that do arise. Barrett *et al.* (1996a) found clinically anxious children were more likely to interpret ambiguous situations as threatening than a group of oppositional children or a non-clinical group. They were also more likely to select avoidant ways of coping with these situations. The tendency for anxious children to be biased towards possible threat was also found by Bogels & Zigterman (2000). In addition, the authors found that anxious children rated themselves as less competent at dealing with threatening situations. Similarly Spence *et al.* (1999) found that socially anxious children had lower expectations of their performance than non-anxious children. The nature of the association between these cognitions and the presence of anxiety, i.e. causal or a consequence, is unclear.

A number of specific cognitions have been found to be associated with particular anxiety disorders. With generalised anxiety disorders, cognitions tend to focus upon worries about future or past events. These could be about what was said ('I hope Nina didn't think I was talking about her when I said that people get on my nerves'), how one behaved ('They will all think I'm stupid for missing that goal') or what might happen ('My teacher will be really cross with me tomorrow'). The cognitive focus in separation anxiety centres around cognitions about being separated from others and in particular whether the child will cope ('I don't think I can go to the shops without Mum') or whether their parents will be safe ('I bet something bad will happen to Mum if I don't stay to look after her'). Phobias tend to involve cognitions specific to the feared object ('That dog will bite me') whereas social phobia is characterised by cognitions associated with negative social evaluation ('They will laugh at these clothes'; 'I know they don't like me').

- Generalised anxiety is associated with negative cognitions about past and future events.
- Separation anxiety is associated with cognitions about safety and ability to cope independently.
- Phobias are associated with cognitions specific to the feared event.
- Social phobia is associated with cognitions about embarrassment and negative evaluation.

■ Depression

Effectiveness

There are a number of randomised trials comparing CBT for depression with controlled conditions or other active interventions. Overall the results are encouraging, at least in the short term, leading to the suggestion that CBT is an effective treatment for mild or moderate depressive disorders (Harrington *et al.* 1998b). However, children with more severe depressive disorders appear to respond less well to CBT than those with mild depression (Jayson *et al.* 1998).

Although significant post-treatment gains are usually reported, the longer-term follow-up data is less promising. A number of studies report that significant depressive symptoms re-emerge or persist (Vostanis *et al.* 1996, 1998; Wood *et al.* 1996). This indicates the need to pay greater attention to relapse prevention and to plan booster or review follow-up sessions into the programme (Harrington 2004).

The two programmes developed by Stark and Lewinsohn are the best-known standardised interventions for depression. Stark *et al.* (1987) developed a group programme for children aged 9–12 based upon the assumption that depression was a product of cognitive distortions and interpersonal and problem-solving skill deficits. The programme focuses firstly upon promoting more positive effect before moving to address important cognitions and processes. The social skill deficits that are assumed to contribute to social problems and depressed mood are then addressed. The Coping with Depression course developed by Lewinsohn *et al.* (1990) is a 14–16-session group-administered programme for adolescents. Once again the programme aims to promote positive affect and coping skills and encourages the development of self-reinforcement.

CBT for depression has involved briefer 6–8-session interventions (Vostanis *et al.* 1996; Wood *et al.* 1996) and some have involved a parent component (Clarke *et al.* 1999), although parental involvement is limited and is largely psychoeducational. Important parental cognitions or behaviours that may contribute to the child's problems are not addressed, as most programmes continue to focus upon the child.

Rationale informing the treatment programme

The theoretical rationales underlying CBT programmes for children with depression are based upon two main models. The skill deficit model assumes that depression is a result of deficits in important areas such as self-reinforcement, social skills or problem solving. These deficits lead to repeated failure, increased unpleasant emotional affect, negative cognitions about performance resulting in avoidance, fewer opportunities to engage in potentially reinforcing activities and the development of depressive symptoms (Seligman *et al.* 2004).

The second is the distortion model and is based upon the cognitive model developed by Beck (1967). Important negative and distorted cognitive processes are viewed as the primary cause of negative affect. The child therefore develops a negative and biased cognitive framework of themselves, their performance and future, characterised by cognitions related to low self-esteem, blame, helplessness and hopelessness. Events are selected and distorted to fit within this framework leading to reduced affect, behavioural avoidance and lack of motivation, which in turn serves to reinforce the child's negative cognitions.

CBT programmes for depression therefore address important emotional and behavioural skill deficits that may lead to repeated failed experiences as well as important cognitive processes that lead to a biased and distorted perception of events.

Core components of the treatment programme

The theoretical model, process and goals of CBT are first explained. Many depressed children have become socially disengaged and inactive, resulting in them spending considerable time listening to their negative thoughts and ruminating about their perceived failings. The intervention therefore aims to promote a sense of mastery and change rather than dwelling upon and rehearsing negative cognitions. Activity monitoring is a relatively undemanding first step and provides a useful overview of the child's daily routine. This can lead to affective monitoring whereby the child rates the strength of their depressed mood throughout each day to identify particularly difficult times. The child's daily activity level is then increased and previously enjoyable activities that had stopped reintroduced, particularly at those times of very low mood. Increased activity often results in an improvement of mood so that the child is able to consider and work at a more cognitive level. Common and important negative thoughts, beliefs, assumptions and cognitive distortions are identified. These are systematically evaluated as the child is helped to develop an alternative, balanced and more helpful cognitive framework. Potential deficits in social and problem-solving skills are identified and solutions are generated, rehearsed and evaluated. This occurs within a positive and supportive relationship where the child is encouraged to identify, acknowledge and reinforce their success.

As previously mentioned, the role of parents in CBT for depression has generally been limited and tends to be psychoeducational. The focus therefore remains the child and their problems and little attention is paid to important parental behaviour that might contribute to their child's problems or interfere with the effectiveness of the intervention. Studies that have compared CBT for depressed children with and without parental involvement have failed to find any additional benefits from parent participation (Clarke *et al.* 1999; Lewinsohn *et al.* 1990).

> CBT programmes for depression typically include:
>
> ■ psychoeducation
>
> ■ activity monitoring
>
> ■ affective monitoring
>
> ■ increasing pleasant activities
>
> ■ identifying important negative cognitions
>
> ■ cognitive evaluation and restructuring
>
> ■ social and problem skill training
>
> ■ self-reinforcement and practice.

Important cognitions

Children with depression tend to present with a number of distorted cognitions. They are more likely to attend to the negative features of an event and to ignore or overlook any positive aspects (Kendall *et al.* 1990). They have negative views and expectations of themselves (Kendall *et al.* 1990), their performance and future, and attribute positive events to external rather than internal causes (Curry & Craighead 1990). They tend to have more negative attributions about events and are likely to report guilt and worthlessness (Kaslow *et al.* 1988; Seligman *et al.* 2004).

Shirk *et al.* (2003) highlight that most interest has been focused upon self-schemas, particularly those related to individual failure. They note that the schemas of children with depression tend to be characterised by over-generalisations where failure in one domain, for example (e.g. school work), is assumed to apply to other areas (e.g. sport). Similarly they note that all-or-nothing thinking is common. Finally there has been some research that suggests that ruminating about depressive mood is associated with symptoms of depression (Abela *et al.* 2002).

> Children with depression present with cognitions that:
>
> ■ are biased towards the negative features of what happens
>
> ■ are overly self-critical
>
> ■ attribute success to external factors
>
> ■ generalise perceived failure in one domain to other areas.

■ Obsessive compulsive disorder (OCD)

Effectiveness

A number of open clinical trials evaluating the effectiveness of individually administered CBT for the treatment of childhood OCD have been reported (Franklin *et al.* 1998; March *et al.* 1994). The results of these and other small-scale studies have led to the clinical consensus that CBT for the treatment of childhood OCD is the treatment of choice (March *et al.* 1997). However, the empirical evidence to support this view is still accumulating since only one randomised controlled treatment trial using a 14-session protocol called the 'Freedom from Obsessions and Compulsions Using Cognitive Behavioural Strategies (FOCUS)' has yet been reported (Barrett *et al.* 2004). This study adapted the best-known programme for OCD, 'How I ran OCD off my Land' (March *et al.* 1994), to deliver as a group intervention with an additional family component. The results from 77 children aged 7–17 demonstrated significant reductions in diagnostic status post-treatment and at six-month follow-up, but no difference between individually or group-administered CBT.

Rationale informing the treatment programme

The treatment programme for children, 'How I ran OCD off my Land' (March *et al.* 1994), is based upon behavioural theory. It assumes that anxiety is elicited by exposure to a feared stimulus and that compulsions serve to reduce anxiety. The programme therefore relies upon three major behavioural strategies. Exposure ensures that the child systematically confronts feared situations and continues in their presence until the associated anxiety decreases. During this time engagement in the previously learned rituals or compulsive behaviours that the child has used to reduce their anxiety are prevented. The child therefore learns that anxiety levels can be reduced without engaging in compulsive behaviours. The third element involves the removal of parental attention and reinforcement of the child's rituals, thereby extinguishing their occurrence.

While behavioural interventions have proven effective, recent interest has turned towards assessing the applicability of the cognitive model of OCD developed from work with adults to children (Salkovskis 1985, 1989). The model emphasises that it is not the obsessional intrusive thoughts themselves that cause distress but rather the way the individual appraises these. Important appraisals involving blame or an inflated responsibility for harm to oneself or others produces intolerable discomfort, which is reduced by engaging in neutralising (compulsive) behaviours. The model suggests that overestimation of both harm probability and harm severity are central to the development and maintenance of OCD. In addition other important cognitive processes associated with the maintenance of OCD include thought–action fusion ('I think it therefore it will happen'), self-doubt (leading to indecisiveness) and a perceived lack of cognitive control (which leads to increased intrusive thoughts) (O'Kearney 1998).

In terms of family characteristics, parents of children with OCD have been found to be less confident in their child's abilities, less rewarding of independence and less likely to use positive problem-solving skills (Barrett *et al.* 2002). Hibbs *et al.* (1991) demonstrated that parents of children with OCD were overly critical of, and over-involved with, their child. Parents and siblings have been found to accommodate and become involved in the child's OCD, which in turn serves to maintain their symptoms (Barrett *et al.* 2004).

Core components of the treatment programme

The first aim of psychoeducation is to externalise OCD as separate from the child. This challenges any parental perceptions that the child's OCD is due to wilful naughtiness and unites the parent and child towards the common goal of beating OCD together. The second aim is to provide an understanding of the treatment rationale, intervention and the role of the parents in the programme. This is followed by a process of mapping where the child identifies and monitors their obsessional thoughts and compulsive behaviours and the degree of distress associated with them. Anxiety management typically follows and provides the child with alternative ways of dealing with their anxious feelings. The FOCUS programme (Barrett *et al.* 2004) pays greater attention to the child's cognitions and highlights and evaluates common thought traps (e.g. cognitions about responsibility and increased probability) and unhelpful cognitive strategies (e.g. thought suppression). The child is encouraged to challenge their unhelpful ways of thinking by positive self-talk, which is used to boss back their obsessional thoughts. Once the child is armed with a range of emotional and cognitive strategies, a hierarchy of the child's obsessions and compulsions is developed. Starting with the least fearful, the child confronts and overcomes each step of their fear hierarchy without engaging in any compulsive behaviours. A series of rewards acknowledge and praise the child's success and increases their motivation to attempt the next step.

The role of parents in the original programme developed by March *et al.* (1994) was limited and was mainly concerned with psychoeducation. The FOCUS programme (Barrett *et al.* 2004) includes a substantial parallel parent and sibling intervention. This involves psychoeducation, developing problem-solving skills and strategies to reduce parental involvement in the child's symptoms, as well as encouragement and support during the exposure and response prevention part of the programme.

Core components of interventions for OCD include:

- psychoeducation
- self-monitoring and mapping
- anxiety management
- identification of key cognitions and thought traps
- bossing back the OCD
- development of a fear hierarchy
- exposure and response prevention
- positive reinforcement.

Important cognitions

The cognitive model of OCD (Salkovskis 1985, 1989) has provided a useful framework for assessing potentially important cognitions and processes in children. Consistent with this model, children with OCD have been found to have significantly higher appraisals of responsibility, harm severity and thought–action fusion and less cognitive control than a group of non-referred children (Barrett & Healy 2003). Similarly, Libby *et al.* (2004) found that young people with OCD had higher scores on measures of inflated responsibility and thought–action fusion and that inflated responsibility predicted OCD symptom severity. However, the findings are not consistent and, although there is some support for the applicability of this model, it may not adequately account for OCD in children (Barrett *et al.* 2003; Libby *et al.* 2004).

Children with OCD tend to:

- have inflated appraisals of responsibility
- have increased expectations that bad things will occur
- demonstrate thought–action fusion.

■ Post-traumatic stress disorder (PTSD)

Effectiveness

A number of RCTs evaluating the effectiveness of trauma-focused CBT have now been reported. Typically these interventions address each of the cardinal features of PTSD, namely trauma re-experiencing, increased arousal and avoidance of events associated with the trauma. The largest trial involving 229 children found that those who received trauma-focused CBT made significantly more post-treatment improvements in terms of PTSD symptomatology, depression, behaviour, shame and abuse-related attributions than those who received child-centred therapy (Cohen *et al.* 2004). Trauma-focused CBT has also been shown to be effective with young children aged 2–8 (Cohen & Mannarino 1996; Deblinger *et al.* 2001). However, some studies failed to find the expected changes in PTSD symptoms (Celano *et al.* 1996) or found that parental involvement resulted in more benefits than child-only CBT (King *et al.* 2000). Finally, the majority of randomised trials have been undertaken with children who have been sexually abused. Further well-controlled studies are required to evaluate the applicability of these programmes to other trauma groups.

Rationale informing the treatment programme

Early models were largely based on learning theory, which assumed that stimuli associated with the trauma became conditioned with emotional reactions. Interventions therefore used exposure (imaginal and in vivo) to facilitate emotional processing of traumatic memories. There has, however, been growing recognition of the importance of cognitive factors in the onset and maintenance of PTSD (Ehlers & Clark 2000) and recent interest has turned towards assessing whether this model developed with adults also applies to children. The model assumes that the traumatic event is not cognitively processed and is poorly integrated into memory. The event is negatively viewed as catastrophic or devastating and the child misinterprets their symptoms (e.g. 'I am going mad'), which creates a sense of current threat. The use of avoidant behaviours and cognitive strategies such as rumination or thought suppression prevent the trauma being processed and serve to reinforce the sense of current threat.

Core components of the treatment programme

Trauma-focused CBT targets the cardinal features of PTSD in the cognitive (trauma re-experiencing), emotional (increased arousal) and behavioural (avoidance) domains.

The cognitive model and process of therapy are explained. Psychoeducation helps the child understand common reactions to traumatic events and begins the process of normalising their reactions and challenging their beliefs about their symptoms ('I must be going mad'). The possibility of achieving positive change is reinforced and the child is encouraged to resume any everyday or pleasant activities that they had stopped. Anxiety-management skills are learned and the child is taught to rate their feelings, skills that will be helpful during the next stage of exposure. The child is helped to process their trauma by developing a narrative in which the event is reconstructed from beginning to end. Important cognitions are elicited and discussed and dysfunctional cognitive processes that prevent processing of the trauma (thought suppression, avoidance) discouraged. Repeated imaginal exposure to those parts of the trauma that are most distressing is undertaken until the associated distress reduces. This may be followed by in vivo exposure through behavioural experiments where the child learns to confront and cope with any events or trauma reminders that are being avoided.

Most programmes involve a parent component. Parents are helped to talk with their child about the trauma and to identify and challenge their own maladaptive cognitions about what happened. They are encouraged to support their child during exposure tasks and to be less protective towards or over-involved with their child.

Core components of CBT programmes for PTSD include:

- psychoeducation
- activity re-engagement
- anxiety management and monitoring
- creating a trauma narrative
- exposure
- cognitive restructuring.

Important cognitions

A number of potentially important cognitions have been identified as contributing to the onset and maintenance of PTSD and should be focused upon during therapy. These include attributions about the event (e.g. as life ruining) or symptoms (e.g. 'I am going mad'). Attributions about perceived responsibility for the trauma happening (e.g. 'I am to blame for this'), shame about how they behaved and guilt about what they should or should not have done need to be elicited and challenged. Finally, the use of dysfunctional cognitive coping strategies such as suppression, rumination and avoidance need to be discouraged.

Cognitions associated with PTSD include:

- negative attributions about the trauma and/or its symptoms
- attributions of responsibility, blame, shame and guilt
- the use of dysfunctional cognitive strategies such as thought suppression, distraction and rumination.

Psychoeducational materials

Included in this book are psychoeducational materials that can be used with children presenting with problems associated with anxiety ('Beating Anxiety'), depression ('Fighting Back Depression'), OCD ('Controlling Worries and Habits') and trauma ('Coping with Trauma'). These materials provide a summary of the common symptoms associated with each problem and an overview of some of the CBT strategies that might be useful. These leaflets are designed as adjuncts to therapy sessions. They provide the child and their carers with an overview and prepare the child for some of the areas that might be addressed in more depth during CBT. The materials are not intended to be prescriptive. The emphasis and focus of the intervention will be determined on the basis of the case formulation.

Beating Anxiety

There are times when we all feel worried, anxious, uptight or stressed. Often there is a reason.

▶ Doing something new or difficult like having a trial for the school sports team.

▶ Telling someone something that they won't like, such as 'I don't want to be your friend any more'.

▶ Preparing for something important like an exam.

Usually, you feel better once you have faced the worry. At other times these uncomfortable feelings seem very strong, come often or seem to last a long time. You may not be able to find a clear reason so it may seem hard to know what is making you feel anxious. You may find that these unpleasant feelings stop you from doing the things you would like to do. At these times it may be useful to learn how you can **beat your anxiety**.

Understand your anxious feelings

When people become anxious or scared they often notice a number of changes in their body. This is called the FLIGHT or FIGHT reaction. Your body prepares itself to run away or to face and fight the scary thing. The main signals are listed below. Understanding which of these are strongest will help you to become better at noticing when you are getting wound up.

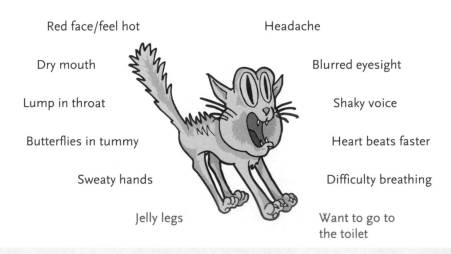

Light-headed/feel faint

Red face/feel hot

Headache

Dry mouth

Blurred eyesight

Lump in throat

Shaky voice

Butterflies in tummy

Heart beats faster

Sweaty hands

Difficulty breathing

Jelly legs

Want to go to the toilet

Learn to relax

You can control your anxious feelings by learning to relax. You can do this in different ways but remember:

▶ There is **no one way** of controlling your anxious feelings.

▶ **Different methods** may be useful at different times.

▶ It is important to **find what works for you**.

Physical exercise

Sometimes you may notice that you have felt anxious for most of the day. You may have had lots of feelings of anxiety and when this happens **physical exercise** can be a good way of relaxing.

A good run, a quick walk, cycle or swim can help you get rid of any anxious feelings and can make you feel better.

Absorbing activities

The second way of relaxing is to find something else to think about and do. Rather than listening to your negative thoughts or focusing on your anxious feelings, try to do something else.

Some people find that they can switch these thoughts and feelings off by becoming totally absorbed in an activity.

Computer games, reading, watching the TV/DVD, playing an instrument, listening to the radio or music may be helpful.

The more you concentrate on what you are doing, the more you drown out any negative thoughts or feelings.

At those times when you become aware that you are listening to your negative thoughts, try one of the activities you find helpful. So, for example,

▶ Instead of lying in bed listening to your negative thoughts, put on your personal stereo and listen to some music.

▶ Instead of worrying whether your friend will call, read a magazine.

The more you practise, the easier you will find it to block out your negative thoughts and the better you will feel.

Controlled breathing

There are times when you may suddenly notice that you have become anxious and need a quick way to relax and regain control.

Controlled breathing is a quick method that can help. The idea is to concentrate on your breathing and this will help you to relax. You can use this method anywhere and often people don't even notice what you are doing!

Slowly draw in a deep breath, hold it for five seconds and then very slowly let it out. As you breathe out say to yourself 'relax'. Doing this a few times will help you regain control of your body and help you feel calmer.

My relaxing place

With this method you chill out by thinking about a special place that you find restful.

Think about your dream place. It could be somewhere you have been or a pretend place. Imagine a picture of it and make the picture as real as you can and think about:

▶ the noise of the waves crashing on the beach or the sound of the wind blowing in the trees

▶ the smell of the sea or the scent of pine forests

▶ the warm sun shining on your face or the wind blowing gently through your hair.

Sometimes we get very anxious before we have to do something new or challenging. This way of relaxing can help you prepare yourself so that you feel more relaxed before you face your problem or difficult situation. Remember, the more you practise, the more it will help.

Identify your worrying thoughts

It is important to identify your negative, critical or worrying thoughts. People who feel anxious often:

▶ have very negative thoughts

▶ find it hard to think, hear or see anything good about themselves

▶ do not recognise their positive skills

- are more likely to expect bad things to happen

- are less likely to think that they can be successful

- have a gloomy view about their future.

For some, this way of thinking takes over. Their thoughts become mainly negative and they often feel **ANXIOUS**.

Are you stuck in a thinking trap?

You may notice that you are thinking in certain negative ways. These are thinking traps and there are four very common traps.

 **Negative glasses** – these only let you see one part of what happens – the negative part! You find it hard to see the good or positive things that happen.

Positive doesn't count – this is where you dismiss as unimportant or put down any positive things that happen.

 **Blowing things up** – this is where the small negative things that happen become bigger than they really are.

Predict that bad things will happen. This happens in two main ways:

 You may become the '**Mind-reader**' who thinks they know what everyone else is thinking.

You may become the '**Fortune-teller**' who thinks they know what is going to happen.

Check and test your thoughts

You can make sure that you haven't become stuck in a negative thinking trap by testing your thoughts. This can help you to find some of the **positive things** that you may have ignored or overlooked and learn that there might be another way of thinking about things.

To test your thoughts, try doing this:

▶ Write down the negative thought you hear most often?

▶ Write down all the evidence that supports this thought?

▶ Write down all the evidence to question this thought?

▶ Ask yourself what your best friend/teacher/parent would say if they heard you thinking this?

▶ What would you say to your best friend if they had this thought?

▶ Now you have done this, is there a more balanced way of thinking about this?

Set up an experiment and test your thoughts

It is sometimes helpful to set up experiments to test your thoughts and see whether what you think will happen comes true. To do an experiment you need to write down:

▶ your **thoughts**

▶ an **experiment** you could set up to test them

▶ your **prediction** (what you expect will happen)

▶ what **actually happened**

Change unhelpful thoughts to helpful thoughts

Sometimes thinking about things in a more positive way can be helpful and may stop you feeling so anxious.

So next time you have to do something that makes you feel worried or anxious, listen to your thoughts and try **changing Negative to Positive**.

Face your fears

 People often learn to cope with worries and anxious feelings by avoiding the thing that makes them worried. This may make you feel better but it doesn't help you to beat your worry. At these times it is useful to **Face your Fears** and learn to overcome these problems.

You can do this as follows:

▶ Identify your challenge – the fear you want to face.

▶ Break your challenge into smaller steps – this will make it easier for you to be successful.

▶ What are the helpful thoughts that will help you to be successful?

▶ Relax, use your helpful thoughts and face the first step towards overcoming your fear.

▶ Don't forget to tell yourself how well you have done!

Once you have been successful, try and face the next step and continue until you have overcome your fears.

Don't forget to praise yourself

We are not always very good at praising ourselves and saying 'well done'. So when you try to **beat your anxiety** and **face your fears**, remember to praise yourself. After all, you deserve it for having a try!

Fighting Back Depression

There are times when everyone feels down, fed-up or unhappy. Most of the time these feelings come and go, but sometimes they last and take over. You can't seem to shift them and end up feeling depressed. You might notice that you:

▶ are often tearful

▶ cry for no clear reason or over small things

▶ wake up early in the morning

▶ have difficulty falling asleep at night

▶ feel constantly tired and lacking in energy

▶ comfort eat or have lost your appetite

▶ have problems concentrating

▶ stopped doing the things you used to enjoy

▶ go out less often and just want to be on your own.

These are some of the many signals that depression has taken over and that it is **time to fight back!**

Getting started is hard work

When you feel down it is very hard to get yourself going again. It feels like you are trying to push an elephant up a hill. Everything seems impossible or feels really hard work and you may feel that you can't be bothered to even try.

This is part of the depression and one of the hardest jobs is to take the first step. Two things might help you to get going.

▶ Tell other people that you are going to start fighting your depression. They can help, support and encourage you.

▶ The other thing to remember is that **you** can make a difference to how you feel. It is hard work but there are things you can do to make yourself feel better.

Check what you do and how you feel

When people feel down they stop doing things. They don't go out so much and may sit around or stay in bed all day. A useful first step is to check what you are doing and to see if there are any times during the day that you feel worse than others.

Each hour, write down on a piece of paper what you did and choose a number from 10 (feel really good) to 1 (feel really low) to rate your mood. Lisa's diary looked like this:

- ▶ 10.00 – In bed. Mood 3
- ▶ 11.00 – In bed. Mood 2
- ▶ 12.00 – Sitting in my room, thinking. Mood 1
- ▶ 1.00 – Downstairs, had lunch with Mum. Mood 6
- ▶ 2.00 – In my bedroom listening to music. Mood 6
- ▶ 3.00 – In my bedroom. Sitting around. Mood 2

This helped Lisa to see that the times she felt worse were when she was sitting in her room not doing anything. When she was downstairs with others or listening to music she felt better.

Find the fun things

When you feel down you stop doing things, even those things that you used to like doing! Hobbies, interests, activities or visiting places you used to like going (e.g. cinema) happen less often.

One of the first things to do is to start having fun again. Try making a list of all the fun things you used to do and enjoy. Mike's list looked like this:

- ▶ Stopped playing my guitar.
- ▶ Don't listen to music as much.
- ▶ Don't phone friends any more – wait for them to phone me.
- ▶ Can't seem to read anything.
- ▶ Not been to town on Saturday afternoon for a few months.

Mike was feeling very down and so even just trying to do something he used to enjoy felt impossible. Because this first step can be so hard it is important that it is **small**.

Mike chose to start by playing his guitar for five minutes each day. Mike felt this was possible and by setting a very small target there was more chance that he would be successful. As soon as he started playing, Mike realised how much fun he used to have and was soon playing his guitar more often and for much longer.

Mike then moved on to his next target. This was to telephone one friend each week. Mike found that the more he did, the more he enjoyed himself and the more he wanted to do.

You may find that you start doing things again but that these things don't seem as much fun as they used to. Don't worry, the fun may take a little longer to return. Keep reminding yourself that you are doing well and remember that being busy gives you less time to listen to your negative thoughts.

Find your negative thoughts

People who feel down and depressed have negative thoughts. They are more likely to:

▶ Look for and find the negative or bad things that happen.

▶ Ignore the good things.

▶ Be very critical of themselves and what they do.

▶ Think that the things that go wrong are due to them.

▶ Apply things that go wrong in one area (e.g. not winning a race) to other parts of their life (e.g. 'I am a loser').

This is the Negative Trap

▶ The more you hear these thoughts

▶ The more you believe them

▶ The less you do and

▶ The worse you feel.

You need to become aware of your negative thoughts and to discover whether you are caught in a thinking trap. The four common traps are:

Negative glasses – these only let you see the negative things that happen!

Jo didn't think people liked her. She noticed that Gemma turned away and carried on talking with Sam when she said 'Hello'. Her negative glasses didn't let her see that Sue, Claire and Becky all smiled and said 'Hello' back.

Positive doesn't count – any positive things that happen are thought of as unimportant or lucky.

Tom's mum told him that he did well in his maths test but Tom replied, 'Everybody did well and anyway these tests don't matter.'

Blowing things up – small negative things become bigger than they really are.

Julie forgot to telephone her friend Mary after school. When Julie remembered she thought to herself, 'I always let my friends down so no one will ever want to be friends with me'.

Predict that bad things will happen. This happens in two main ways:

The '**Mind-reader**' thinks they know what everyone else is thinking – 'I don't think Scott likes me'.

The '**Fortune-teller**' thinks they know what is going to happen – 'I know that I will say something stupid and that everyone will laugh at me'.

Challenge your negative thoughts

Once you find your negative thoughts and know the negative trap you have fallen into, you can learn to **fight back**.

▶ If you have negative glasses, you need to learn to stop, look again and find any positives that you have overlooked.

▶ If you think that positive doesn't count, you need to learn to accept and celebrate your successes.

▶ If you blow things up, you need to learn to stop things getting on top of you and to stop them growing too big.

▶ If you predict bad things will happen, you need to stop gazing into your crystal ball and check out what really happens!

Learn to cope with any problems

People who feel depressed sometimes feel that they don't know how to deal with their problems. Difficulties with friends, family or teachers can feel so big that you just don't know how to cope with them.

Think about *ALL* the possible solutions

Think about your problem and write down all the possible solutions. It is sometime useful to keep asking yourself I could do this **OR, ...**

Sade wanted to go to the cinema but she didn't want to go on her own. She kept putting it off, thinking that no one would be interested in the film. She tried the 'OR' question to look for solutions:

> I could ask my friend Mandy **OR**
> I could see if Sally wanted to go **OR**
> I could ask Gemma **OR**
> I could see if Mum or Dad wanted to go **OR**
> I could ask my sister Lucy **OR**
> I could invite my cousin Jade

This helped Sade realise that there were quite a few people she could go to the cinema with, so there was no need to put it off any longer.

Practise being successful

When faced with a challenge or new situation it is easy to expect to fail or think that things will go wrong. This is one of the negative traps where we predict bad things will happen. A useful way forward is to imagine a picture of yourself being successful.

Imagine a picture of your challenge and talk yourself through what will happen. Think about the steps involved but this time imagine yourself coping and being successful. Make your picture as real as possible and describe your scene in lots of detail.

Practising this a few times will help you to see that, while it might be difficult, you can be successful.

Watch what other people do

Another helpful way of solving problems is to watch someone who is successful and learn what they do.

Susheela was always getting teased at school and she often ended up getting upset or angry and storming off. The more she reacted, the more the other children teased her.

Susheela decided to watch how her friend Nina coped with the teasing. Nina had been badly teased at the start of school and although she was still called names she didn't get teased so much. Susheela watched what happened. When the other children started to call Nina names she just smiled and agreed with them. She did not argue back or over-react. After a minute the children got bored and moved off to find someone else to tease.

Positive self-talk

A useful way of helping yourself through a difficult or worrying situation is by using self-talk. Positive self-talk helps you to feel more relaxed and confident by keeping doubts and worries under control. You do this by saying positive things to yourself when you feel worried or unsure if you will be successful.

▶ **I am** going to go back to that place again.

▶ **I have** managed to get to the door and now I am going in.

Repeat your positive message and praise yourself as you face your challenge.

Praise yourself for having a go

When you are feeling down it can be hard to praise yourself and say 'well done'.

There always seems to be so many things that you would like to do or that could be done better that it becomes difficult to notice what you have achieved.

You may not always be successful but that doesn't matter. What is important is that you have tried and that you have started to **fight back**. So don't overlook it, praise yourself for having a go.

Controlling Worries and Habits

We often have **obsessional thoughts** that go round and round in our heads. Sometimes these thoughts keep happening and are about worrying things like germs, danger or bad things such as:

▶ Thinking that people will be hurt or involved in accidents.

▶ Catching or giving others germs or diseases.

▶ Thinking that you will be rude or behave inappropriately.

Obsessional thoughts like these can be difficult to stop. Because they are very worrying you may feel uncomfortable or anxious. To feel better, people often try to stop or cancel these thoughts by doing something to make them better. These are called '**safety behaviours**', **habits** or **compulsive behaviours** and could be anything such as:

▶ Washing hands or clothes.

▶ Checking things like doors, light switches, windows.

▶ Doing things (like getting washed or dressed) in a special way.

▶ Repeating words, phrases or numbers a set number of times.

Compulsive behaviours like these can take over. Each day becomes a struggle as more and more time is spent doing these compulsive behaviours. This is called **Obsessional Compulsive Disorder** or **OCD** for short. When this happens you need to learn how to **regain control of your life**.

Dealing with obsessional thoughts

We all have worrying thoughts

We don't usually tell anyone that we have worrying thoughts. We keep them a secret. We may worry that other people won't understand, will become cross, or think that we are silly, and so we keep them locked up in our heads.

The first thing you need to know is that **you are not silly**. We all have worrying thoughts at some time or another.

▶ You may spill or touch something and wonder if you might catch any germs.

▶ You may forget to unplug the TV and worry that it will catch fire.

▶ You may have an argument with somebody and wish that something horrible happens to them.

So **everybody has bad or worrying thoughts**.

Just because you think something doesn't mean that it will happen

Worrying thoughts are very common but the difference for people with OCD is that they **believe their thoughts will come true**. So, someone with OCD might:

▶ think that their mum will have a car crash and believe that this will happen.

▶ think that they have a serious illness and believe that they will give it to other people if they touch them.

It is only the bad things we believe we can make happen. Thinking that you will win the National Lottery or that you will get an 'A' grade in your maths doesn't make it happen.

So the second thing we need to know is that **just because we think something doesn't mean it will happen!**

Check the 'chain of events'

Because you hear your obsessional thoughts so often you simply believe them and don't bother to check them out. Sometimes it is useful to test them and check whether they really can be true.

Mike worried that he would pass germs to other people and make them seriously ill. He was worried that if he touched a door handle he would pass germs to the next person who touched the handle. Mike worked through the **chain of events** that needed to happen before this could come true.

- ► Mike must have a serious illness.

- ► This illness has to be passed to others through touch.

- ► Germs would have to be on his hand when he touched the door.

- ► The germs would have to move from his hand to the door handle.

- ► The germs would have to stay 'alive' on the door handle.

- ► The germs would be picked up by the next person who touched the door.

- ► The germs would have to get inside their body.

- ► The germs would have to be strong enough to beat their body defences.

- ► They would then become ill.

Writing down the steps involved is useful and can show how many things need to happen before the worry could possibly come true.

How likely is it that each step will happen?

The big problem with OCD is that it tricks you into thinking that bad things **will definitely** happen. We need to watch out for this trick and check it out.

Look at your **chain of events** and rate how likely it is that each step could happen. For each step ask yourself '**How likely is it that ...**' and choose a number between 1 and 100 to show how likely it is to happen. 100 means absolutely certain and 0 means extremely unlikely. Mike did this to rate his chain of events:

- ► How likely I have serious illness (60)

- ► How likely I can pass this on by touch (40)

- ► How likely I have germs on my hands when I touch the door (74)

- ► How likely that the germs would move to the door handle (70)

- ► How likely that germs would stay 'alive' on the door handle (25)

- ► How likely that germs would be picked up by the next person (20)

- ► How likely that germs would get inside their body (18)

- ► How likely that the germs would be stronger than their body's defence (45)

- ► How likely that they would become ill (60)

This helped Mike to see that the chances of him making someone seriously ill were actually very, very small.

Don't try to stop your thoughts

Some people try very hard not to think about their obsessional thoughts. It may seem to make sense but we know that this doesn't work. The harder you try not to think about them, the more they will happen.

Don't try to stop them. Let them happen but **learn to live with them**.

Learn to control anxious feelings

Obsessional and worrying thoughts will make you feel anxious or uncomfortable. You can try to control these feelings by learning to relax. You can do this in different ways but remember:

▶ There is **no one way** of controlling your anxious feelings.

▶ **Different methods** may be useful at different times.

▶ It is important to **find what works for you**.

Physical exercise

Physical exercise can be a good way of relaxing. A good run, a quick walk, cycle or swim can help you to get rid of any anxious feelings and can make you feel better.

Absorbing activities

There might be some things that you really get into which take over your mind and make you forget about everything else. These can help you switch off and relax.

Computer games, reading, watching the TV/DVD, playing an instrument, listening to the radio or music may be helpful.

If you notice yourself feeling anxious or uncomfortable, then try to become lost in one of the activities you really enjoy.

Controlled breathing

There are times when you may suddenly notice that you have become anxious and need a quick way to relax and regain control.

Controlled breathing is a quick method that can help. The idea is to concentrate on your breathing and this will help you to relax. You can use this method anywhere and often people don't even notice what you are doing!

Slowly draw in a deep breath, hold it for five seconds and then very slowly let it out. As you breathe out, say to yourself 'relax'. Doing this a few times will help you regain control and help you feel calmer.

My relaxing place

With this method you chill out by thinking about a special place that you find restful. Think about your dream place. It could be somewhere you have been or a pretend place. Imagine a picture of it and make the picture as restful and peaceful as possible. Try to make the picture as real as you can and think about:

- ▶ the colour of the sand, sea, sky
- ▶ the noise of the waves crashing on the beach
- ▶ the sound of the wind blowing in the trees
- ▶ the smell of the sea
- ▶ the warm sun shining on your face
- ▶ the wind blowing gently in your hair.

This way of relaxing can help you prepare yourself so that you feel more relaxed before you face your problem or difficult situation. Remember, the more you practise, the more it will help.

Learn to beat your compulsive behaviours

To beat OCD you need to learn that you don't have to do your compulsive behaviours or habits when you have a worrying thought.

List all your compulsive behaviours

Make a **list of all your compulsive behaviours** – the habits or routines you use to make your worrying thoughts safe. Write each one down on a piece of paper. Choose a number between 1 and 10 (1 not at all upset – 10 very upset) and for each behaviour rate how upset you would be if you couldn't do it.

Put them in order

Now arrange your pieces of paper so that they go from the lowest numbers (least distress) to the highest (most distress).

Nisha was very worried that her parents would – have a serious accident if she left them. She listed all the compulsive safety behaviours she used to make sure that this didn't happen and rated how distressed she would be if she didn't do it.

▶ Say to my parents 'I love you very much' three times when I go out to my friends (Distress 4)

▶ Say to my parents 'I love you very much' three times when I go to school (Distress 6)

▶ When they go out, check the time they will be home and repeat it three times (Distress 7)

▶ Phone them every 15 minutes when they go out to check that they are OK (Distress 8)

Start with the easiest and STOP doing it

Take the habit that causes you the least distress and **STOP** it.

▶ If you have to say things three times, then try saying them only once or twice.

▶ If you have to wash your hands as soon as you touch something you think is dirty, then try waiting 5, 10 or 15 minutes before you wash.

▶ If you have to change all your clothes after bumping into someone, then try changing only your jumper.

You can break habits in different ways so choose the way **you think you can do it**. For Nina the habit she started with was saying 'I love you very much' to her parents three times when she went to her friends. Nina tried to break her habit by saying this only once.

Face your fears

People often learn to cope with worries and anxious feelings by avoiding the thing that makes them worried.

▶ Mike, worried about catching germs from door handles, might avoid touching them.

▶ Nina, worried that bad things might happen to her parents, might avoid going out to friends or school so that she can stay with them.

This may make you feel better but it doesn't help you learn that you actually don't need to do habits. You need to **face your fears**.

▶ Mike has to learn that he can touch doors and that bad things won't happen.

▶ Nina has to learn that she can go out and that her parents are safe.

You will feel anxious but ... it will get easier

When you face your fears and try to stop your habits you will feel anxious or uncomfortable. You will worry that your obsessive thoughts will become true and this will make you feel very anxious.

Don't give in! What you will find is that these feelings will get less. You can check this out by rating your feelings and seeing them **get less over time**:

▶ Immediately after you have stopped your habit, rate how you feel (10 very anxious/worst ever felt – 1 calm and relaxed).

▶ After 5 minutes rate yourself again and keep doing this and see how you feel after 30 minutes.

You will find that even though you haven't done your habits, the unpleasant anxious feelings get less.

Use positive self-talk

A way of helping yourself through a difficult or worrying situation is by using self-talk. **Self-talk** helps you to feel more relaxed and confident. By repeating encouraging and positive messages to yourself you can **boss back your worries**.

▶ **I am** going to beat my habits.

▶ **I have** managed not to do this for 5 minutes so I can do another 5.

▶ **I will** be able to do this.

Remember to praise yourself as you beat your habits. You may want to give yourself a special treat – after all, you do deserve it.

Coping with Trauma

 Being involved in a trauma can be very frightening and it is not surprising that most children and young people will be upset for a few days afterwards. You may notice a number of changes and find that:

▶ You can't stop thinking about the trauma.

▶ There are times when it feels like the trauma is happening all over again.

▶ You have difficulty sleeping at nights.

▶ You have bad dreams.

▶ You become very frightened or upset by things that remind you of your trauma.

▶ You feel angry or irritable with friends and family.

▶ You don't want to think or talk about what happened.

▶ You are reluctant to go out or be with others.

For most people these changes last only a couple of weeks, although some children find that the effects of the trauma last longer. If this happens you may want to try some of these ideas to see if they help.

They don't always work but if you practise enough there will be some times when they may make you feel better and more in control.

Stopping trauma thoughts and pictures

 There may be times when you find that you cannot stop thinking about your trauma. Thoughts and memories may keep going round and round in your head like a videotape which you cannot switch off. You may find that this happens more when you are not very busy or if something reminds you about it.

You could try to control your thoughts by teaching yourself to think about something else. Rather than listening to worrying thoughts about the trauma you can try to learn how to switch the videotape off. This can be done in different ways and you will need to experiment to see what works for you.

Describe what you see

Describe to yourself in a lot of detail what is going on around you. Describe what you see as quickly as you can and think about colours, shapes, size, textures, what things are made of, etc. By concentrating on the things you see you stop thinking about the trauma. You will need to practise and, remember, it probably won't work straight away.

Thinking puzzles

You may want to squeeze out trauma memories by setting yourself thinking puzzles. This could be done in lots of ways, such as:

▶ counting backwards from 123 in 9's

▶ spelling the names of your family backwards

▶ naming the records of your favourite group

▶ naming all the players in your favourite sports team.

The puzzles have to be hard enough to challenge you and make you think; so don't make them too easy.

Activities

Some people find that activities are a good way of switching off. The idea is that the activity takes over and drowns out any thoughts or memories about the trauma. When you notice that you are thinking about your trauma, try one of the activities you find helpful.

Crosswords, reading, watching the TV/video, listening to the radio or music or whatever you find useful.

The more you concentrate on what you are doing, the more you drown out any trauma thoughts.

Turn the video off

People involved in traumas sometimes find that pictures of it keep popping into their minds. It is almost like part of the trauma has been videotaped and is played over and over again. Learning how to turn the video off can be useful.

Imagine a picture of a video player. You may find that looking at your own video player at home can help you get a good picture.

Concentrate on this, and imagine yourself putting a video in the machine and turning the player on. As you turn it on, the video will start and you will see the pictures of your chosen video. Now imagine yourself turning the video off. Really concentrate on the 'off' switch and, as you touch the button, notice how the video stops. Practise turning the video player in your mind on and off. When the video starts playing pictures from your trauma, imagine yourself turning the video off and watching the screen go blank.

Write your worries down

You may have lots of memories about the trauma and see pictures of it time and time again. Some people have a different sort of memory and may feel responsible, guilty, angry or somehow to blame for what happened. These thoughts are very troubling and, because no one hears or questions them, they tend to stay racing around in your head.

Sometimes it is useful to empty out your head and clear them away. Seeing them written down on paper can help you to think more clearly and make you feel better.

Write down your trauma worries on a piece of paper.

Think of them all and write them down.

Once you have finished, scrunch up your paper tightly and throw them in the bin!

Sleeping

Night-times can be difficult as it is often the time when thoughts about the trauma seem to happen most. The more you listen, the worse they seem to become and so it is helpful to try to break out of this cycle.

Settling at night

A relaxing night-time routine may help you to fall asleep easier and give you less chance to think about your trauma. Think about the things that help you relax and see if they can become part of your night-time routine:

▶ Have a quiet 'wind down' time before going to bed.

▶ A warm drink or a bath may make you feel relaxed.

▶ A comfortable room (not too hot or cold).

▶ Leave the light on if it helps.

▶ Put the radio or TV on a timer switch, so they turn off after you fall asleep.

▶ If you find it takes a long time before you fall asleep, then try to go to bed later. Staying up later may help you to settle quicker.

Waking at nights and bad dreams

Sometimes you may find that you wake in the middle of the night and can't get back to sleep again. This is a time when you may be troubled by thoughts about your trauma. The more you listen to your thoughts, the worse you feel. Once again it may be useful to try to concentrate on something else:

▶ Put on your personal stereo and listen to your favourite CD. If you fall asleep the machine will turn itself off.

▶ Try reading a chapter of a book or a favourite magazine for a few minutes to settle you again.

Learn to relax

Thinking about your trauma or reminders of it may make you feel frightened or worried. Learning to relax might help you to feel better. There are lots of different ways to relax and you will have to find what way works best for you.

Controlled breathing

There are times when you may suddenly start to become tense or worked up and won't have time to go through any relaxation exercises. Controlled breathing is a quick method to help you regain control and relax. You can use this method anywhere and often people don't even notice what you are doing!

 Slowly draw in a deep breath, hold it for 5 seconds and then very slowly let it out. As you breathe out, say to yourself 'relax'. Doing this a few times will help you regain control of your body and help you feel calmer.

Calming pictures

With this method you make yourself feel more pleasant by thinking about those things you find nice or restful.

Try thinking about your dream place. It could be somewhere you have been or your fantasy. Imagine a picture of it in your mind, making the picture as restful and peaceful as possible. Try to make the picture as real as you can and think about:

▶ the noise of the waves crashing on the beach

▶ the wind blowing in the trees

▶ the smell of the sea or pine forests

▶ the warm sun shining on your face

▶ the wind blowing gently through your hair.

You need to practise so that you can really imagine your dream place. If you start to feel unpleasant, then try turning the picture on. Really concentrate hard on your restful scene and see if it helps you to relax.

Physical exercise

Some people find that physical exercise is a helpful way to relax. If physical exercise works for you, then use it. If possible it may be particularly useful to try at those times you notice strong unpleasant feelings.

 A good run, brisk walk or swim can help you get rid of any angry or anxious feelings.

Facing your fears

 You may find that you become very worried about things that remind you of your trauma. You may become very worried if you go past the place where the trauma happened or if you are reminded about events or people involved in the trauma. This is very understandable and most people feel like this for a short time afterwards. For others this feeling becomes very strong and may stop you from doing the things you would really like to do. You may:

▶ give up trying to do things

▶ become reluctant to try anything new

▶ avoid situations you think will be difficult.

When this happens you need to face your fears and learn to overcome them. The following ideas might help.

Practise being successful

When faced with difficult challenges we often think that we will not be successful. We are very good at predicting failure and thinking that things will go wrong. Thinking like this means that you will feel more anxious and more reluctant to try.

 A useful way forward is to imagine a picture of your challenge in your mind and to talk yourself through what will happen. Think about the steps involved and imagine yourself coping and being successful. Make your picture as real as possible and describe your scene in lots of detail.

Practising this a few times will help you to recognise that, while it might be difficult, you can be successful.

Small steps

Sometimes challenges seem too big to tackle in one go. At these times it might be useful to break the task down into smaller steps. Someone who is feeling very frightened about travelling in a car might, for example, break this down into the following steps.

▶ Sit for a minute in a stationary car.

▶ Sit in a stationary car with the engine running.

▶ Go for a very short ride on a quiet road.

▶ Go for a slightly longer ride on a quiet road.

▶ Go for a short ride on a busier road.

▶ Go for a longer ride.

Because each step is small it increases the chances of success and moves you closer to your overall target. Practise each step a few times until you feel confident enough to go on to the next. Remember, praise yourself when you have been successful – you have done well!

Positive self-talk

A useful way of helping yourself through a difficult or worrying situation is by using self-talk. Positive self-talk helps you to feel more relaxed and confident by keeping doubts and worries under control. You do this by saying positive things to yourself when you feel worried or unsure if you will be successful.

▶ **I am** going to go back to that place again.

▶ **I have** managed to get to the door and now I am going in.

Repeat your positive message and praise yourself as you face your challenge.

Talk about it

You may find it difficult to talk with other people about your trauma. You may want to try to forget about it. At other times you may feel that people aren't interested in what happened or you may worry that they will become upset if you talk about how you are feeling. This isn't always helpful and, although it might be hard, it is often good to try to talk about what happened.

Traumas are very frightening and upsetting events. They are difficult to understand. Talking about it may help you make sense of what happened.

References

Abela, J.R.Z., Brozina, K. & Haigh, E.P. (2002). An examination of the response styles theory of depression in third- and seventh-grade children: a short longitudinal study. *Journal of Abnormal Child Psychology*, **30**, 515–527.

Bailey, V. (2001). Cognitive-behavioural therapies for children and adolescents. *Advances in Psychiatric Treatment*, **7**, 224–232.

Barrett, P.M. (1998). Evaluation of cognitive behavioural group treatments for childhood anxiety disorders. *Journal of Clinical Child Psychology*, **27**, 4, 459–468.

Barrett, P.M. (2000). Treatment of childhood anxiety: developmental aspects. *Clinical Psychology Review*, **20**, 4, 479–494.

Barrett, P.M. & Healy, L.J. (2003). An examination of the cognitive processes involved in childhood obsessive-compulsive disorder. *Behaviour Research and Therapy*, **41**, 3, 285–299.

Barrett, P.M. & Turner, V.M. (2001). Prevention of anxiety symptoms in primary school children: preliminary results from a universal school based trial. *British Journal of Clinical Psychology*, **40**, 399–410.

Barrett, P.M., Dadds, M.R. & Rapee, R.M. (1996b). Family treatment of childhood anxiety: a controlled trial. *Journal of Consulting and Clinical Psychology*, **64**, 2, 333–342.

Barrett, P., Healey-Farrell, L. & March, J.S. (2004). Cognitive behavioural treatment of childhood obsessive compulsive disorder: a controlled trial. *Journal of the American Academy of Child and Adolescent Psychiatry*, **43**, 1, 46–62.

Barrett, P.M., Short, A. & Healy, L. (2002). Do parent and child behaviours differentiate families whose children have obsessive compulsive disorder for other clinic and non-clinic families? *Journal of Child Psychology and Psychiatry*, **43**, 5, 597–607.

Barrett, P., Webster, H. & Turner, C. (2000a). FRIENDS prevention of anxiety and depression for children. Children's workbook. Australia: Australian Academic Press.

Barrett, P., Webster, H. & Turner, C. (2000b). The FRIENDS group leader's manual for children. Australia: Australian Academic Press.

Barrett, P.M., Duffy, A.L., Dadds, M.R. & Ryan, S.M. (2001). Cognitive-behavioural treatment of anxiety disorders in children; long term (6 year) follow-up. *Journal of Consulting and Clinical Psychology*, **69**, 1–7.

Barrett, P.M., Healey-Farrell, L., Piacentini, J. & March, J. (2003). Obsessive-compulsive disorder in childhood and adolescence: description and treatment. In P.M. Barrett & T.H. Ollendick (Eds), *Handbook of interventions that work with children and adolescents; prevention and treatment*. Chichester: Wiley.

Barrett, P.M., Rapee, R.M., Dadds, M.R. & Ryan, S.M. (1996a). Family enhancement of cognitive style in anxious and aggressive children. *Journal of Abnormal Child Psychology*, **24**, 187–203.

Beck, A.T. (1967). *Depression: clinical, experimental and theoretical aspects*. New York: Harper & Row.

Beck, A.T. (1976). *Cognitive therapy and the emotional disorders*. New York: International Universities Press.

Bogels, S. & Zigterman, D. (2000). Dysfunctional cognitions in children with social phobia, separation anxiety and generalised anxiety disorders. *Journal of Abnormal Child Psychology*, **28**, 205–211.

Bolton, D. (2004). Cognitive behaviour therapy for children and adolescents: some theoretical and developmental issues. In P. Graham (Ed), *Cognitive behaviour therapy for children and families* (second edition). Cambridge: Cambridge University Press.

Brandell, J.R. (1984). Stories and story telling in child psychotherapy. *Psychotherapy*, **21**, 54–62.

Braswell, L. (1991). Involving parents in cognitive-behavioural therapy with children and adolescents. In P. Kendall (Ed), *Child and adolescent therapy: cognitive behavioural procedures*. New York: Guilford Press.

Brestan, E.V. & Eyberg, S.M. (1998). Effective psychosocial treatment of conduct disordered children and adolescents; 29 years, 82 studies and 5,272 kids. *Journal of Clinical Child Psychology*, **27**, 2, 180–189.

British Psychological Society (2002). *Drawing on the evidence*. Leicester: BPS.

Bugental, D.B., Ellerson, P.C., Lin, E.K., Rainey, B., Kokotovic, A. & O'Hara, N. (2002). A cognitive approach to child abuse prevention. *Journal of Family Psychology*, **16**, 3, 243–258.

Butler. G. (1998). Clinical formulation. In A.S. Bellack & M. Hersen (Eds), *Comprehensive clinical psychology*. New York: Pergamon Press.

Celano, M., Hazzard, A., Webb, C. & McCall, C. (1996). Treatment of traumagenic beliefs among sexually abused girls and their mothers: an evaluation study. *Journal of Abnormal Child Psychology*, **24**, 1–16.

Chalder, T. & Hussain, K. (2002). *Self-help for chronic fatigue syndrome: a guide for young people*. Oxford: Blue Stallion Publications.

Chambless, D.I. & Ollendick, T.H. (2001). Empirically supported psychological interventions: controversies and evidence. *Annual Review of Psychology*, **52**, 685–716.

Chang, J. (1999). Collaborative therapies with young children and their families: developmental, pragmatic and procedural issues. *Journal of Systemic Therapies*, **14**, 44–64.

Charlesworth, G.M. & Reichelt, F.K. (2004). Keeping conceptualisation simple: examples with family carers of people with dementia. *Behavioural and Cognitive Psychotherapy*, **32**, 4, 401–409.

Chu, B.C. & Kendall, P.C. (2004). Positive association of child involvement and treatment outcome within a manual based cognitive-behavioural treatment for children with anxiety. *Journal of Consulting and Clinical Psychology*, **72**, 5, 821–829.

Clark, G., Lewinsohn, P. & Hops, H. (1990). Adolescent Coping with Depression Course. Available from http://www.kpchr.org/

Clarke, G.N., Rhode, P., Lewinsohn, P.M., Hops, H. & Seeley, J.R. (1999). Cognitive behavioural treatment of adolescent depression: efficacy of acute group treatment and booster sessions. *Journal of the American Academy of Child and Adolescent Psychiatry*, **38**, 3, 272–279.

Clarke, G.N., Hornbrook, M., Lynch, F., Polen, M., Gale, J., O'Connor, E., Seeley, J.R. & Debar, L. (2002). Group cognitive-behavioural treatment for depressed adolescent offspring of depressed patients in a health maintenance organisation. *Journal of the American Academy of Child and Adolescent Psychiatry*, **41**, 3, 305–313.

Cobham, V.E., Dadds, M.R. & Spence, S.H. (1998). The role of parental anxiety in the treatment of childhood anxiety. *Journal of Consulting and Clinical Psychology*, **66**, 6, 893–905.

Cohen, J.A. & Mannarino, A.P. (1996). A treatment outcome study for sexually abused preschool children: initial findings. *Journal of the American Academy of Child and Adolescent Psychiatry*, **35**, 42–50.

Cohen, J.A. & Mannarino, A.P. (1998). Interventions for sexually abused children: initial treatment outcome findings. *Child Maltreatment*, **3**, 1, 17–26.

Cohen, J.A., Deblinger, E., Mannarino, A.P. & Steer, R.A. (2004). A multisite, randomised controlled trial for children with sexual abuse-related PTSD symptoms. *Journal of the American Academy of Child and Adolescent Psychiatry*, **43**, 4, 393–402.

Compton, S.N., March, J.S., Brent, D., Albano, A.M., Weersing, V.R. & Curry, J. (2004). Cognitive-behavioural psychotherapy for anxiety and depressive disorders in children and adolescents: an evidence based medicine review. *Journal of the American Academy of Child and Adolescent Psychiatry*, **43**, 8, 930–959.

Curry, J.F. & Craighead, W.E. (1990). Attributional style in clinically depressed and conduct disordered adolescents. *Journal of Clinical and Consulting Psychology*, **58**, 109–116.

Dadds, M.R. & Barrett, P.M. (2001). Practitioner Review: Psychological management of anxiety disorders in childhood. *Journal of Child Psychology and Psychiatry*, **42**, 8, 999–1011.

Deblinger, E., Lippmann, J. & Steer, R. (1996). Sexually abused children suffering posttraumatic stress symptoms: initial treatment outcome findings. *Child Maltreatment*, **1**, 310–321.

Deblinger, E., Stauffer, L.B. & Steer, R.A. (2001). Comparative efficacies of supportive and cognitive behavioural group therapies for young children who have been sexually abused and their non-offending mothers. *Child Maltreatment*, **6**, 4, 332–343.

Durlak, J.A., Fuhrman, T. & Lampman, C. (1991). Effectiveness of cognitive-behaviour therapy for maladapting children: a meta analysis. *Psychological Bulletin*, **110**, 204–214.

Durlak, J.A., Rubin, L.A. & Kahng, R.D. (2001). Cognitive behaviour therapy for children and adolescents with externalizing problems. *Journal of Cognitive Psychotherapy*, **15**, 3, 183–194.

Ehlers, A. & Clark, D.M. (2000). A cognitive model of post-traumatic stress disorder. *Behaviour Research and Therapy*, **38**, 319–345.

Ehlers, A., Mayou, R.A. & Bryant, B. (2003). Cognitive predictors of posttraumatic stress disorder in children. Results of a prospective longitudinal study. *Behaviour Research and Therapy*, **41**, 1–10.

Ellis, A. (1977). The basic clinical theory of rational-emotive therapy. In A. Ellis & R. Grieger (Eds), *Handbook of rational-emotive therapy*. New York: Springer.

Feehan, C.J. & Vostanis, P. (1996). Cognitive-behavioural therapy for depressed children: children's and therapist's impressions. *Behavioural and Cognitive Psychotherapy*, **24**, 171–183.

Flannery-Schroeder, E. & Kendall, P.C. (2000). Group and individual cognitive-behavioural treatments for youth with anxiety disorders: a randomized clinical trial. *Cognitive Therapy and Research*, **24**, 251–278.

Flavell, J.H., Flavell, E.R. & Green, F.L. (2001). Development of children's understanding of connections between thinking and feeling. *Psychological Science*, **12**, 430–432.

Forehand, R. & MacMahon, R.J. (1981). *Helping the noncompliant child: a clinician's guide to effective parent training*. New York: Guilford Press.

Franklin, M.E., Kozak, M.J., Cashman, L.A., Coles, M.E., Rheingold, A.A. & Foa, E.B. (1998). Cognitive behavioural treatment of pediatric obsessive compulsive disorder: an open clinical trial. *Journal of the American Academy of Child and Adolescent Psychiatry*, **37**, 412–419.

Friedberg, R.D. & McClure, J.M. (2002). *Clinical practice of cognitive therapy with children and adolescents: the nuts and bolts*. New York: Guilford Press.

Friedberg, R.D., Crosby, L.E., Friedberg, B.A., Rutter, J.G. & Knight, K.R. (2000). Making cognitive behavioural therapy user-friendly to children. *Cognitive and Behavioural Practice*, **6**, 189–200.

Garcia, J.A. & Weisz, J.R. (2002). When youth mental health care stops: therapeutic relationship problems and other reasons for ending outpatient treatment. *Journal of Consulting and Clinical Psychology*, **70**, 439–443.

Gardner, R. (1971). *Therapeutic communication with children: the mutual storytelling technique*. New York: Science House.

Ginsburg, G.S. & Schlossberg, M.C. (2002). Family-based treatment of childhood anxiety disorders. *International Review of Psychiatry*, **14**, 143–154.

Ginsburg, G.S., Silverman, W.K. & Kurtines, W.K. (1995). Family involvement in treating children with phobic and anxiety disorders: a look ahead. *Clinical Psychology Review*, **15**, 5, 475–473.

Graham, P. (1998). *Cognitive behaviour therapy for children and families*. Cambridge: Cambridge University Press.

Graham, P. (2005). Jack Tizard lecture: cognitive behaviour therapy for children: passing fashion or here to stay? *Child and Adolescent Mental Health*, **10**, 2, 57–62.

Grave, J. & Blissett, J. (2004). Is cognitive behaviour therapy developmentally appropriate for young children? A critical review of the evidence. *Clinical Psychology Review*, **24**, 399–420.

Harrington, R. (2004). Depressive disorders. In P. Graham (Ed), *Cognitive behaviour therapy for children and families* (second edition). Cambridge: Cambridge University Press.

Harrington, R., Wood, A. & Verduyn, C. (1998a). Clinically depressed adolescents. In P. Graham (Ed), *Cognitive behaviour therapy for children and families*. Cambridge: Cambridge University Press.

Harrington, R.C., Whittaker, J., Shoebridge, P. & Campbell, F. (1998b). Systematic review of the efficacy of cognitive behaviour therapies in child and adolescent depressive disorder. *British Medical Journal*, **316**, 1559–1563.

Henggeler, S.W., Clingempeel, G.W., Brodino, M.J. & Pickrel, S.G. (2002). Four year follow-up of Multisystemic Therapy with substance-abusing and substance-dependent juvenile offenders. *Journal of the American Academy of Child and Adolescent Psychiatry*, **41**, 868–874.

Heyne, D., King, N.J., Tonge, B., Rollings, S., Young, D., Pritchard, M. & Ollendick, T.H. (2002). Evaluation of child therapy and caregiver training in the treatment of school refusal. *Journal of the American Academy of Child and Adolescent Psychiatry*, **41**, 6, 687–695.

Hibbs, E.D., Hamburger, S.D., Lenane, M., Rapport, J.L., Kruesi, M.J.P., Keysor, C.S. & Goldstein, M.J. (1991). Determinants of expressed emotion in families of disturbed and normal children. *Journal of Child Psychology and Psychiatry*, **32**, 757–770.

Howard, K., Lueger, R., Maling, M. & Martinovich, Z. (1993). A phase model of psychotherapy outcome. Causal mediation of change. *Journal of Consulting and Clinical Psychology*, **61**, 678–685.

Hudson, J.L. & Rapee, R.M. (2001). Parent–child interactions and the anxiety disorders. An observational analysis. *Behaviour Research and Therapy*, **39**, 1411–1427.

Ironside,V. (2003). *The huge bag of worries*. London: Hodder Children's Books.

Jayson, D., Wood, A.J., Kroll, L., Fraser, J. & Harrington, R.C. (1998). Which depressed patients respond to cognitive behavioural treatment? *Journal of the American Academy of Child and Adolescent Psychiatry*, **37**, 35–39.

Johnston, C. (1996). Addressing parent cognitions in interventions with families of disruptive children. In K. Dobson & K. Craig (Eds), *Advances in cognitive behaviour therapy*. London: Sage.

Kane, M.T. & Kendall, P.C. (1989). Anxiety disorders in children: a multiple baseline evaluation of a cognitive behavioural treatment. *Behaviour Therapy*, **20**, 499–508.

Kaslow, N.J., Rehm, I.P., Pollack, S.L. & Siegel, A.W. (1988). Attributional style and self-control behaviour in depressed and non-depressed children and their parents. *Journal of Abnormal Child Psychology*, **16**, 163–175.

Kazdin, A.E. (1997). Parent management training: evidence, outcomes, and issues. *Journal of the American Academy of Child and Adolescent Psychiatry*, **36**, 10–18.

Kazdin, A.E. & Kendall, P.C. (1998). Current progress and future plans for developing effective treatments. Comments and perspectives. *Journal of Clinical Child Psychology*, **27**, 217–226.

Kazdin, A.E. & Weisz, J. (1998). Identifying and developing empirically supported child and adolescent treatments. *Journal of Consulting and Clinical Psychology*, **66**, 19–36.

Kendall, P.C. (1990). *The coping cat workbook*. Philadelphia, PA: Temple University.

Kendall, P.C. (1992). *Stop and think workbook* (second edition). Ardmore, PA: Workbook Publishing.

Kendall, P.C. (1994). Treating anxiety disorders in children: results of a randomized clinical trial. *Journal of Consulting and Clinical Psychology*, **62**, 100–110.

Kendall, P.C. & Panichelli-Mindel, S.M. (1995). Cognitive-behavioural treatments. *Journal of Abnormal Child Psychology*. **23**, 1, 107–124.

Kendall, P.C. & Southam-Gerow, M.A. (1996), Long-term follow-up of cognitive-behavioural therapy for anxiety-disordered youth. *Journal of Consulting and Clinical Psychology*, **64**, 724–730.

Kendall, P.C., Stark, K.D. & Adam, T. (1990). Cognitive deficit or cognitive distortion in childhood depression. *Journal of Abnormal Child Psychology*, **18**, 3, 255–270.

Kendall, P.C., Flannery-Schroeder, E., Panichelli-Mindel, S.M., Southam-Gerow, M., Henin, A. & Warman, M. (1997). Therapy for youths with anxiety disorders: a second randomized clinical trial. *Journal of Consulting and Clinical Psychology*, **65**, 3, 366–380.

King, N.J., Tonge, B.J., Heyne, D., Pritchard, M., Rollings, S., Young, D., Myerson, N. & Ollendick, T.H. (1998). Cognitive behavioural treatment of school-refusing children: a controlled evaluation. *Journal of the American Academy of Child and Adolescent Psychiatry*, **37**, 4, 395–403.

King, N.J., Tonge, B.J., Mullen, P., Myerson, N., Heyne, D., Rollings, S., Martin, R. & Ollendick, T.H. (2000). Treating sexually abused children with posttraumatic stress symptoms: a randomized clinical trial. *Journal of the American Academy of Child and Adolescent Psychiatry*, **39**, 11, 1347–1355.

Knell, S.M. & Ruma, C.D. (2003). Play therapy with a sexually abused child. In M.A. Reinecke, F.M. Dattilio & A. Freeman (Eds), *Cognitive therapy with children and adolescents: a casebook for clinical practice* (second edition). New York: Guilford Press.

Krain, A. & Kendall, P. (1999). Cognitive behavioural therapy. In S. Russ & T. Ollendick (Eds), *Handbook of psychotherapies for children and families*. New York: Plenum.

Krohnc, H.W. & Hock, M. (1991). Relationships between restrictive mother–child interactions and anxiety of the child. *Anxiety Research*, **4**, 109–124.

Kuyken, W. & Beck, A.T. (2004). Cognitive therapy. In V. Freeman, & M.J. Power (Eds), *Handbook of evidence-based psychotherapy: a guide for research and practice*. Chichester: Wiley.

Lazarus, A.A. & Abramovitz, A. (1962). The use of 'emotive imagery' in the treatment of children's phobias. *Journal of Mental Science*, **108**, 191–195.

Lewinsohn, P.M., Clarke, G.N., Hops, H. & Andrews, J. (1990). Cognitive behavioural treatment for depressed adolescents. *Behaviour Therapy*, **21**, 385–401.

Libby, S., Reynolds, S., Derisley, J. & Clark, S. (2004). Cognitive appraisals in young people with obsessive-compulsive disorder. *Journal of Child Psychology and Psychiatry*, **45**, 1076–1084.

March, J.S., Mulle, K. & Herbel, B. (1994). Behavioural psychotherapy for children and adolescents with obsessive-compulsive disorder: an open clinical trial of a new protocol driven treatment package. *Journal of the American Academy of Child and Adolescent Psychiatry*, **33**, 333–341.

March, J., Frances, A., Kahn, D. & Carpenter, D. (1997). Expert consensus guidelines: treatment of obsessive compulsive disorder. *Journal of Clinical Psychology*, **58**, 4, 1–72.

Mendlowitz, S.L., Manassis, M.D., Bradley, S., Scapillato, D., Miezitis, S. & Shaw, B.F. (1999). Cognitive behaviour group treatments in childhood anxiety disorders: the role of parental involvement. *Journal of the American Academy of Child and Adolescent Psychiatry*, **38**, 10, 1223–1229.

Nauta, M.H., Scholing, A., Emmelkamp, P.M.G. & Minderaa, R.B. (2001). Cognitive behaviour therapy for anxiety disordered children in a clinical setting: does additional cognitive parent training enhance treatment effectiveness? *Clinical Psychology and Psychotherapy*, **8**, 300–340.

Nauta, M.H., Scholing, A., Emmelkamp, P.M.G. & Minderaa, R.B. (2003). Cognitive behaviour therapy for children with anxiety disorders in a clinical setting: no additional effect of a cognitive parent training. *Journal of the American Academy of Child and Adolescent Psychiatry*, **42**, 11, 1270–1278.

Nelson, W.M. & Finch, A.J. (1996). *'Keeping your cool': the anger management workbook*. Ardmore, PA: Workbook Publishing.

O'Kearney, R. (1998). Responsibility appraisals and obsessive-compulsive disorder. A critique of Salkovskis's cognitive theory. *Australian Journal of Psychology*, **50**, 1, 43–47.

Overholser, J.V. (1993a). Elements of the Socratic method: I. Systematic questioning. *Psychotherapy*, **30**, 1, 67–74.

Overholser, J.V. (1993b). Elements of the Socratic method: II. Inductive reasoning. *Psychotherapy*, **30**, 1, 75–85.

Overholser, J.C. (1994). Elements of the Socratic method: III. Universal definitions. *Psychotherapy*, **31**, 2, 286–293.

Padesky, C. Audio tape – *Socratic process* (SQ1).

Padesky, C. & Greenberger, D. (1995), *Clinician's guide to mind over mood*. New York: Guilford Press.

Patterson, G.R. (1982). *Coercive family process*. Eugene, OR: Castalia.

Phillips, N. (1999). *The panic book*. Australia: Shrink-Rap Press.

Piacentini, J. & Bergman, R.L. (2001). Developmental issues in cognitive therapy for childhood anxiety disorders. *Journal of Cognitive Psychotherapy*, **15**, 3, 165–182.

Piaget, J. (1952). *The origins of intelligence in the child*. London: Routledge & Kegan Paul.

Prinz, R.J. & Miller, G.E. (1994). Family-based treatment for childhood antisocial behaviour: experimental influences on dropout and engagement. *Journal of Consulting and Clinical Psychology*, **62**, 645–650.

Prochaska, J.O., DiClemente, C.C. & Norcross, J.C. (1992). In search of how people change. *American Psychologist*, **47**, 1102–1104.

Quakley, S., Reynolds, S. & Coker, S. (2004). The effects of cues on young children's abilities to discriminate among thoughts, feelings and behaviours. *Behaviour Research and Therapy*, **42**, 343–356.

Rapee, R.M. (1997). The potential role of childrearing practices in the development of anxiety and depression. *Clinical Psychology Review*, **17**, 47–67.

Reinecke, M.A., Dattilio, F.M. & Freeman, A. (2003). *Cognitive therapy with children and adolescents; a casebook for clinical practice* (second edition). New York: Guilford Press.

Rollnick, S. & Miller, W.R. (1995). What is motivational interviewing? *Behavioural and Cognitive Psychotherapy*, **23**, 325–334.

Rollnick, S., Mason, P. & Butler, C. (1999). *Health behaviour change: a guide for practitioners*. London: Churchill Livingstone.

Ronen, T. (1992). Cognitive therapy with young children. *Child Psychiatry and Human Development*, **23**, 1, 19–30.

Ronen, T. (1997). *Cognitive developmental therapy with children*. Chichester: Wiley.

Russell, R.L. & Shirk, S.R. (1998). Child psychotherapy process research. *Advances in Clinical Child Psychology*, **20**, 93–124.

Rutter, J.G. & Friedberg, R.D. (1999). Guidelines for the effective use of Socratic dialogue in cognitive therapy. In L. VandeCreek, S. Knapp & T.L. Jackson (Eds), *Innovations in clinical practice: a sourcebook*. Sarasota, FL: Professional Resource Process.

Salkovskis, P.M. (1985). Obsessional compulsive problems: a cognitive-behavioural analysis. *Behaviour Research and Therapy*, **23**, 5, 571–583.

Salkovskis, P.M. (1989). Cognitive behavioural factors and the persistence of intrusive thoughts in obsessional problems. *Behaviour Research and Therapy*, **27**, 6, 677–682.

Salmon, K. & Bryant, R.A. (2002). Posttraumatic stress disorder in children: the influence of developmental factors. *Clinical Psychology Review*, **22**, 163–188.

Sanders, M.R., Shepherd, R.W., Cleghorn, G. & Woolford, H. (1994). The treatment of recurrent abdominal pain in children: a controlled comparison of cognitive-behavioural family intervention and standard paediatric care. *Journal of Consulting and Clinical Psychology*, **62**, 306–314.

Schmidt, N.B., Joiner, T.E., Young, J.E. & Telch, M.J. (1995). The schema questionnaire: investigation of the psychometric properties and the hierarchical structure of a measure of maladaptive schemas. *Cognitive Therapy and Research*, **19**, 295–321.

Schmidt, U. (2004). Engagement and motivational interviewing. In P. Graham (Ed), *Cognitive behaviour therapy for children and families* (second edition). Cambridge: Cambridge University Press.

Scott, S., Spender, Q., Doolan, M., Jacobs, M. & Aspland, H. (2001). Multicentre controlled trial of parenting groups for childhood antisocial behaviour in clinical practice. *British Medical Journal*, 323, 194–198.

Seligman, L.D., Goza, A.B. & Ollendick, T.H. (2004). Treatment of depression in children and adolescents. In P.M. Barrett & T.H. Ollendick (Eds), *Handbook of interventions that work with children and adolescents: prevention and treatment*. Chichester: Wiley.

Shirk, S. (1999). Developmental therapy. In W. Silverman & T. Ollendick (Eds), *Developmental issues in clinical treatment of children*. Boston: Allyn & Bacon.

Shirk, S.R. (2001). Development and cognitive therapy. *Journal of Cognitive Psychotherapy*, **15**, 3, 155–163.

Shirk, S. & Russell, R. (1996). *Change processes in child psychotherapy*. New York: Guilford Press.

Shirk, S.R. & Saiz, C.C. (1992). Clinical, empirical and developmental perspectives on the therapeutic relationship in child psychotherapy. *Development & Psychopathology*, **4**, 713–728.

Shirk, S.R., Burwell, R. & Harter, S. (2003). Strategies to modify low self-esteem in adolescents. In M.A. Reinecke, F.M. Dattilio & A. Freeman (Eds), *Cognitive therapy with children and adolescents: a casebook for clinical practice* (second edition). New York: Guilford Press.

Siegal, M. (1997). *Knowing children: experiments in conversation and cognition* (second edition). Hove: Lawrence Erlbaum.

Silverman, W.K., Kurtines, W.M., Ginsburg, G.S., Weems, C.F., Rabian, B. & Serafini, L.T. (1999a). Contingency management, self-control and educational support in the treatment of childhood phobic disorders: a randomized clinical trial. *Journal of Consulting and Clinical Psychology*, **67**, 5, 675–687.

Silverman, W.K., Kurtines, W.M., Ginsburg, G.S., Weems, C.F., Lumpkin, P.W. & Carmichael, D.H. (1999b). Treating anxiety disorders in children with group cognitive behavioural therapy: a randomised clinical trial. *Journal of Consulting and Clinical Psychology*, **67**, 6, 995–1003.

Spence, S.H. (1995). *Social skills training: enhancing social competence in children and adolescents*. Windsor, UK: NFER Nelson.

Spence, S.H., Donovan, C. & Brechman-Toussaint, M. (1999). Social skills, social outcomes and cognitive features of childhood social phobia. *Journal of Abnormal Psychology*, **108**, 211–221.

Spence, S.H., Donovan, C. & Brechman-Toussaint, M. (2000). The treatment of childhood social phobia: the effectiveness of a social, skills training based, cognitive-behavioural intervention, with and without parental involvement. *Journal of Child Psychology and Psychiatry*, **41**, 6, 713–726.

Stallard, P. (2002a). *Think good – feel good. A cognitive behaviour therapy workbook for children and young people*. Chichester: Wiley.

Stallard, P. (2002b). Cognitive behaviour therapy with children and adolescents: a selective review of key issues. *Behavioural and Cognitive Psychotherapy*, **30**, 321–333.

Stallard, P. (2004). Cognitive behaviour therapy with prepubertal children. In P. Graham (Ed), *Cognitive behaviour therapy for children and families* (second edition). Cambridge: Cambridge University Press.

Stallard, P. & Rayner, H. (2005). The development and preliminary evaluation of a schema question-naire for children. *Behavioural and Cognitive Psychotherapy*, **33**, 217–224.

Stark, K.D., Reynolds, W.M. & Kaslow, N. (1987). A comparison of the relative efficacy of self-control therapy and a behavioural problems solving therapy for depression in children. *Journal of Abnormal Child Psychology*, **15**, 91–113.

Stark, K.D., Swearer, S., Kurowski, C., Sommer, D., & Bowen, B. (1996). Targeting the child and family: a holistic approach to treating child and adolescent disorders. In E.D. Hibbs & P.S. Jensen (Eds), *Psychosocial treatments for child and adolescent disorders: empirically based strategies for clinical practice*. Washington, DC: American Psychological Association.

Stulemeijer, M., de Jong, L.W.A.M., Fiselier, T.J.W., Hoogveld, S.W.B. & Bleijenberg, G. (2005). Cognitive behaviour therapy for adolescents with chronic fatigue syndrome: randomised controlled trial. *British Medical Journal*, **330**, 14–17.

Tarrier, N. & Calam, R. (2002). New developments in cognitive-behavioural case formulation. Epidemiological, systemic and social context: an integrative approach. *Behavioural and Cognitive Psychotherapy*, **30**, 311–328.

Thornton, S. (2002). *Growing minds: an introduction to cognitive development*. Basingstoke: Palgrave Macmillan.

Toren, P., Wolmer, L., Rosental, B., Eldar, S., Koren, S., Lask, M., Weizman, R. & Laor, N. (2000). Case series: brief parent–child group therapy for childhood anxiety disorders using a manual based cognitive-behavioural technique. *Journal of the American Academy of Child and Adolescent Psychiatry*, **39**, 10, 1309–1312.

Vernberg, E.M. & Johnston, C. (2001). Developmental considerations in the use of cognitive therapy for posttraumatic stress disorder. *Journal of Cognitive Psychotherapy*, **15**, 3, 223–237.

Vostanis, P., Feehan, C. & Grattan, E. (1998). Two year outcome of children treated for depression. *European Child and Adolescent Psychiatry*, **7**, 12–18.

Vostanis, P., Feehan, C., Grattan, E. & Bickerton, W. (1996). Treatment for children and adolescents depression: lessons from a controlled trial. *Clinical Child Psychology and Psychiatry*, **1**, 199–212.

Webster-Stratton, C. (1992). *The incredible years: a trouble-shooting guide for parents of children aged 3–8*. Ontario: Umbrella Press.

Wellman, H.M., Hollander, M. & Schult, C.A. (1996). Young children's understanding of thought bubbles and thoughts. *Child Development*, **67**, 768–788.

Wever, C. (1999). *The school wobblies*. Australia: Shrink-Rap Press.

Wever, C. (2000). *The secret problem*. Australia: Shrink-Rap Press.

White, C., McNally, D. & Cartwright-Hatton, S. (2003). Cognitively enhanced parent training. *Behavioural and Cognitive Psychotherapy*, **31**, 99–102.

Wood, A., Harrington, R. & Moore, A. (1996). Controlled trial of a brief cognitive-behavioural intervention in adolescent patients with depressive disorders. *Journal of Child Psychology and Psychiatry*, **37**, 737–746.

Young, J. (1990). *Cognitive therapy for personality disorder: a schema-focused approach*. Sarasota, FL: Professional Resource Press.

Index